D0812733

STATIC
DEMAND
THEORY

MACMILLAN SERIES IN ECONOMICS

LAWRENCE R. KLEIN, Consulting Editor

STATIC DEMAND THEORY

Donald W. Katzner

Wharton School of Finance and Commerce
University of Pennsylvania

THE MACMILLAN COMPANY
COLLIER-MACMILLAN LIMITED, LONDON

Library
I.U.P.
Indiana, Pa.

330.1 K159a
c.1

© Copyright, Donald W. Katzner, 1970

All rights reserved.
No part of this book may be reproduced
or transmitted in any form or by any means,
electronic or mechanical, including photocopying,
recording,
or by any information storage and retrieval system,
without permission in writing from the Publisher.

First Printing

Library of Congress catalog card number: 74-96742

The Macmillan Company
866 Third Avenue, New York, New York 10022

Collier-Macmillan Canada, Ltd., Toronto, Ontario

Printed in the United States of America

SYLVIA WAHL KATZNER

Preface

This book was written in the belief that many of the scattered threads of argument loosely amalgamated under the heading of demand theory are, in fact, fragments of a single unit, and that it is worthwhile combining them into a tightly knit, unified whole. Economic literature strongly suggests that such diverse concepts as constant marginal utility of income, revealed preference, separable preference orderings, expected utility, and so on, are small parts of an overall effort to link individual preferences and a maximization process with market behavior. The elucidation of such relationships under a wide variety of circumstances is the central theme pursued in the following pages.

Unfortunately one cannot begin to study demand theory today without quickly becoming involved in rather sophisticated mathematical reasoning. It is only too obvious why: the subject matter is so complex that there is no other satisfactory language in which research can be conducted and reported. Thus, in preparing a book of this sort a choice must be made between two alternatives: either the difficult mathematics can be skirted or it has to be faced head on. Although the former permits a more fluid and flexible approach, it suffers from a lack of the precision which is crucial to many of the problems with which the theory deals and it is therefore inappropriate here.

I am keenly aware of the fact that many readers may have difficulty with several of the more advanced mathematical arguments. As a result an effort has been made to present the major development so as to require minimal mathematical background. Geometry often is employed to illustrate and clarify points. By using the formal theorem–proof style of exposition, it has been possible to relegate many of the hardest points to proofs which can be overlooked without critically impairing an understanding of what is going on.

Even so, the minimal prerequisites are high. The text should not be attempted by anyone who does not know at least a little bit about advanced calculus and matrix theory.

A rather lengthy Appendix is included which serves not only to develop many strictly mathematical results required by the text, but also to present in a fairly complete way many theorems which are not readily available in the economics literature. It is hoped that the detailed discussion of properties of convex functions will be especially useful in this regard. The author can take little credit for these propositions. Many are no more than a reworking of the original sources referred to in the footnotes.

Both the text and Appendix are almost entirely self-contained. All notation and concepts are explicitly defined, and results are either rigorously proved or a method of proof is indicated for the interested reader to follow up. However, formality of style is relaxed somewhat in later chapters where the frequent repetition it requires would tend to add unnecessary camouflage to the issues at hand.

Exercises are provided at the ends of Chapters 2 through 7 which contain many examples and proofs omitted from the text. There is a wide range of difficulty with hints supplied for the hardest exercises. Somewhat abbreviated answers follow the Appendix.

It is obvious that a work such as this relies heavily on the efforts of a great many people. I can only acknowledge a few of them here. Parts of the book began as M.A. and Ph.D. theses under the kind and very patient tutelage of Leonid Hurwicz at the University of Minnesota. It is no exaggeration to say that his ideas and influence pervade virtually every paragraph. For this I am most deeply grateful. Along the way Hukukane Nikaidô, Robert A. Pollak, and Marcel K. Richter provided help with solutions to many problems. Daniel McFadden and Hugo Sonnenschein read the manuscript, and what follows has benefited considerably from their suggestions. In addition to aiding with the manuscript itself, Lawrence R. Klein gave warm and continued encouragement. The faults which remain, and perhaps only these, can I claim as truly my own.

I would also like to thank the Institute of Social and Economic Research at Osaka University for generously making available their excellent research facilities during the completion of a rough draft; the Ford Foundation, the National Science Foundation, the Social Science Research Council, and the Kansai Economic Federation for financial support; and, finally, Ruth, my wife, who, along with helping in many ways, provided the necessary atmosphere in which to accomplish this task.

D. W. K.

Contents

STATIC
DEMAND
THEORY

1

Introduction

1.1 PROLOGUE

The purpose of demand theory is to explain consumer market behavior. Thus answers must be provided for at least two distinct but related questions. (1) Given various market parameters such as price, income, etc., what commodities will the consumer purchase and in what quantities? (2) How are these decisions affected by changes in the original parameters? A convenient mathematical device for summarizing all relevant information about a consumer's behavior is to construct demand functions, which show for each possible set of market parameters that collection of commodities he buys. Stated in these terms, the purpose of demand theory is to explain the general properties of such functions.

The world to which demand theory addresses itself has specific physical limitations. A consumer is either an individual or a group with common purpose (for example, a family) who purchase commodities in a market. Commodities include all goods and services among which consumers may choose: ice cream, entertainment, medical care, etc. Every item exists in all nonnegative, finite quantities. Commodities are therefore perfectly divisible; there is a lower bound on what may be purchased but no upper limit. Markets are competitive. No consumer is powerful enough to influence prices in any way and thus acts as if they were fixed. Sometimes his funds available to spend may also be fixed; at others he can increase them by, say, working longer hours. In the latter case the market still dictates the wage returned for his labor.

Nevertheless the consumer is sovereign: it is the sole purpose of all economic activity to satisfy him. He chooses among available consumables and his choices indicate to sellers how supplies should be altered to meet his needs. His decisions are based on preferences among various quantities of commodities in the absence of any market considerations. Although subject to outside pressures such as advertising, they are entirely his own; their source is wrapped up in the psychological constructs of his personality. Now, if the consumer is rational, he will be guided in his choices by Adam Smith's invisible hand and will attempt to purchase the most preferred collection of commodities possible. This principle is the vehicle by which personal tastes are translated into action.

The properties of a consumer's demand functions, then, are derived from his preferences and assumed desire to buy the most satisfactory bundle of goods once market constraints are introduced. Demand theory can handle in this manner a large class of varied sets of preferences, although, unlike demand functions, none are capable of empirical observation. Naturally, different sets of preferences within the class generate different demand functions. But the importance of the theory lies in that whenever the latter are derived from the former as prescribed by it, they must exhibit certain properties which are the same for every set of preferences. Thus by observing any individual's demand functions it is possible to tell if his behavior is consistent with demand theory without knowing anything about his preferences at all. Moreover, if his behavior is that which the theory predicts, then there will be a set of preferences in the original class which could be taken as his. They need not, in fact, be his but they can still be used to predict his behavior.

None of these assertions, of course, should be accepted at face value; all require proof. Indeed, a good portion of this book is devoted to such matters. The idea underlying the above approach, however, may be further illuminated by drawing a parallel with molecular theory, which serves as the basis for modern physics and chemistry. In that theory it is hypothesized that all matter consists of combinations of atoms, molecules, and smaller particles which behave in certain assumed ways. Now no one has ever seen an atom, and no one ever will. But it is useful to suppose that the world is made up of these kinds of particles, even though, in reality, it might not be so, because it then becomes possible to predict more or less accurately a wide variety of physical phenomena. So, too, the economist makes assumptions about what might not exist (preference orderings) in the hope that it will lead to reasonable predictions of observed behavior. If his results are not yet very startling, he can be forgiven for the relative infancy of his theory and inadequacy of his laboratory. These will certainly improve with time.

Of course, if a consumer's observed demand functions do not exhibit the required properties, demand theory does not provide an adequate description of his behavior. But apart from providing a basis for testing the theory as such, properties of demand functions frequently are relevant in more general empirical contexts. Suppose, for example, one were asked to analyze a large collection of data describing an individual's market behavior. This would involve organization of the observations along systematic guidelines and comparisons of the results to specific standards or norms. But unless instructions indicating what to look for were included with the request, how should one proceed? What guidelines and norms should be used? To answer these questions an appeal could be made to the theory of demand, obtaining thereby precisely the kind of instructions sought after: organize the data into demand functions and compare with those of a rational consumer. For several reasons, then, it is important to know something about the properties of rational behavior. Not surprisingly, the latter are a major concern in the following chapters.

An important limitation of the analysis of this book is that it is static rather than dynamic. In a dynamic environment the consumer would choose his most satisfying sequence or stream of commodities over a finite or infinite number of periods. Decisions for one period could not be made independently of those for others. Choices would be studied more for their implications over time than for their instantaneous properties at any particular moment. Statics, on the other hand, takes each period separately. The consumer is thought of as making decisions and purchasing commodities once per period: demand functions describe his choices under all market contingencies at that time. There are links between periods of course. Bonds held last year provide income this year and abstaining from consumption now permits greater purchases in the future. But such links can be treated either as fixed parameters or as current decision variables having only vague reference to other periods. An individual might save, for example, not to have any specific sum ten years later, but just to have "something" available if and when it is needed and for retirement. Savings decisions, then, are based on his preferences at the moment and made independently each period. Although certain kinds of problems are obviously ruled out by ignoring dynamics, there is still much to say about the static world.

Briefly, the plan of the following pages is to present, in a self-contained manner, the theory of demand interpreted in this light. At the outset justification is needed for general use of utility representations in place of the preference orderings mentioned above. In Chapter 2 it is shown that for all practical purposes these notions are equivalent ways of looking at the same thing; the properties of each are uniquely characterized in terms of properties of the other.

What is frequently referred to as "traditional" or "classical" theory comprises the material of Chapter 3. Here implications for market behavior of maximizing twice continuously differentiable, increasing utility functions with strictly convex indifference surfaces are explored in rigorous detail. Chapter 4 is devoted to the reverse question: given demand functions exhibiting properties implied by maximization, does there exist an appropriate utility generator of them? The development of these chapters is next extended in two directions. First the scope of traditional theory is narrowed so that special kinds of utility functions such as homogeneous and separable ones may be studied (Chapter 5); and second it is widened by weakening hypotheses to include and even go beyond revealed preference analysis (Chapter 6). Thus the fundamental problems raised by static demand theory are analyzed under a broad spectrum of differing circumstances.

There are many applications of demand theory to economic questions outside its realm. Several of the more important ones are discussed in Chapter 7 along with various miscellaneous topics convenient to include at that point. Chapter 8 returns to the general theme of analysis to consider demand problems in the face of different kinds of uncertainty. Included here are two approaches to portfolio selection. By way of summary, Chapter 9 outlines a relatively complete theoretical description of the behavior of economic man as he reacts to his market environment. Several of his decision-making processes involving commodities, savings, bonds, etc., are incorporated into one maximization model.

A short historical survey tracing the development of these ideas is presented in Section 1.2.

Finally, a word about notation. In a work such as this it is very difficult to construct a system of symbolic representation which is at the same time both practical and readable. Many compromises had to be made. The reader may therefore find it useful to keep the following rules in mind. Subscripts on symbols such as x, y, z denote components of vectors, superscripts denote different fixed vectors. Subscripts on symbols such as u, f, h denote derivatives, superscripts denote components of functional vectors. [For example, f_j^i is the derivative of f^i with respect to its jth argument, f^i is a component of $f = (f^1, \ldots, f^n)$, and u_{ij} is a second-order partial derivative of u.] Frequently (but not always), capital letters are sets or matrices whose respective elements are denoted by corresponding lowercase letters. The notation of Chapter 3 is more or less standard throughout; important symbols appearing there are listed here.

n	number of commodities ($n > 1$ unless otherwise stated).
x	vector of quantities of commodities, $x = (x_1, \ldots, x_n)$.
P	vector of prices, $P = (P_1, \ldots, P_n)$.
p	vector of normalized prices, $p_i = P_i/P_n$.
M	income.
m	normalized income, $m = M/P_n$.
E	interior of the commodity space.
$\bar{E}$	closure of E.
u	utility function (derivatives u_i, u_{ij}).
$x_{(i)}$	the vector x with its ith component deleted.

w^i indifference surface as a function of $x_{(i)}$ (derivatives w^i_j, w^i_{jk}).

U bordered Hessian matrix associated with u.

Δ subset of E on which U is nonsingular.

Γ^* price-income space, $\Gamma^* = \{(P, M): P > 0, M > 0\}$.

Γ normalized price-income space, $\Gamma = \{(p, m): p > 0, m > 0\}$.

f inverse demand functions defined on E, $f = (f^1, \ldots, f^n)$ (derivatives f^i_j).

h^* demand functions defined on Γ^*, $h^* = (h^{*1}, \ldots, h^{*n})$ (derivatives h^{*i}_j, h^{*i}_M).

h demand functions defined on Γ, $h = (h^1, \ldots, h^n)$ (derivatives h^i_j, h^i_m).

Ω^* set on which h^* is differentiable.

Ω set on which h is differentiable.

a_{ij} Antonelli function defined on E.

s^*_{ij} Slutsky (substitution) function defined on Ω^*.

s_{ij} Slutsky (substitution) function defined on Ω.

A $n - 1 \times n - 1$ matrix of terms a_{ij}.

S^* $n - 1 \times n - 1$ matrix of terms s^*_{ij}.

S $n - 1 \times n - 1$ matrix of terms s_{ij}.

l indirect utility function.

λ^* marginal utility of income.

$B^=(P, M)$ budget hyperplane, $B^=(P, M) = B^=(p, m) = \{x: P \cdot x = M\}$.

$B^{\leq}(P, M)$ budget set, $B^{\leq}(P, M) = B^{\leq}(p, m) = \{x: P \cdot x \leq M\}$.

1.2 HISTORICAL DEVELOPMENT

The following is intended as a very brief chronology of important developments in the theory of demand. Since many of the ideas included are studied rigorously in later chapters, they are not pursued in great detail here.

The historical origins of demand theory lie in the discovery of two concepts: utility and demand. For a long time these generally appeared only in separate contexts; focusing on one seemed to preclude consideration of the other. However, during the second half of the nineteenth century a link between them became apparent, and at this point theoretical content was given to the study of demand.

In the beginning, a necessity to distinguish between "value in use" and "value in exchange" seems to have given rise to the notion of utility. Although traceable to Aristotle,[1] the distinction was placed in economic

_____

[1] See J. A. Schumpeter, *History of Economic Analysis* (New York: Oxford University Press, 1954), p. 60.

perspective by Davanzati[2] (1588), Law[3] (1705), and others who applied it to explain the paradox that usefulness is not necessarily reflected in price. Law, in fact, argued in terms of the diamond–water example which Smith[4] (1776) later made famous: although of little practical use, diamonds are dear because they are scarce, while water, being a necessity of life, is cheap due to its abundance. For these people "utility" meant precisely value in use. Bentham[5] (1789, 1802), on the other hand, thought of utility as an explicit measure of pleasure and pain. His original purpose was to rationalize civil and criminal codes of law, but a subsequent application dealt with the distribution of wealth. Small reductions of a rich man's wealth would lower his pleasure less than the increase experienced by a poor man receiving a similar amount. Therefore, equal distributions of wealth provide the most "aggregate happiness." Although hardly successful, this argument clearly anticipates the notion of marginal utility and the principle that it diminishes.

Actually these ideas, if in somewhat different form, had already been invented by Bernoulli[6] (1738) to resolve the St. Petersburg paradox. Suppose A tosses a fair coin until the first head appears. If it occurs after one throw he pays \$1 to B, after a second, \$2, and in general, after n tosses he pays $\$2^{n-1}$. Now B's expected winnings in such a game are the infinite sum $(\frac{1}{2})(1) + (\frac{1}{2})^2(2) + \cdots + (\frac{1}{2})^n(2)^{n-1} + \cdots$. The paradox arises because it is clearly not necessary for B to advance A such a large bribe to induce him to play. Bernoulli's solution was to compute, under the assumption that marginal utility of wealth diminishes, expected utility rather than expected winnings. The bribe then became a reasonable number which depended on B's initial wealth. Interestingly enough, Bernoulli also suggested that for games with finite expected winnings, if wealth were very large and the sums at stake small, then the marginal utility of wealth could be taken as constant. Marshall[7] (1890), who knew Bernoulli's work well, introduced a similar concept to obtain demand functions one and one-half centuries later.

Marginal utility and the principle that it diminishes, however, did not become important tools of economic analysis until the time of Dupuit[8] (1844) and Gossen[9] (1854). By then Bentham's concept of utility had been

---

[2] *Lezione delle moneta* (1588).

[3] *Money and Trade Considered, with a Proposal for Supplying the Nation with Money* (1705).

[4] *An Inquiry into the Nature and Causes of the Wealth of Nations* (1776).

[5] *Introduction to the Principles of Morals and Legislation* (1789), *Theory of Legislation* (1802).

[6] "Specimen theoriae novae de mensura sortis," in *Commentarii academiae scientiarum imperialis Petropolitanae* (1738); English translation, "Exposition of a New Theory on the Measurement of Risk," *Econometrica* (1954), pp. 23–26.

[7] *Principles of Economics* (London: Macmillan, 1890).

[8] His important essays are collected and reprinted in *De l'utilité et de sa mesure* (Turin: La Riforma Sociale, 1934).

[9] *Entwicklung der Gesetze des menschlichen Verkehrs* (Berlin: Prager, 1854).

narrowed to more or less reflect satisfaction associated with consumption of various economic quantities. Out of the difference between total and marginal utility Dupuit created consumers' surplus to aid him in obtaining the optimal toll charge for crossing a bridge. The surplus was measured by what today would be called the area under a demand curve minus appropriate expenditure, and he concluded that the optimum rate was zero. Implicitly Dupuit had identified utility with demand but he never made any serious effort to define or construct a theory of the latter. Ten years later Gossen, dealing with an additive utility function, i.e., one for which total utility is found by summing independent utilities of quantities of separate commodities, argued that at constrained maxima, marginal utilities per dollar are equal for all commodities.

The early forms utility functions were permitted to take were rather restrictive. Additivity and diminishing marginal utility ruled the day and cardinality, the assumption that utility can be measured, was never seriously questioned. This was true even of Walras[10] (1874). It was Edgeworth[11] (1881) who finally wrote utility as a general function of quantities of all commodities and introduced the indifference map in order to geometrically analyze barter in the nonadditive case. Although he somewhat redundantly assumed both, the door was now open for the replacement of diminishing marginal utility with convexity of indifference contours. Furthermore, Edgeworth employed indifference curves only as an expositional device; he did not see, as did no one before him, that their use renders cardinality an unnecessary requirement. The observation that an increasing transformation of the utility function has no effect on demand had to wait for Fisher[12] (1892) and Pareto[13] (1896).

The concept of demand goes back at least to King[14] (1696), who actually computed a demand schedule for wheat. From it he derived "King's law": an inverse statistical relationship between price and quantity. However, Verri[15] (1760) was the first to give a precise formulation of a demand function by writing $pq = c$, where p represents price, q quantity, and c a constant. Such exactitude in defining demand then seems to have been forgotten until Cournot[16] (1838) reestablished it many years later. Shortly

[10] *Éléments d'économie politique pure* (Lausanne: Carbay, 1874); English translation, *Elements of Pure Economics* (Homewood, Ill.: Irwin, 1954).

[11] *Mathematical Psychics* (London: Kegan Paul, 1881).

[12] "Mathematical Investigations in the Theory of Value and Prices," *Transactions of the Connecticut Academy of Arts and Sciences*, v. 9 (1892).

[13] *Cours d'économie politique* (Lausanne: Rouge, 1896).

[14] *Natural and Political Observations and Conclusions upon the State and Condition of England in 1696.*

[15] *Elementi del commercio* (1760).

[16] *Recherches sur les principes mathématiques de la théorie des richesses* (Paris: Hachette, 1838); English translation, *Researches into the Mathematical Principles of the Theory of Wealth* (New York: Macmillan, 1897).

thereafter another "law" associated with demand was discovered by Engel[17] (1857): among families of similar taste who face identical prices, percentage expenditure on food declines as income rises. Thus loci of tangencies between indifference and budget surfaces for fixed prices and variable income have become known as Engel curves.

Jevons[18] (1871) perhaps made the initial attempt to bridge the gap between utility and demand, though Walras (1874) was the first to succeed. This is the point at which it becomes possible to speak of a "theory" of demand. From utility maximization Walras derived demand as a function of all prices and initial endowment; however, he failed to deduce any limitations implied by his hypotheses—in particular by the combination of additivity and diminishing marginal utility. Marshall's (1890) demand functions depended only on the price of the commodity in question (all other prices held constant) and income, but with the additional assumption of a "constant" marginal utility of income (anticipated by Bernoulli's constant marginal utility of wealth) was able to demonstrate that such hypotheses imply demand curves are downward sloping. Pareto[19] (1892) achieved the same result without requiring constancy. Later W. E. Johnson[20] (1913) showed in the general (nonadditive) case upward-sloping demand curves are consistent with convex indifference contours; and finally Slutsky[21] (1915) brilliantly put all these pieces together, transforming "classical" demand theory into what it is today.

Slutsky posited an ordinal utility function reflecting merely an objective ranking of preferences and gave it enough properties to permit its maximization subject to linear constraints. If the consumer does, in fact, purchase utility maximizing bundles of commodities while limited by his budget, then certain characteristics of his behavior are implied which observation can contradict. These implications include negativity of diagonal elements and symmetry of the matrix of compensated price derivatives obtained from demand. The distinction between income and substitution effects is also due to him.

The relationship between demand and utility goes both ways and so it is not surprising that while Walras was explaining the former in terms of the

---

[17] "Die Produktions und Consumtionsverhältnisse des Königreiches Sachsen," *Zeitschrift des statistischen Büreaus des Königlich Sächsischen Ministeriums des Innern* (1857).

[18] *The Theory of Political Economy* (London: Macmillan, 1871).

[19] "Considerazoni sui principi fondamentali dell'economia politica pura," *Giornale degli economisti* (May, 1892), pp. 389–420.

[20] "The Pure Theory of Utility Curves," *Economic Journal* (1913), pp. 483–513.

[21] "Sulla teoria del bilancio del consumatore," *Giornale degli economisti* (1915), pp. 1–26; English translation, "On the Theory of the Budget of the Consumer," in G. J. Stigler and K. E. Boulding (eds.), *Readings in Price Theory* (Homewood, Ill.: Irwin, 1952), pp. 27–56.

latter, Antonelli[22] (1886) was examining the construction of indifference curves from demand. His technique was to integrate a system of marginal rates of substitution derived from inverse demand functions, i.e., prices expressed in terms of quantities. For three or more commodities this requires an integrability condition which often is equivalent to the symmetry obtained by Slutsky above. Antonelli's work seems to have slipped by unnoticed until recently,[23] but the problem was independently discovered by Fisher (1892) and frequently discussed thereafter by Pareto. It is interesting that in the earlier Italian version of his *Manuale* (1906), Pareto's analysis for three or more commodities conspicuously ignores the integrability condition. This now-famous error was pointed out by Volterra[24] (1906) and acknowledged by Pareto several months later.[25] More recently, Samuelson[26] (1947) proposed the concept of revealed preference in an attempt to avoid mathematical integration; nevertheless Houthakker[27] (1950) still had to integrate a system of partial differential equations to solve the problem in that context. Uzawa[28] (1960) then did for the two-way relationship between utility and demand in terms of revealed preference what Slutsky had done for the classical approach forty-four years earlier, and Richter[29] (1966) finally succeeded in dispensing with Houthakker's integration altogether.

Because it is difficult to produce explicitly a given individual's utility function, the concept itself has come under serious question. Cassel[30] (1918) and Moore[31] (1929) wanted to do away with utility completely, the latter attempting to replace it with a statistical theory of demand. Moore's work resulted in statistical analyses not seen since King (1696), although

---

[22] *Teoria mathematica della economica politica* (Pisa, 1886); English translation, "On the Mathematical Theory of Political Economy," in J. S. Chipman et al. (eds.), *Studies in the Mathematical Foundations of Utility and Demand Theory* (New York: Harcourt, Brace & World, forthcoming).

[23] See P. A. Samuelson, "The Problem of Integrability in Utility Theory," *Economica* (1950), p. 355, n. 3.

[24] Review of Pareto's *Manuale, Giornale degli economisti*, v. 32 (1906), pp. 296–301; English translation, "Mathematical Economics and Professor Pareto's New Manual," in J. S. Chipman et al. (eds.), *Studies in the Mathematical Foundations of Utility and Demand Theory* (New York: Harcourt, Brace & World, forthcoming).

[25] "L'Ofelimita nei cicili non chiusi," *Giornale degli economisti*, v. 33 (1906), pp. 15–30; English translation, "Ophelimity in Non-closed Cycles," in J. S. Chipman et al. (eds.), *Studies in the Mathematical Foundations of Utility and Demand Theory* (New York: Harcourt, Brace & World, forthcoming).

[26] *Foundations of Economic Analysis* (Cambridge, Mass.: Harvard University Press, 1947).

[27] "Revealed Preference and the Utility Function," *Economica* (1950), pp. 159–174.

[28] "Preference and Rational Choice in the Theory of Consumption," in K. J. Arrow, S. Karlin, and P. Suppes (eds.), *Mathematical Methods in the Social Sciences* (Stanford, Calif.: Stanford University Press, 1960).

[29] "Revealed Preference Theory," *Econometrica* (1966), pp. 635–645.

[30] *Theoretische Sozialökonomie* (Leipzig: Scholl, 1918).

[31] *Synthetic Economics* (New York: Macmillan, 1929).

many economists involved in such studies; e.g., Schultz[32] (1938), did not share his view. An alternative approach suggested by Evans[33] (1930) and later taken up by Allen[34] (1932) and Georgescu-Roegen[35] (1936) was to build a theory of demand which did not rely on integrability conditions. Hence a utility function might not exist and so consumer decisions could not be based on its maximization. In place of utility their analyses focused on properties of nonintegrable marginal rates of substitution and "directions" of preference and antipreference.

For those willing to accept the utility hypothesis different problems arose. To identify the precise relationship between preference and ordinal utility, Wold[36] (1943–44) and Debreu[37] (1954) explored conditions on the former which permit its representation as a real-valued, continuous function. A similar problem had already been studied from a purely mathematical point of view by Eilenberg[38] (1941). Ichimura[39] (1951) was concerned with the impact of changes in an individual's preferences on his behavior. He showed that a particular kind of variation in the marginal rates of substitution between, say, commodity i and all other goods $j \neq i$ (with no alteration in the remaining marginal rates of substitution) changed demand for $j \neq i$ proportionately to the compensated cross-price derivative between them. In a somewhat different vein, economists have also noted that the demand for certain commodities exhibits special traits when combined into groups such as food and clothing. The issue has been approached in two distinct ways. Hicks[40] (1939) proved if prices of goods within any group always move in the same proportion, then an individual's demand for the group as a whole has properties identical to that for a single commodity. Notions of separability, introduced independently by Sono[41] (1945) and Leontief[42] (1947), attacked the problem in terms of tastes. Thus if an individual's preferences

[32] *Theory and Measurement of Demand* (Chicago: University of Chicago Press, 1938).

[33] *Mathematical Introduction to Economics* (New York: McGraw-Hill, 1930).

[34] "The Foundations of a Mathematical Theory of Exchange," *Economica* (1932), pp. 197–226.

[35] "The Pure Theory of Consumer's Behavior," *The Quarterly Journal of Economics* (1936), pp. 545–593.

[36] "A Synthesis of Pure Demand Analysis," *Skandinavisk Aktuarietidskrift* (1943), pp. 85–118, 221–263; (1944), pp. 69–120.

[37] "Representation of a Preference Ordering by a Numerical Function," in R. M. Thrall, C. H. Coombs, and R. L. Davis (eds.), *Decision Processes* (New York: Wiley, 1954).

[38] "Ordered Topological Spaces," *American Journal of Mathematics* (1941), pp. 39–45.

[39] "A Critical Note on the Definition of Related Goods," *Review of Economic Studies*, v. 18 (1950–51), pp. 179–183.

[40] *Value and Capital* (London: Oxford University Press, 1939).

[41] "The Effect of Price Changes on the Demand and Supply of Separable Goods," *Kokumin Keizar Zasski* (1945), pp. 1–51; English translation, *International Economic Review* (1961), pp. 239–271.

[42] "Introduction to a Theory of the Internal Structure of Functional Relationships," *Econometrica* (1947), pp. 361–373.

within a particular group do not depend on quantities of commodities outside it, his demand for that group often can be defined with similar properties regardless of price proportionality. Furthermore, in that case the consumer's decision-making process can be broken down into two steps: he may first decide how much to spend on the group itself and then determine the way expenditure is to be allocated within it.

During the same period alternative forms of the utility explanation of consumer behavior also were proposed. By substituting demand equations into their utility generator, Hotelling[43] (1932) defined indirect utility as a function of prices and income, and from it Roy[44] (1943) succeeded in deriving Slutsky's properties of demand. What Roy established was that demand could be expressed as a ratio of appropriate partial derivatives of the indirect utility function and hence the latter could legitimately serve as a basis for the theory of demand. Meanwhile Court[45] (1941) had demonstrated that maximizing utility with respect to commodities gives the same result as minimizing indirect utility with respect to prices and income, the identical budget constraint imposed in both instances. Still a third possible point of departure for demand theory is the expenditure or support function introduced by McKenzie[46] (1957). It is defined as the minimum expenditure necessary to achieve a given level of utility at specified prices and may be obtained by inversion of the indirect utility function. McKenzie showed that partial price derivatives of expenditure functions are demand functions and proceeded to establish the Slutsky properties from that relationship. Returning to the original direct utility model, Lancaster[47] (1966) has suggested focusing on characteristics of commodities along with commodities themselves. The idea, traceable to Hicks[48] (1956), is to maximize utility as a function of characteristics, subject to the budget constraint and a "technological" relation between characteristics and commodities. This approach, however, has not yet added any new restrictions on market behavior.

The thought that relationships may be defined between commodities seems to have intrigued economists for quite some time. Although distinctions between complements and substitutes were anticipated by Jevons (1871) in his discussion of "equivalent" commodities, Auspitz and Leiben[49] (1889)

---

[43] "Edgeworth's Taxation Paradox and the Nature of Demand and Supply Functions," *Journal of Political Economy* (1932), pp. 577–616.

[44] *De l'utilité, contribution à la théorie des choix* (Paris: Hermann, 1943).

[45] "Entrepreneurial and Consumer Demand Theories for Commodity Spectra," *Econometrica* (1941), pp. 135–162.

[46] "Demand Theory without a Utility Index," *Review of Economic Studies*, v. 24 (1956–57), pp. 185–189.

[47] "A New Approach to Consumer Theory," *The Journal of Political Economy* (1966), pp. 132–157.

[48] *A Revision of Demand Theory* (London: Oxford University Press, 1956).

[49] *Untersuchungen über die Theorie des Preises* (Leipzig: Duncker and Humblot, 1889).

provided the first formal analysis. Their approach, also attributed to Edge-worth[50] (1897) and Pareto[51] (1906), is stated in terms of signs of cross-partial derivatives of the utility function—two commodities are complements, independent, or substitutes according as the appropriate derivative is positive, zero or negative—and hence rests on a rigid interpretation of cardinality. The latter was avoided when Fisher (1892) and W. E. Johnson (1913) ex-pressed these notions as properties of indifference curves, and Hicks and Allen[52] (1934) as traits of demand. Thus Fisher called two goods perfect complements if the indifference curves between them consisted of two straight lines meeting at right angles. They were substitutes if the curves were nega-tively sloped straight lines. Johnson's definition depended on the rate of change of marginal rates of substitution: i and j are complements provided that increasing i increases the increment of i needed to compensate the consumer for a unit of j. Hicks and Allen referred to them as complements, independent, and substitutes according as the compensated cross-price derivative between them is negative, zero, or positive.

Because of their applications in empirical research and index number theory, particular kinds of utility functions have received special attention. Additivity and separability have been discussed above, and, like the former, quadratic utility (i.e., a utility function consisting of sums of terms such as $\alpha_i x_i$ and $\theta_{ij} x_i x_j$, where α_i and θ_{ij} are constants) also goes back to Gossen (1854). Additivity of the indirect utility function was introduced by Konus[53] (1939) and studied, along with direct additivity, by Houthakker[54] (1960). Bergson[55] (1936) considered linearly homogeneous utility functions—ones for which multiplication of all quantities of commodities by a constant multiplies utility by that constant. Bergson also explored the implications of simulta-neous additivity and homogeneity as did Samuelson[56] (1965) those of simul-taneous direct and indirect additivity. Klein and Rubin[57] (1947) showed that demand functions linear in price and income–price ratios are consistent with utility maximization. There are many interrelationships among these cases. For example, additivity is a special form of separability, and quadratic utility, homogeneous utility, and linear demand all imply linear Engel curves.

[50] "La teoria pura del monopolio," *Giornale degli economisti* (July, 1897), pp. 13–31; English translation, "The Pure Theory of Monopoly," in F. Y. Edgeworth, *Papers Related to Political Economy*, v. 1 (London: Macmillan, 1925).

[51] *Manuale di economia politica* (Milan: Società Editrice Libraria, 1906).

[52] "A Reconsideration of the Theory of Value," *Economica* (1934), pp. 52–76, 196–219.

[53] "On the Theory of Means," *Acta Universitatis Asiae Mediae*, Series Va, no. 24 (1939).

[54] "Additive Preferences," *Econometrica* (1960), pp. 244–257.

[55] "Real Income, Expenditure Proportionality and Frish's 'New Methods of Measur-ing Marginal Utility'," *Review of Economic Studies*, v. 4 (1936), pp. 33–52.

[56] "Using Full Duality to Show that Simultaneous Additive Direct and Indirect Utilities Implies Unitary Price Elasticity of Demand," *Econometrica* (1965), pp. 781–796.

[57] "A Constant-Utility Index of the Cost of Living," *Review of Economic Studies*, v. 15 (1947), pp. 84–87.

Analysis of the consumer under various environments of uncertainty seems to have stemmed from Bernoulli's (1738) discussion of the St. Petersburg paradox mentioned earlier. His solution stimulated an immense literature in mathematics which is of little relevance here. For economists, the next important step came two centuries later when, in different contexts, Allen and Bowley[58] (1935) and Georgescu-Roegen (1936) permitted random errors to disturb choice and preference patterns. The former were trying to explain variations in family expenditure in terms of stochastic perturbations of preferences, while the latter's interest lay in studying a consumer who is not entirely sure of his tastes. Subsequent developments focusing on still different aspects of uncertainty include von Neumann and Morgenstern's[59] (1944) analysis of conditions on preferences under which the utility of a gamble is the expected utility of the prizes it offers, Tobin's[60] (1958) derivation of the demand for speculative cash from choices among probability distributions, and Markowitz's[61] (1959) rules for optimal portfolio selection.

---

[58] *Family Expenditure: A Study of Its Variation* (London: Staples, 1935).
[59] *Theory of Games and Economic Behavior* (Princeton, N.J.: Princeton University Press, 1944).
[60] "Liquidity Preference as Behavior Towards Risk," *Review of Economic Studies*, v. 25 (1958), pp. 65–86.
[61] *Portfolio Selection* (New York: Wiley, 1959).

2

Foundations

It is quite reasonable to suppose that the characteristics of an individual's likes and dislikes determine the purchases he makes in the market. And so the theory of demand naturally begins with a description of consumer preferences. This chapter is primarily concerned with these so-called "foundations." It deals specifically with the conditions under which preferences may be represented by a numerical function and the way in which various properties of the former appear in the latter. The reason for such an undertaking is that using functions in place of preferences affords considerable mathematical convenience since all the rules and techniques for dealing with the former can then be applied. The study of consumer behavior thereby gains both depth and analytical simplification.

In what follows it is shown that preference orderings and their functional representations are two equivalent ways of describing the same thing. A knowledge of set theory is an essential prerequisite to understand the basic results. For those with limited experience in this field, the important concepts and theorems used below are discussed in Appendix A.

2.1 PREFERENCE ORDERINGS AND REPRESENTABILITY

Consider an economy with n commodities and let x_i vary over quantities of commodity i, where $i = 1, \ldots, n$. Bundles or baskets of commodities are then represented by vectors $x - (x_1, \ldots, x_n)$. The universe of discourse (commodity space) is the nonnegative orthant of Euclidean n-space $\bar{E} = \{x : x \geq 0\}$ with interior $E = \{x : x > 0\}$. [The term $x \geq y$ (or $x > y$) will always mean $x_i \geq y_i$ (or $x_i > y_i$) for each i.] A consumer's *preference ordering* is a binary relation $\gtrless$ defined on $\bar{E}$ which is reflexive and transitive.

Such an ordering immediately gives rise to two additional relations, $\overset{\circ}{>}$ and $\overset{\circ}{=}$, defined as follows. For all x' and x'' in $\bar{E}$,

(1) $x' \overset{\circ}{>} x''$ if and only if $x' \overset{\circ}{\geq} x''$ and $x'' \overline{\overset{\circ}{\geq}} x'$.

(2) $x' \overset{\circ}{=} x''$ if and only if $x' \overset{\circ}{\geq} x''$ and $x'' \overset{\circ}{\geq} x'$.

Here $\overline{\overset{\circ}{\geq}}$ denotes the complement of $\overset{\circ}{\geq}$. Clearly $\overset{\circ}{>}$ is irreflexive and transitive while $\overset{\circ}{=}$ is an equivalence relation. It is assumed that there is at least one pair of points x' and x'' in $\bar{E}$ for which $x' \overset{\circ}{>} x''$. The usual interpretations of $x' \overset{\circ}{>} x''$, $x' \overset{\circ}{=} x''$, and $x' \overset{\circ}{\geq} x''$ are, respectively, "x' is preferred to x''," "x' is indifferent to x''," and "x' is preferred or indifferent to x''."

A preference ordering is *weakly representable* whenever there exists a real-valued function u defined on $\bar{E}$ such that for any x' and x'', $x' \overset{\circ}{\geq} x''$ implies $u(x') \geq u(x'')$, and for at least one pair of points, $x' \overset{\circ}{>} x''$ implies $u(x') > u(x'')$. It is *representable* provided for all x' and x'',

(1) $x' \overset{\circ}{>} x''$ if and only if $u(x') > u(x'')$.

An equivalent definition of representability is

(2) $x' \overset{\circ}{\geq} x''$ if and only if $u(x') \geq u(x'')$.

In either case, u is called a *utility function* representing $\overset{\circ}{\geq}$. Note that any function u generates a preference ordering which it represents according to (1) or (2). Of course, the literary definition of utility as "anticipated satisfaction" can be thought of as a possible interpretation of the functional values of u when $\overset{\circ}{\geq}$ is representable.

Let T be a function of the scalar variable μ defined on the range of u. If T is *increasing* [i.e., $\mu_1 > \mu_2$ if and only if $T(\mu_1) > T(\mu_2)$], then $T(u)$ is called an *increasing transformation* of u. It is clear that u represents $\overset{\circ}{\geq}$ if and only if every increasing transformation of u also represents $\overset{\circ}{\geq}$.

The fundamental theorem asserting the existence of utility functions representing preference orderings is due to Cantor. It asserts that representability is possible whenever the set on which the ordering is defined is a chain containing a countable, order-dense subset (see Theorem A-2 in Appendix A). Since $\bar{E}$ does not satisfy this requirement, the problem is to construct an appropriate set which does. A technique suggested by Richter [11] is used below.

Theorem 2.1-1   *Every preference ordering is weakly representable.*

PROOF:

Let $\overset{\circ}{\geq}$ be reflexive and transitive. By Corollary A-5 (Appendix A), $\overset{\circ}{\geq}$ may be extended to a reflexive, transitive, and total relation, ρ, on $\bar{E}$. Let K be a countable subset of $\bar{E}$ such that $x^0 \overset{\circ}{>} z^0$ for some x^0 in $\bar{E}$ and z^0 in K. For any x' and x'' in $\bar{E}$, set $x' \rho^* x''$ if and only if either

(1) $x' \rho x''$ and $x'' \rho x'$, or

(2) x' and x'' are not in K and there is no y in K such that both $x' \rho y$ and $y \rho x''$ or both $x'' \rho y$ and $y \rho x'$.

It is not hard to show that ρ^* is an equivalence relation. Thus ρ^* partitions $\bar{E}$ into equivalence classes $[x]$.

The next thing to demonstrate is that for any two equivalence classes $[x]$ and $[z]$, either they are identical or all elements of one are in the same ρ-relation to all elements of the other. Thus suppose the contrary, i.e., $[x] \neq [z]$, and there exist x', x'' in $[x]$ but not in $[z]$ and z', z'' in $[z]$ but not in $[x]$ such that $x' \rho z'$ and $z'' \rho x'$. Now it is impossible to have both $x'' \rho x'$ and $z' \rho z''$, for otherwise all four points would be in both $[x]$ and $[z]$. On the other hand, if $x'' \bar{\rho} x'$ (recall $\bar{\rho}$ is the complement of ρ), then from (2), x' and x'' are not in K. Furthermore, $x' \rho z'$, $z' \rho z''$, and $z'' \rho x''$ imply, again by (2), that z' and z'' are not in K. A similar argument shows that none of these four points is in K if $z' \bar{\rho} z''$ or if both $x'' \bar{\rho} x'$ and $z' \bar{\rho} z''$. But since ρ is total, either $x' \rho z''$ or $z'' \rho x'$. In the former case, $x' \bar{\rho}^* z''$ and neither x' nor z'' is in K. By the negation of (2) there is a y in K such that $x' \rho y$ and $y \rho z''$. Hence $x' \rho y$ and $y \rho x''$, which is a contradiction. The case $z'' \rho x'$ is argued similarly.

The preceding paragraph legitimizes the following definition of $\bar{\rho}$: for any $[x]$ and $[z]$, $[x] \bar{\rho} [z]$ if and only if $x \rho z$. It follows that the set of all equivalence classes is a chain under $\bar{\rho}$ and $\{[y]: y$ is in $K\}$ is a countable, order-dense subset. By Theorem A-2 (Cantor) there exists a real-valued function u such that $[x] \bar{\rho} [z]$ if and only if $u([x]) \geq u([z])$. Define u on $\bar{E}$ by

$$u(x') = u([x]),$$

for all x' in $[x]$. Clearly, if $x \geqq z$, then $x \rho z$ and hence $u(x) \geq u(z)$. Furthermore, the choice of x^0 and z^0 ensures $u(x^0) > u(z^0)$. Therefore, $\geqq$ is weakly representable.

Q.E.D.

The converse of Theorem 2.1-1 certainly does not hold. There may exist distinct points x' and x'' in the same equivalence class such that $x' \geqq x''$ and these would be given the same utility value by u. Thus u may not reveal much about $\geqq$ since it possibly hides many "interesting" points by treating them identically. This is also the reason why u can represent preference orderings different from $\geqq$ and why weakly representable orderings are not necessarily representable. It is clear that the particular countable set chosen in the proof of Theorem 2.1-1 determines u and the class of all preference orderings it represents. To illustrate these points consider the so-called *lexicographic* case. With $n = 2$, let $x \geqq z$ if and only if either:

(1) $x_1 = z_1$ and $x_2 \geq z_2$, or

(2) $x_1 > z_1$.

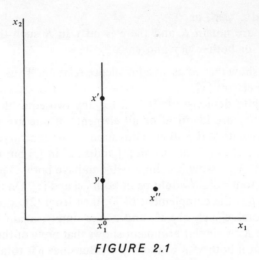

FIGURE 2.1

Thus $x' \gtrsim y$ and $x'' \gtrsim y$ in Figure 2.1. Now if K is the set of all points in $\bar{E}$ of the form $(x_1, 0)$, where x_1 is rational, then the utility function of Theorem 2.1-2 will assign to each point on the vertical line through, say, x_1^0 the same utility value. Even though $\gtrsim$ is weakly representable, it is not representable. For if it were, let x_2^0 and $\bar{x}_2$ be fixed with $x_2^0 < \bar{x}_2$. Then for each $x_1 \geq 0$ there must correspond one and only one open interval $(u(x_1, x_2^0), u(x_1, \bar{x}_2))$. But for $x_1' \neq x_1''$, these intervals are disjoint. Hence there is a $1:1$ correspondence between the real numbers and a set of disjoint, open intervals on the real line. This, however, is impossible,[1] so $\gtrsim$ cannot be representable.

To examine further the difference between weak representability and representability, consider the sets

$$L_{x^0}^> = \{x: x \gtrsim x^0\},$$

$$L_{x^0}^< = \{x: x^0 \gtrsim x\},$$

$$C_{x^0}^> = \{x: u(x) > u(x^0)\},$$

$$C_{x^0}^< = \{x: u(x^0) > u(x)\},$$

for x^0 and x in $\bar{E}$. Sets such as $C_{x^0}^{\geq}$, $C_{x^0}^{=}$, and $L_{x^0}^{=}$ can be defined similarly. It is clear that if $\gtrsim$ is weakly representable, then $L_{x^0}^>$ and $L_{x^0}^<$ are respective subsets of $C_{x^0}^>$ and $C_{x^0}^<$. The sets are respectively equal if and only if $\gtrsim$ is

---

[1] Let I be a set of disjoint, open intervals. Then every element of I contains a rational point not contained in any other element. Since the set of rationals is countable, I must be, too. But the reals are not countable and cannot be placed in a $1:1$ correspondence with any countable set. See Rudin [13, ch. 2].

representable. These conclusions are true for any u representing $\gtreqqless$. When $C_{x^0}^{=} = L_{x^0}^{=}$ and this set forms a surface, it is called the *indifference surface* through x^0. In this case $C_{x^0}^{\geq}$ is frequently referred to as the *upper contour set* of u with respect to x^0. The collection of all indifference surfaces in $\bar{E}$ is the *indifference map*.

The relation $\gtreqqless$ is *increasing* if for all x' and x'' in $\bar{E}$, $x' > x''$ implies $x' \gtreqqless x''$. It is now possible to give sufficient conditions for representability. The following proof is due to Rader [10].

Theorem 2.1-2 *Let $\gtreqqless$ be a total preference ordering on $\bar{E}$. If $L_{x^0}^{<}$ is open relative to $\bar{E}$ for every x^0, then $\gtreqqless$ is representable.*

PROOF:

There exists a countable collection of relatively open sets $\{G_k\}$, where $k = 1, 2, \ldots$, such that any relatively open subset of $\bar{E}$ is the union of all the G_k it contains [13, p. 28]. In particular this is true for each $L_{x^0}^{<}$. Let $N(x^0)$ be the set of all integers k for which G_k is contained in $L_{x^0}^{<}$. Define

$$u(x^0) = \sum_{k \text{ in } N(x^0)} (\tfrac{1}{2})^k,$$

for all x^0 in E. If x^0 is on the boundary of $\bar{E}$ and $L_{x^0}^{<}$ is not open, then since $\gtreqqless$ is total, $x \gtreqqless x^0$ for every x in E. In this case set $u(x^0) = 0$. Thus for any x' and x'', if $x' \gtreqqless x''$, then $L_{x''}^{<}$ is contained in $L_{x'}^{<}$, so $u(x') \geq u(x'')$. The converse assertion is equally trivial and therefore $\gtreqqless$ is representable.

Q.E.D.

Note that the u of Theorem 2.1-2 can define only one preference ordering, namely, that which it represents. Also the sufficient conditions stated in this result are not necessary, as the example in Figure 2.2 shows. In this case x^0 lies on the indifference curve labeled 1. Curves like 2 and 3 would be tangent to 1 at x^0 if they were defined there, but they are not. Each has a "hole" at this point. The remaining curves are of the ordinary variety. Such an indifference map is derived from a utility function which has a discontinuity at x^0. (A utility function can be constructed along the lines suggested in the proof of Theorem 2.2-2 in the next section.) It also may be used to define a preference ordering which is total on $\bar{E}$. However, $L_{x'}^{<}$ contains the point x^0 and cannot, therefore, be open. Finally, Theorem 2.1-2 remains valid if the $L_x^{>}$ are assumed open in place of the $L_x^{<}$. That the conditions of this altered theorem are also not necessary is demonstrated by placing x^0 on the "upper" indifference curve in Figure 2.2 and leaving the "lower" ones with holes. The example in Figure 2.3 is also a counterexample to this proposition.

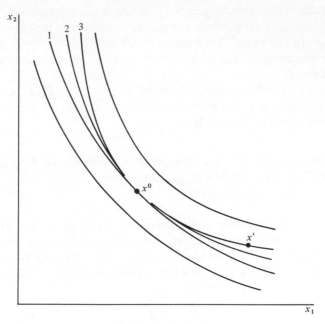

FIGURE 2.2

2.2 CONTINUOUS REPRESENTABILITY

A preference ordering is said to be *continuously representable* whenever there exists a continuous utility function representing it. An example of Uzawa's [16] demonstrates that the hypotheses of Theorem 2.1-2 are not strong enough to guarantee the existence of a continuous function. Suppose $n = 2$ and

$$u(x) = \begin{cases} \left[\sqrt{2} - \dfrac{\sqrt{2} - \sqrt{1 + x_2}}{\sqrt{x_1}}\right]^2, & \text{if } x_1 \geq 1, x_2 < 1, \\ x_1(1 + x_2), & \text{otherwise.} \end{cases}$$

The indifference map corresponding to this function is pictured in Figure 2.3. It is clear that the preference ordering defined by u implies that $\geqq$ is total and $L_x^<$ is open for all x in $\bar{E}$. But if, say, $x^0 = (1, 2)$, then $L_{x^0}^> = C_{x^0}^>$ is not open. Hence the inverse image under u of the open interval $(u(x^0), \infty)$ is not open. Since this is true for any representation, the preference ordering cannot be continuously representable.

It is also true that $\geqq$ need not be continuously representable if all $L_x^>$ are open but some of the $L_x^<$ are not. This is illustrated by the example in

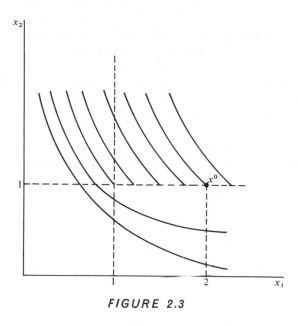

FIGURE 2.3

Figure 2.2. Hence it is necessary that both $L_x^>$ and $L_x^<$ be open for every x. This suggests the following definition due to Eilenberg [6]: the relation $\geqslant$ is said to be *continuous* on $\bar{E}$ provided that for all x in $\bar{E}$, both $L_x^>$ and $L_x^<$ are open in $\bar{E}$. Continuity of $\geqslant$ has a simple consequence needed below.

Lemma 2.2-1 *Suppose $\geqslant$ is total and continuous on $\bar{E}$. Then for any x', x'', and x''' such that $x' \geqslant x''$ and $x'' \geqslant x'''$, there exists a number θ between 0 and 1 such that $\theta x' + (1 - \theta)x''' \ominus x''$.*

PROOF:

Let $x' \geqslant x''$ and $x'' \geqslant x'''$. Then x' is in $L_{x''}^>$ and x''' is in $L_{x''}^<$. But $L_{x''}^>$ and $L_{x''}^<$ are disjoint open sets and hence there must be a point on the line segment connecting them, $\theta x' + (1 - \theta)x''$, where $0 < \theta < 1$, which is not contained in either. Since $\geqslant$ is total, the conclusion follows.

Q.E.D.

Continuity of $\geqslant$ is, in fact, equivalent to continuous representability. But as suggested by Wold [17], the proof can be simplified considerably if it is further assumed that $\geqslant$ is increasing. Theorem 2.2-2 takes his approach. The more general argument may be found in Debreu [4] and Rader [10].

Theorem 2.2-2 *Let $\geqslant$ be a total preference ordering on $\bar{E}$ such that $\geqslant$ is increasing. Then $\geqslant$ is continuously representable if and only if it is continuous.*

PROOF:

If $\geqq$ is continuously representable, then it is obviously continuous. If $\geqq$ is continuous, then by Theorem 2.1-2, it is representable and hence for any x and any utility representation, $C_x^{\geqq} = L_x^{\geqq}$ and $C_x^{\leqq} = L_x^{\leqq}$ are both open. Now let $[x]$ denote the equivalence classes defined by $\ominus$, and Q the 45° ray from the origin into E, $Q = \{x: x_i = x_1$ for $i = 1,\dots, n-1$, and x in $\bar{E}\}$. The next step is to show that for any x in $\bar{E}$, $[x] \cap Q$ contains exactly one point. Clearly $[x] \cap Q$ cannot contain more than one point since $\geqq$ is increasing. Now consider any x in $\bar{E}$. If $[x]$ contains the origin there is nothing to prove. Otherwise choose q' and q'' in Q such that

$$q_1' < \min_i x_i,$$

$$q_1'' > \max_i x_i.$$

This is illustrated in Figure 2.4. Then $q'' > x > q'$, so $q'' \ominus x$ and $x \ominus q'$. By Lemma 2.2-1, there is a point q^0 in Q such that q^0 is in $[x]$.

Define

$$u(x) = q_n,$$

where q is the unique point in $[x] \cap Q$. It is easy to verify that u represents $\geqq$. To prove that u is continuous, first note that u is continuous on Q. Hence inverse images of intervals of the form $(-\infty, \alpha)$ and (α, ∞) must be, respectively, $\{q: q < q^0\}$ and $\{q: q > q^0\}$ for some q^0 in Q. Therefore, the inverse images of these intervals under u must be $C_{q^0}^{\leqq}$ and $C_{q^0}^{\geqq}$, both of which are assumed open in $\bar{E}$. Since any open interval (α, β) be written as $(-\infty, \beta) \cap$

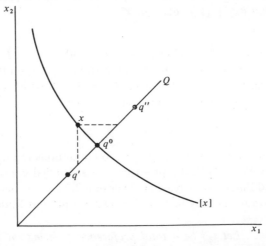

FIGURE 2.4

(α, ∞) and since the intersection of open sets is open, it follows that the inverse images of open intervals under u are open in $\bar{E}$. Therefore, u is continuous.

Q.E.D.

It is possible to prove the results of Sections 2.1 and 2.2 with weaker topological restrictions on the commodity space, but this will not be investigated here. The interested reader is referred to Debreu [4], Chipman [3], and Rader [10].

With rare but notable exceptions, most of demand analysis requires assumptions which, among other things, imply an increasing $\ominus$ and continuous representability, and it is from the properties of an associated utility function that behavior of the "rational" man has been traditionally deduced. Of course, different utility properties imply different kinds of behavior. The remainder of this chapter is concerned with the relationship between these properties and those of $\ominus$. It is assumed that $\ominus$ is continuously representable and $\ominus$ is increasing.

2.3 PROPERTIES OF PREFERENCE ORDERINGS AND REPRESENTATIONS

Continuity having been the subject matter of the preceding section and separability being reserved for the one that follows, this section is concerned with somewhat simpler properties of preference orderings and representations. The notion of an increasing relation has already been introduced in Section 2.1. In addition, the ordering $\ominus$ is said to be

(1) *convex* if for any x' and x'' in $\bar{E}$ and any θ where $0 \le \theta \le 1$, $x' \ominus x''$ implies $\theta x' + (1 - \theta)x'' \ominus x'$.

(2) *strictly convex* if for any distinct x' and x'' in E and any θ where $0 < \theta < 1$, $x' \ominus x''$ implies $\theta x' + (1 - \theta)x'' \ominus x'$.

(3) *homothetic* if for any x' and x'' in $\bar{E}$, $x' \ominus x''$ implies $\alpha x' \ominus \alpha x''$ for any real number $\alpha \ge 0$.

(4) *quasi-linear with respect to x_n* if for any x' and x'' in $\bar{E}$, $x' \ominus x''$ implies $(x'_{(n)}, x'_n + \alpha) \ominus (x''_{(n)}, x''_n + \alpha)$ for any α such that $x'_n + \alpha \ge 0$ and $x''_n + \alpha \ge 0$, where $x_{(n)} = (x_1, \ldots, x_{n-1})$.

(5) *linear* if for any x' and x'' in $\bar{E}$, $x' \ominus x''$ implies $\alpha x' + \beta x \ominus \alpha x'' + \beta x$ for any x in $\bar{E}$ and any real $\alpha > 0$ and $\beta > 0$.

The corresponding properties of utility representations are defined in the usual manner. Thus u will be called

(1) *increasing* if for any x' and x'' in $\bar{E}$, $x' > x''$ implies $u(x') > u(x'')$.

(2) *quasi-concave* if for any x' and x'' in $\bar{E}$ and any θ where $0 \le \theta \le 1$, $u(x') = u(x'')$ implies $u(\theta x' + (1 - \theta)x'') \ge u(x')$.

(3) *strictly quasi-concave* if for any distinct x' and x'' in E and any θ where $0 < \theta < 1$, $u(x') = u(x'')$ implies $u(\theta x' + (1 - \theta)x'') > u(x')$.

(4) *linearly homogeneous* if $u(\alpha x) = \alpha u(x)$ for all x in $\bar{E}$ and any real $\alpha > 0$.

(5) *quasi-linear with respect to x_n* if there exists a function η and constant $\delta \geq 0$ such that $u(x) = \eta(x_{(n)}) + \delta x_n$ on $\bar{E}$.

(6) *linear* if $u(\alpha x' + \beta x'') = \alpha u(x') + \beta u(x'')$ for all x' and x'' in $\bar{E}$ and any real $\alpha > 0$ and $\beta > 0$.

Concave and strictly concave functions are defined in the Appendix (Section B.1).

When $\gtreqless$ is representable, it is obvious that increasingness of $\gtrdot$ and convexity and strict convexity of $\gtreqless$ are respectively equivalent to increasingness, quasi-concavity, and strict quasi-concavity of all representations. Convexity of $\gtreqless$ is also equivalent to $L_x^{\gtreqless} = C_x^{\gtreqless}$ being convex sets[2] for every x. With regard to representations, note that linear functions are concave. If u is concave, then it is quasi-concave, but the converse is not true [counterexample: $u(x_1, x_2) = (x_1 x_2)^2$]. On the other hand, if u is quasi-concave but not concave, sometimes there may exist an increasing transformation of u which is concave [in the above example take $T(\mu) = \mu^{1/4}$]. The discussion in Section B.7, however, shows that this is not true in general.

Homotheticity and linearity of $\gtreqless$ are now related to homogeneity and linearity of its representations, respectively. The proof of the former uses the function, d, which assigns to each x its distance from the origin:

$$(2.3\text{-}1) \qquad\qquad d(x) = \sqrt{\sum_{i=1}^{n} x_i^2}.$$

Note that d is linearly homogeneous.

Theorem 2.3-2   *Let $\gtreqless$ be continuously representable and $\gtrdot$ increasing. Then $\gtreqless$ is homothetic if and only if there exists a linearly homogeneous representation of it.*

PROOF:

If u is a linearly homogeneous representation and $u(x') = u(x'')$, then $u(\gamma x') = u(\gamma x'')$ for any $\gamma \geq 0$. It follows that $\gtreqless$ is homothetic.

If $\gtreqless$ is homothetic, consider any ray q from the origin into E. Since $\gtreqless$ is continuously representable and $\gtrdot$ is increasing, for any x in $\bar{E}$ there is a unique q in Q such that $x \ominus q$. For this x define the representation u by

$$u(x) = d(q),$$

[2] Convex sets are defined in Section B.1.

Library
I.U.P.
Indiana, Pa.

330.1 K159ω
c. 1

where d is given by (2.3-1). Then, using the homotheticity of $\succeq$, for any $\alpha > 0$,

$$
\begin{aligned}
u(\alpha x) &= d(\alpha q) \\
&= \alpha d(q) \\
&= \alpha u(x),
\end{aligned}
$$

so u is linearly homogeneous.

Q.E.D.

Let $E^* = \{(x_{(n)}, 0): x_{(n)} > 0\}$, where $x_{(n)} = (x_1, \ldots, x_{n-1})$. Write $Q_k = \{x: x = (1/k, \ldots, 1/k, x_n)$ and $x_n \geq 0\}$ for $k = 1, 2, \ldots$. The Q_k represent lines in space perpendicular to E^* and parallel to the x_n-axis. Denote elements of Q_k by $q^k = (q_1^k, \ldots, q_n^k)$ and set $\bar{q}^k = (1/k, \ldots, 1/k, 0)$.

Theorem 2.3-3 *Let $\succeq$ be continuously representable and $\succ$ increasing. Then $\succeq$ is quasi-linear with respect to $x_{(n)}$ if and only if there exists a representation which is also quasi-linear with respect to $x_{(n)}$.*

PROOF:

It is clear that if a quasi-linear representation exists, $\succeq$ is also quasi-linear.

Conversely, if $\succeq$ is quasi-linear, all indifference surfaces intersect E^*. Furthermore, if $x \geq q^k$ for some k and q^k in Q_k, then the indifference surface $C_x^=$ intersects uniquely each Q_i where $i \geq k$. Evidently every indifference surface intersects infinitely many Q_k. This and the following argument are illustrated in Figure 2.5.

To construct a quasi-linear representation, if $x \geq q^1$ for some q^1, define

$$ u(x) = q_n^{*1}, $$

where q_n^{*1} is the last component of the unique intersection point of $C_x^=$ and Q_1. Of course, $u(\bar{q}^1) = 0$.

Now $C_{\bar{q}^1}^=$ intersects Q_2 at, say, $\tilde{q}^2$. All indifference surfaces intersecting Q_2 above $\tilde{q}^1$ have been assigned utility values and so it is only necessary to consider those intersecting below. Thus for x not in $C_{\bar{q}^1}^\geq$ and $x \geq q^2$, where q^2 is in Q_2, define

$$ u(x) = q_n^{*2} - \tilde{q}_n^2, $$

where q_n^{*2} is the last component of the intersection point of $C_x^=$ and Q_2. Note $u(\tilde{q}^2) = 0$ and $u(\bar{q}^2) = -\tilde{q}_n^2$.

Continuing in this manner for each k and similarly chosen x, q^{*k} and $\tilde{q}^i$, set

$$ u(x) = q_n^{*k} - \sum_{i=2}^{k} \tilde{q}_n^i. $$

Then u is defined on E and, as in Theorem 2.2-2, is continuous. It may be continuously extended to $\bar{E}$. Clearly u represents $\succeq$.

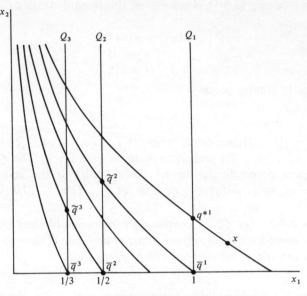

FIGURE 2.5

It remains to show that u is quasi-linear with respect to x_n. Consider any x in $\bar{E}$. Then $u(x) = \mu$, where μ is chosen according to the above specifications. But from the quasi-linearity of $\gtreqqless$,

$$u(x_{(n)}, x_n + t) = \mu + t$$

for all t such that $(x_{(n)}, x_n + t)$ is in $\bar{E}$. The quasi-linear form of u is therefore clear.

Q.E.D.

Theorem 2.3-4 *Let $\gtreqqless$ be continuously representable and $\gtrdot$ increasing. Then $\gtreqqless$ is linear if and only if there exists a linear representation of it.*

PROOF:

If u is a linear representation and $u(x') = u(x'')$, then for any positive α and β and any x in $\bar{E}$,

$$u(\alpha x' + \beta x) = u(\alpha x'' + \beta x).$$

Hence $\gtreqqless$ is linear.

If $\gtreqqless$ is linear, then it is clearly homothetic and indifference surfaces are hyperplanes whose normals have positive direction cosines. But homotheticity implies that the indifference surfaces are all parallel. Hence there is a ray Q from the origin into E which is perpendicular to each of them. Let q^0 be a positive vector in Q. For any x in $\bar{E}$ define the representation

$$u(x) = q^0 \cdot q,$$

where q is the unique point in Q such that $x \ominus q$ and the dot denotes "inner product."[3] Since x and q lie on the same hyperplane, $x - q$ and q^0 are orthogonal. Hence

$$q^0 \cdot x - q^0 \cdot q = q^0 \cdot (x - q) = 0,$$

so

$$u(x) = q^0 \cdot x.$$

Therefore, u is linear.

Q.E.D.

2.4 SEPARABILITY

Because the discussion of separability presented below requires considerable notational machinery which has not yet been introduced, it has been avoided until now. The concepts analyzed here have also been studied by Leontief [8], Sono [14], and Strotz [15]. Previous assumptions that $\ominus$ is continuously representable and $\oslash$ is increasing are continued.

The first step is to partition the n commodities into m mutually exclusive and exhaustive subsets. Let this partition be

$$N_1 = \{1, \ldots, k_1\},$$
$$\vdots$$
$$N_i = \{k_{i-1} + 1, \ldots, k_i\},$$
$$\vdots$$
$$N_\pi = \{k_{m-1} + 1, \ldots, n\},$$

where $\pi > 1$. Next split up the vectors x and commodity space $\bar{E}$ correspondingly by letting

$$x_{\bar{i}} = (x_{k_{i-1}+1}, \ldots, x_{k_i}),$$
$$\bar{E}^i = \{x_{\bar{i}}: x_{\bar{i}} \geq 0\}.$$

Thus $x = (x_{\bar{1}}, \ldots, x_{\bar{\pi}})$ and $\bar{E}$ is the cartesian product $\bar{E}^1 \times \cdots \times \bar{E}^\pi$. Finally, it is necessary to define,

$$x_{(\bar{i})} = (x_{\bar{1}}, \ldots, x_{\overline{i-1}}, x_{\overline{i+1}}, \ldots, x_{\bar{\pi}}),$$
$$\bar{E}^{(i)} - \bar{E}^1 \times \cdots \times \bar{E}^{i-1} \times \bar{E}^{i+1} \times \cdots \times \bar{E}^\pi.$$

The vector $(x_{\bar{i}}, x_{(\bar{i})})$ for any i will be thought of as x even though the order of appearance of the x_j's are different.

---

[3] That is, $q^0 \cdot q = \sum_{i=1}^{n} q_i^0 q_i$.

Now the preference ordering $\geqq$ induces an ordering on $\bar{E}^i$ which in general depends on points of $\bar{E}^{(i)}$. If $x_{(i)}^0$ is such a point, then the induced ordering, written $\geqq_{x_{(i)}^0}$, is defined by

$$x_{\bar{i}}' \underset{x_{(i)}^0}{\geqq} x_{\bar{i}}'' \text{ if and only if } (x_{\bar{i}}', x_{(i)}^0) \geqq (x_{\bar{i}}'', x_{(i)}^0),$$

for any $x_{\bar{i}}'$ and $x_{\bar{i}}''$ in $\bar{E}^i$. With the analogous concept of conditional probability in mind, $\geqq_{x_{(i)}}$ may be referred to as the *conditional ordering* on $\bar{E}^i$ given $x_{(i)}$. All forms of separability considered here are based on the notion of conditional orderings. Thus $\geqq$ is called

(1) *weakly separable* with respect to the partition $\{N_1, \ldots, N_\pi\}$ if for every $i = 1, \ldots, \pi, x_{\bar{i}}' \underset{x_{(i)}^0}{\geqq} x_{\bar{i}}''$ implies $x_{\bar{i}}' \underset{x_{(i)}}{\geqq} x_{\bar{i}}''$ for any $x_{(i)}^0$ and $x_{(i)}$ in $\bar{E}^{(i)}$.

(2) *strongly separable* with respect to $\{N_1, \ldots, N_\pi\}$ if it is weakly separable with respect to $\{N_1, \ldots, N_\pi\}$ and each of the partitions consisting of all possible unions of $N_1, \ldots, N_\pi$ except $\{1, \ldots, n\}$ itself.

(3) *additive* if it is strongly separable with respect to the pointwise partition $\{\{1\}, \ldots, \{n\}\}$.

Note the analogy between separability and independence in probability theory.

A continuous utility function u is said to be

(1) *weakly separable* with respect to $\{N_1, \ldots, N_\pi\}$ if there exist continuous functions $V, v^1, \ldots, v^\pi$ such that for all x in $\bar{E}$,

$$u(x) = V(v^1(x_{\bar{1}}), \ldots, v^\pi(x_{\bar{\pi}})).$$

(2) *strongly separable* with respect to $\{N_1, \ldots, N_\pi\}$ if there exist continuous functions $V, v^1, \ldots, v^\pi$ such that for all x in $\bar{E}$,

$$u(x) = V\left(\sum_{i=1}^{\pi} v^i(x_{\bar{i}})\right).$$

(3) *additive* if there exist continuous functions $v^1, \ldots, v^n$ such that for all x in $\bar{E}$,

$$u(x) = \sum_{i=1}^{n} v^i(x_i).$$

These definitions have the peculiar property that although there is no difference between weakly and strongly separable preference orderings when $\pi = 2$, weakly separable representations still may not be strongly separable. This fact is reflected in Theorem 2.4-2 and Corollary 2.4-3, which demonstrate equivalence for $\pi > 2$ only. Such an approach, then, leads to a finer distinction between separable representations than between separable orderings. A similar phenomenon occurs when considering separability in terms of demand functions (Chapter 5).

Theorem 2.4-1 *Let $\gtrsim$ be continuously representable and $\gtrsim$ increasing. Then $\gtrsim$ is weakly separable if and only if every continuous representation is also.*

PROOF:

If u is a weakly separable representation of $\gtrsim$, then

$$x'_{\bar{1}} \underset{x_{(\bar{1})}}{\gtrsim} x''_{\bar{1}} \quad \text{if and only if} \quad v^i(x'_{\bar{1}}) \geq v^i(x''_{\bar{1}}),$$

and the conditional ordering does not depend on $x_{(\bar{1})}$. Therefore, $\gtrsim$ is weakly separable.

If $\gtrsim$ is weakly separable, then $\gtrsim_{x_{(\bar{1})}}$ is a preference ordering on $\bar{E}^i$ which is independent of $x_{(\bar{1})}$ and inherits all the properties of $\gtrsim$. By Theorem 2.2-2, there exists a continuous function v^i defined on $\bar{E}^i$ representing it. Write

$$z_i = v^i(x_{\bar{1}}), \quad i = 1, \ldots, \pi.$$

Let u be any continuous representation of $\gtrsim$. Define V by the equation

$$u(x) = V(v^1(x_{\bar{1}}), \ldots, v^{\pi}(x_{\bar{\pi}})).$$

Since for each $z = (z_1, \ldots, z_n)$ there is a unique collection of sets of the form $\{x_{\bar{1}} \colon v^i(x_{\bar{1}}) > z_i\}$, it is easy to show that V is continuous.

Q.E.D.

Note in the preceding theorem that if V were defined by, say, $u(x) = V(v^1(x_{\bar{1}}) + \cdots + v^{\pi}(x_{\bar{\pi}}))$, then the collection of sets $\{x_{\bar{1}} \colon v^i(x_{\bar{1}}) > z_i\}$ associated with $z_1 + \cdots + z_{\pi}$ is not unique. Hence the continuity of V need not follow. A different method of proof is therefore needed to demonstrate the corresponding relationship (originally proved by Debreu [5]) between strongly separable preference orderings and their representations. As a preliminary step observe that since, in Theorem 2.4-1, u and the v^i are increasing, V as a function of z is also.

Theorem 2.4-2 *Let $\gtrsim$ be continuously representable and $\gtrsim$ increasing. Suppose $\pi > 2$. Then $\gtrsim$ is strongly separable if and only if every continuous representation is also.*

PROOF:

If u is a strongly separable representation, then repeated applications of Theorem 2.4-1 show that $\gtrsim$ is also strongly separable.

If $\geqslant$ is strongly separable, consider first the case $\pi = 3$. Again by repeated applications of Theorem 2.4-1, there exist continuous, increasing functions V^i and v^{ij} such that for all x in $\bar{E}$,

$$u(x) = \begin{cases} V^1(v^{11}(x_{\bar{1}}),\ v^{12}(x_{\bar{2}},\ x_{\bar{3}})), \\ V^2(v^{21}(x_{\bar{2}}),\ v^{22}(x_{\bar{1}},\ x_{\bar{3}})), \\ V^3(v^{31}(x_{\bar{3}}),\ v^{32}(x_{\bar{1}},\ x_{\bar{2}})), \end{cases}$$

and continuous, increasing functions v^1 and v^3 such that

$$v^{12} = v^1(v^{21},\ v^{31}),$$

$$v^{32} = v^3(v^{11},\ v^{21}).$$

Letting $z_i = v^{i1}(x_{\bar{i}})$ this becomes

$$u(x) = \begin{cases} V^1(z_1,\ v^1(z_2,\ z_3)), \\ V^3(z_3,\ v^3(z_1,\ z_2)). \end{cases}$$

It follows from the general theory of solutions of functional equations [1, p. 312 (Corollary 1)] that there exist continuous increasing functions R, r^1, r^2, and r^3 such that

$$u(x) = R\left(\sum_{i=1}^{3} r^i(z_i) \right).$$

The proof concludes with an induction argument on π. Suppose the result valid for $\pi - 1$ and consider the case $N_1, \ldots, N_\pi$. Then there exist continuous, increasing functions R^i and r^{ij} such that

$$u(x) = \begin{cases} R^1\left(r^{10}(z_1,\ z_2) + \sum_{j=3}^{\pi} r^{1j}(z_j) \right), \\ R^2\left(r^{20}(z_{\pi-1},\ z_\pi) + \sum_{j=1}^{\pi-2} r^{2j}(z_j) \right). \end{cases}$$

Holding z_j for $j \neq 1,\ 2$ fixed, it follows that r^{10} is an increasing transformation of $r^{21} + r^{22}$. But since R^1 is also increasing, it is possible to find a continuous, increasing R such that

$$u(x) = \left(Rr^{21}(z_1) + r^{22}(z_2) + \sum_{j=3}^{\pi} r^{1j}(z_j) \right).$$

Q.E.D.

The relationship between the two concepts of additivity is a trivial corollary of Theorem 2.4-2. Its proof is omitted.

Corollary 2.4-3 *Let* $\gtrless$ *be continuously representable,* $\gtrless$ *increasing, and* $n > 2$. *Then* $\gtrless$ *is additive if and only if there exists a continuous, additive representation of it.*

This section concludes with a discussion of a special class of utility representations due to Bergson [2]. Recall that if u is additive it may be written in the form $u(x) = \sum_{i=1}^{n} v^i(x_i)$. Denote the first and second derivatives of u and v^i with respect to the ith variable (when they exist) by, respectively, u_i, u_{ii}, v^i_i, and v^i_{ii}. The next theorem is proved only for the case in which the representations required for the proof exist as twice continuously differentiable functions.

Theorem 2.4-4 *Let* $\gtrless$ *be continuously representable, convex, and* $\gtrless$ *increasing. Then* $\gtrless$ *is additive and homothetic if and only if there exists a real number* $b \leq 1$ *and a representation* u *such that*

$$(2.4\text{-}5) \qquad u(x) = \begin{cases} \displaystyle\sum_{i=1}^{n} \alpha_i x_i^b + \gamma_i, & \text{if } b \neq 0, \\ \displaystyle\sum_{i=1}^{n} \alpha_i (\log x_i) + \gamma_i, & \text{if } b = 0, \end{cases}$$

where the α_i *and* γ_i *are constants,* $b\alpha_i > 0$ *if* $b \neq 0$, *and* $\alpha_i > 0$ *if* $b = 0$. *If* $\gtrless$ *is strictly convex, then* $b < 1$.

PROOF:

If $\gtrless$ is additive and homothetic, then by Theorem 2.3-2 and Corollary 2.4-3 there exists a representation of the form $u(x) = \sum_{i=1}^{n} v^i(x_i)$ which is also an increasing transformation of a linearly homogeneous representation. It follows that for all $\zeta > 0$,

$$\frac{v^i_i(\zeta x_i)}{v^j_j(\zeta x_j)} = \frac{v^i_i(x_i)}{v^j_j(x_j)},$$

for any i and j. Differentiating with respect to ζ, noting that the derivative of the right-hand side is zero, and setting $\zeta = 1$ yields

$$\frac{v^i_{ii}(x_i)}{v^i_i(x_i)} x_i = \frac{v^j_{jj}(x_j)}{v^j_j(x_j)} x_j,$$

for all $x_i > 0$ and $x_j > 0$. Hence there exists a constant b such that

$$(2.4\text{-}6) \qquad \frac{u^i_{ii}(x)}{u^i_i(x)} x_i = \frac{v^i_{ii}(x_i)}{v^i_i(x_i)} x_i = b - 1$$

on E. If $\gtrless$ is strictly convex, then so are indifference surfaces. By differentiating (3.1-8) and applying Theorem B.5-5, $v^i_{ii}(x_i) < 0$ on some open interval of the positive real line. But v^i is increasing on that interval and hence

$v_i^i(x) > 0$ for some x contained in it (Lemma B.2-1). Therefore, $b - 1 < 0$ or $b < 1$. If $\gtreqless$ is only convex, a similar argument shows $b \leq 1$.

Now write $z_i = \log u_i^i(x)$ and $y_i = \log x_i$. Then (2.4-6) becomes the differential equation

$$\frac{dz_i}{dy_i} = b - 1,$$

whose unique solution is

$$z_i = (b - 1)y_i + \beta_i,$$

where β_i is an arbitrary constant. Therefore,

$$u_i^i(x) = \beta_i' x_i^{b-1},$$

where β_i' is another constant. But the unique solution of this differential equation is

$$u^i(x) = \begin{cases} \alpha_i x_i^b + \gamma_i, & \text{if } b \neq 0, \\ \alpha_i(\log x_i) + \gamma_i, & \text{if } b = 0, \end{cases}$$

where γ_i is arbitrary and

$$\alpha_i = \begin{cases} \dfrac{\beta_i'}{b}, & \text{if } b \neq 0, \\ \beta_i', & \text{if } b = 0. \end{cases}$$

Since $\gtreqless$ is increasing, $b\alpha_i > 0$ for $b \neq 0$ and $\alpha_i > 0$ otherwise. This proves (2.4-5).

The converse assertion is trivial.

Q.E.D.

The collection of all preference orderings representable by functions of the form of (2.4-5) is referred to as the *Bergson class*. The representations are *Bergson utility functions*. Note that linearity is the special case in which $b = 1$.

2.5 CLASSICAL HYPOTHESES

The purpose of this section is to discuss briefly some of the more important assumptions made by the classical economists concerning the nature of utility representations. These hypotheses are placed in historical perspective in the survey of Section 1.2.

One assumption, additivity, has already been considered in the previous section. A second, constancy of the marginal utility of income, can take at least two forms: (1) constancy with respect to all prices but not income, and

(2) constancy with respect to income and all prices but one. In Chapter 5 the former is shown to be equivalent to linear homogeneity of u and the latter to quasi-linearity. Hence Theorems 2.3-2 and 2.3-3 apply. Diminishing marginal utility is a third assumption, which frequently appears as

$$(2.5\text{-}1) \qquad u_{ii}(x) < 0, \quad i = 1, \ldots, n,$$

for all x in E. It is not necessary to investigate the implications of this restriction with respect to preference orderings, but it is interesting to note that, in general, diminishing marginal utility does not imply strict quasi-concavity [counterexample: $u(x_1, x_2) = \sqrt{x_1 + x_2}$]. On the other hand, diminishing marginal utility plus additivity do imply strictly convex indifference surfaces but not conversely. For additivity implies that the second-order cross-partial derivatives $u_{ij}(x) = 0$ for $i \neq j$ on E. This together with (2.5-1) and Lemma 3.1-9 may be used to show that W (also defined in Chapter 3) is positive definite on E. By Theorem B.5-2, u is strictly quasi-concave. The counterexample $u(x_1, x_2) = x_1^2 x_2^2$ demonstrates that the converse assertion is false.

Although the distinction between ordinal and cardinal utility has lost much of its importance today it still appears often enough to warrant its inclusion here. An *ordinal* utility function is defined simply as a representation of a preference ordering (recall Section 2.1). The notion of cardinality requires, in addition, that the numbers assigned to each commodity bundle have a special meaning not recorded in the ordering itself. In its most general form, a utility function u is *cardinal* provided that for any four points x^1, x^2, x^3, and x^4 in E, $u(x^1) - u(x^2) \geq u(x^3) - u(x^4)$ if and only if $T(u(x^1)) - T(u(x^2)) \geq T(u(x^3)) - T(u(x^4))$ for every increasing transformation T of u.

Theorem 2.5-2 *u is cardinal if and only if every increasing transformation T of u takes the form*

$$T(\mu) = \alpha\mu + \beta,$$

where α and β are constants and $\alpha > 0$.

PROOF:

If T has the required form, then u is clearly cardinal.

If u is cardinal, then $u(x^1) - u(x^2) = u(x^3) - u(x^4)$ if and only if $T(u(x^1)) - T(u(x^2)) = T(u(x^3)) - T(u(x^4))$. But T is increasing and therefore has a derivative T' almost everywhere in its domain [12, p. 5]. It follows that for any two μ and μ^0 for which T' exists,

$$T'(\mu) = T'(\mu^0) = \alpha,$$

where α is a positive constant. Therefore, T has the required form.

Q.E.D.

Thus ordinal utility functions are determined up to arbitrary, increasing transformations while cardinal ones are unique only up to increasing, linear transformations.

An equivalent way of looking at cardinality, and one which gives further insight into what is involved, is in terms of the scale on which utility is measured. Thus given a representation, u, its range is measured on a scale, the μ-axis, whose zero is fixed and whose unit length is one. Denote this scale by ϵ and consider the unit length expressed as

(2.5-3) $$(\mu_\epsilon + 1) - \mu_\epsilon,$$

where μ_ϵ are points of the ϵ scale. Note that (2.5-3) is invariant over all μ_ϵ. Now any transformation, T, maps the ϵ scale into a new one, say, δ, also having a fixed zero and unit length. But, in general, the ϵ unit length need not be constant over the δ scale. If, for example, $T(\mu) = \mu^2$, then (2.5-3) becomes

$$(\mu_\epsilon + 1)^2 - \mu_\epsilon^2 = 2\mu_\epsilon + 1,$$

which depends on μ_ϵ. Thus although T leaves the position of the ϵ zero fixed, the ϵ unit length varies over the δ scale. On the other hand, if $T(\mu) = \alpha\mu + \beta$ as in Theorem 2.5-2, the position of the ϵ zero changes (unless $\beta = 0$) and the ϵ unit length from (2.5-3) becomes α. The latter being constant over the entire δ scale is the unique aspect of cardinality implicit in its definition: the unit length of utility on any given scale does not vary over scales obtained by applying admissible transformations.

Thus the notion of cardinality is a property of utility scales only; it cannot be expressed in terms of personal preferences. Since all previous results in this chapter are concerned with properties of representations which do appear in underlying preference orderings, the representations themselves may be considered as either ordinal or cardinal. But in most analyses, the additional assumption of cardinality does not turn out to be very useful. Examples in which it is required appear in Sections 7.5 and 8.1.

EXERCISES

2.1 Show that definitions (1) and (2) of representability are equivalent.

2.2 Assume that $\ominus$ is increasing and prove Theorem 2.1-2 using an argument similar to that of Theorem 2.1-1. (HINT: Take K to be the set of all points of $\bar{E}$ with rational coordinates and apply Cantor's theorem to the chain of equivalence classes under $\ominus$.)

2.3 If $\ominus$ is quasi-linear with respect to x_n, demonstrate that the associated indifference map must have the properties asserted in the proof of Theorem 2.3-3. (Recall Figure 2.5.)

2.4 Let $\geqq$ be continuously representable and $\geqslant$ increasing. Show that if $\geqq$ is linear, then indifference surfaces are parallel hyperplanes whose normals have positive direction cosines. State and prove the corresponding relationship between indifference surfaces when $\geqq$ is homothetic.

2.5 Prove that V defined in Theorem 2.4-1 is continuous.

2.6 A preference ordering is called *Pearce separable* (see [9]) with respect to the partition $N_1, \ldots, N_\pi$, whenever it is weakly separable with respect to $N_1, \ldots, N_\pi$, and the conditional ordering induced on each $\bar{E}^i$ is strongly separable with respect to the pointwise partition of N_i. Deduce the equivalent functional form of u.

REFERENCES

[1] Aczél, J., *Lectures on Functional Equations and Their Applications* (New York: Academic Press, 1966).

[2] Burk (Bergson), A., "Real Income, Expenditure Proportionality and Frish's 'New Methods of Measuring Marginal Utility'," *Review of Economic Studies*, v. 4 (1936), pp. 33–52.

[3] Chipman, J. S., "The Foundations of Utility," *Econometrica* (1960), pp. 193–224.

[4] Debreu, G., "Representation of a Preference Ordering by a Numerical Function," in R. M. Thrall, C. H. Coombs, and R. L. Davis (eds.), *Decision Processes* (New York, Wiley, 1954), pp. 159–165.

[5] Debreu, G., "Topological Methods in Cardinal Utility Theory," in K. J. Arrow, S. Karlin, and P. Suppes (eds.), *Mathematical Methods in the Social Sciences* (Stanford, Calif.: Stanford University Press, 1960), pp. 16–26.

[6] Eilenberg, S., "Ordered Topological Spaces," *American Journal of Mathematics* (1941), pp. 39–45.

[7] Herstein, I. N., and J. Milnor, "An Axiomatic Approach to Measurable Utility," *Econometrica* (1953), pp. 291–297.

[8] Leontief, W. W., "Introduction to a Theory of the Internal Structure of Functional Relationships," *Econometrica* (1947), pp. 361–373.

[9] Pearce, I. F., "An Exact Method of Consumer Demand Analysis," *Econometrica* (1961), pp. 499–516.

[10] Rader, T., "The Existence of a Utility Function to Represent Preferences," *Review of Economic Studies*, v. 30 (1963), pp. 229–232.

[11] Richter, M. K., "Revealed Preference Theory," *Econometrica* (1966), pp. 635–645.

[12] Riesz, F., and B. Sz.-Nagy, *Functional Analysis* (New York: Ungar, 1955).

[13] Rudin, W., *Principles of Mathematical Analysis* (New York: McGraw-Hill, 1953).

[14] Sono, M., "The Effect of Price Changes on the Demand and Supply of Separable Goods," *Kokumin Keizai Zasshi* (1945), pp. 1–51; English translation, *International Economic Review* (1961), pp. 239–271.

[15] Strotz, R. H., "The Empirical Implication of a Utility Tree," *Econometrica* (1957), pp. 269–280.

[16] Uzawa, H., "A Comment on Newman's 'Complete Ordering and Revealed Preference'," *Review of Economic Studies*, v. 28 (1961), pp. 140–141.

[17] Wold, H. O. A., "A Synthesis of Pure Demand Analysis," *Skandinavisk Aktuarietidskrift* (1943), pp. 85–118, 221–263; (1944), pp. 69–120.

3

Utility
Maximization

As remarked earlier, tradition and convenience often dictate that hypotheses of the theory of demand be stated in terms of an ordinal utility function. Hypotheses essentially are of two types. First are technical restrictions on the utility function which limit admissible preference orderings under consideration. Some freedom prevails in choosing these assumptions, particular choices depending on the special circumstances in question. But in one way or another they necessarily provide an appropriate framework in which the analysis can be carried out. Maximization, for example, is hardly meaningful if conditions do not guarantee the existence of at least one maximum. Thus whenever utility is to be maximized, these hypotheses must make that guarantee. The theory evolved from the technical restrictions employed below may be called "classical." It is primarily due to Slutsky [12].

The second type of hypothesis is a "postulate of rationality." It is a decision rule by which consumer purchases are made under given market conditions. It establishes a link between desires and action and provides the means for transforming utility restrictions into properties of demand. Rationality is the motivating force behind all individual activity. Without a vehicle of this sort, utility could not possibly be used as the basis for an explanation of consumer behavior.

These two kinds of hypotheses serve as the point of departure for Slutsky's theory. Together they permit a complete description of consumer activity: demand functions can be meaningfully defined and their properties deduced. And, as Slutsky argued, since demand is observable and utility is not, any empirical check on the theory requires translating assumptions on the latter into properties of the former. Then, if an individual's observed demands do not have these properties, the theory does not give an adequate explanation of his behavior. The classical theory and its empirical implications are examined here in considerable detail.

The analysis itself requires a moderate degree of mathematical sophistication. Definitions of mathematical concepts not given in the text may frequently be found in the Appendix. Important theorems not proved in either are given references in brackets when they appear for the first time.

3.1 RATIONAL BEHAVIOR

Let u be a utility function mapping $\bar{E}$ into the extended real line. Denote its first- and second-order partial derivatives by, respectively, u_i and u_{ij} for $i, j = 1, \ldots, n$. Suppose that

3.1-1. u has continuous, second-order partial derivatives on E and is continuous where finite on $\bar{E}$.
3.1-2. $u_i(x) > 0$ for $i = 1, \ldots, n$, and all x in E.
3.1-3. u is strictly quasi-concave.
3.1-4. For any distinct x' and x'' in $\bar{E}$ such that $u(x') = u(x'')$, if $x' > 0$, then $x'' > 0$.

Now 3.1-3 is equivalent to strict convexity of $\gtrless$ but 3.1-2 is slightly stronger than increasingness of $\gtrless$. Loosely speaking, the latter states that a larger bundle of commodities always is preferred to a smaller one. Differentiability of u and 3.1-4 were not characterized in terms of $\gtrless$ in Chapter 2, but it is the presence of both of these restrictions which distinguishes classical from nonclassical theory. In the classical case, as will be demonstrated shortly, all consumer purchases occur at interior tangency points easily located by applying the Lagrangean theorem. The meaning and use of 3.1-1–3.1-4 are discussed further in Section 3.3. They will be systematically strengthened in Chapter 5 and weakened in Chapter 6. Immediate consequences of them are that for any x, $C_x^{\geqq}$ is closed and convex, $C_x^{=}$ is the boundary of $C_x^{\geqq}$, and if $C_{x'}^{=}$ and $C_{x''}^{=}$ have any point in common, then they are identical.

By applying the implicit function theorem [1, p. 146] at each point of E to the equation $\mu = u(x)$, there exist twice continuously differentiable functions w^i defined on an appropriate subset of $E^{(i)}$ for each μ such that

$$(3.1-5) \qquad\qquad x_i = w^i(x_{(i)}, \mu), \quad i = 1, \ldots, n,$$

where $x_{(i)}$ is x without its ith component and $E^{(i)}$ is the corresponding subset[1] of E. Thus, if $u(x^0) = \mu^0$, where x^0 is in E, the expressions $C_{x^0}^{=}$, $\mu^0 = u(x)$, $x_i = w^i(x_{(i)}, \mu^0)$, and $x_i = w^i(x_{(i)}, u(x^0))$ are all different ways of looking at the same thing: the indifference surface through x^0. It is also true that

$$(3.1-6) \qquad\qquad x_i = w^i(x_{(i)}, u(x)),$$

---

[1] $x_{(i)}$ is the same as $x_{(i)}$ of Section 2.4 when the latter is defined with respect to the partition $\{\{1\}, \ldots, \{n\}\}$. The same is true of the difference between $E^{(i)}$ and $\bar{E}^{(i)}$.

for $i = 1, \ldots, n$, and all x in E. Let w_j^i be the partial derivative of w^i with respect to x_j and w_{jk}^i the second-order cross derivative with respect to x_j and x_k.

Theorem 3.1-7 *For any x in E, w^i as a function of $x_{(i)}$ alone is strictly convex and $w_j^i(x_{(i)}, \mu) < 0$, where $j \neq i$.*

PROOF:

Holding μ constant in (3.1-5), it follows from the implicit function theorem that

$$(3.1\text{-}8) \qquad w_j^i(x_{(i)}, \mu) = -\frac{u_j(x_{(i)}, w^i(x_{(i)}, \mu))}{u_i(x_{(i)}, w^i(x_{(i)}, \mu))}, \quad i = 1, \ldots, n, j \neq i.$$

Therefore, w_j^i is negative by 3.1-2.

To show strict convexity, recall that $C_x^{\geq}$ is convex. Hence it suffices to prove that for any distinct x' and x'' on its boundary (i.e., in $C_x^{=}$), $\theta x' + (1 - \theta)x''$ lies in the interior, where $0 < \theta < 1$. But this is immediate from 3.1-3.

Q.E.D.

Thus in the familiar two-dimensional context, indifference curves are downward sloping and strictly convex; curves higher and to the right provide greater utility than those lower and to the left.

Consider the matrices

$$U(x) = \begin{bmatrix} 0 & u_1(x) & \cdots & u_n(x) \\ u_1(x) & u_{11}(x) & \cdots & u_{1n}(x) \\ \vdots & \vdots & & \vdots \\ u_n(x) & u_{n1}(x) & \cdots & u_{nn}(x) \end{bmatrix},$$

$$W(x_{(n)}, \mu) = \begin{bmatrix} w_{11}^n & \cdots & w_{1n-1}^n \\ \vdots & & \vdots \\ w_{n-11}^n & \cdots & w_{n-1n-1}^n \end{bmatrix},$$

where, as is frequently done to simplify notation, the arguments of the w_{ij}^n have been omitted. Let $U^k(x)$ be obtained from $U(x)$ by deleting its last $n - k$ rows and columns. Define $W^k(x_{(n)}, \mu)$ by deleting the last $n - k$ rows and columns of W. Denote determinants of these matrices by vertical bars so that, for example, $|U^k(x)|$ is the determinant of U^k. Let $\Delta = \{x : |U(x)| \neq 0\}$. The following lemma asserts an important relationship between the derivatives of u and those of w^n. Its proof is somewhat terse and the reader may therefore wish to consider first the simplified case in which $n = 2$ and $k = 1$ (see Exercise 3.1).

Lemma 3.1-9   *For all x in E and $k = 1, \ldots, n - 1$,*

$$|U^{k+1}(x)| = (-1)^{k+1}(u_n(x))^{k+2}|W^k(x_{(n)}, \mu)|,$$

where $u(x) = \mu$.

PROOF:

Let x be in E and $u(x) = \mu$. Then differentiating (3.1-8) gives

$$w_{ij}^n = -\frac{u_n u_{ij} - u_i u_{nj} + (u_n u_{in} - u_i u_{nn})w_j^n}{(u_n)^2}$$

for $i, j = 1, \ldots, n - 1$. By using the familiar rules for manipulating determinants [4, pp. 46–56],

$$W^k = -\frac{(-1)^k}{(u_n)^{2k}}\begin{vmatrix} 0 & -w_1^n & \cdots & -u_k^n & 1 \\ 0 & u_n u_{11} - u_1 u_{n1} & \cdots & u_n u_{1k} - u_1 u_{nk} & u_n u_{1n} - u_1 u_{nn} \\ \vdots & \vdots & & \vdots & \vdots \\ 0 & u_n u_{k1} - u_k u_{n1} & \cdots & u_n u_{kk} - u_k u_{nk} & u_n u_{kn} - u_k u_{nn} \\ 1 & u_{n1} & \cdots & u_{nk} & u_{nn} \end{vmatrix},$$

from which the right-hand determinant may be shown to be U^{k+1} for an appropriate permutation of the last rows and columns of U.

Q.E.D.

Theorem 3.1-10   *Let x be in E and $k = 1, \ldots, n$. Then for all permutations of the rows and columns containing u_{ij} of $U(x)$,*

$$|U^k(x)| \begin{cases} \leq 0, & \text{if } k \text{ is odd,} \\ \geq 0, & \text{if } k \text{ is even,} \end{cases}$$

and these inequalities are strict on Δ. Furthermore, Δ is at least a dense, open subset of E.

PROOF:

First note $|U^1| = -(u_1)^2$, which is always negative. Suppose now that $k > 1$. From the convexity of w^n and Theorems B.5-1 and B.5-5, as a function of $x_{(n)}$, W is positive semidefinite on $E^{(n)}$ and positive definite except possibly on a nowhere-dense subset. Using interpretation (3.1-6), this result is easily extended to E. Now the complement of nowhere-dense sets are dense and open. Hence $|W^k| \geq 0$ on E for $k = 1, \ldots, n - 1$, and any permutation of the rows and columns of W [2, pp. 296, 298], and all inequalities are strict on at least a dense, open subset. By Lemma 3.1-9, the latter implies $|U(x)| \neq 0$ if and only if $|U^k(x)| \neq 0$ for each k. Further application of Lemma 3.1-9 completes the proof.

Q.E.D.

It is now convenient to introduce market variables. Let $P = (P_1, \ldots, P_n)$ be a vector of prices where P_i varies over the price of commodity i. Write M for the consumer's income. Only points of the set $\Gamma^* = \{(P, M): P > 0, M > 0\}$ are considered. The consumer has no control over the elements of Γ^*, but once one is selected (by a market or dictator), the set of all purchases available to him,

$$B^{\leq}(P, M) = \{x: P \cdot x \leq M\},$$

is fixed. Set

$$B^{=}(P, M) = \{x: P \cdot x = M\}.$$

The equation $P \cdot x = M$ is called the *budget constraint*, while the set $B^{\leq}(P, M)$ is the *budget set* given (P, M). Note that $B^{\leq}(\gamma P, \gamma M) = B^{\leq}(P, M)$ for any $\gamma > 0$. Hence to have price–income vectors correspond uniquely to budget sets the former must be suitably normalized. The normalization chosen here is to put

$$p_j = \frac{P_j}{P_n}, \quad j = 1, \ldots, n - 1,$$

(3.1-11)

$$m = \frac{M}{P_n},$$

$p = (p_1, \ldots, p_{n-1})$, and $\Gamma = \{(p, m): p > 0, m > 0\}$. The budget constraint becomes $(p, 1) \cdot x = m$ and the budget set $B^{\leq}(p, m)$ is defined accordingly. With this kind of normalization, the nth commodity is frequently called the *numéraire*.

Now for each (p, m) in Γ the consumer chooses at least one x in $B^{\leq}(p, m)$ he would like to purchase. This act of choice thus defines a function from Γ to E called the consumer's *demand function*. In principle, demand functions are easily observed; all that is required is to place the consumer in various market situations and watch what he buys. But different individuals may choose their purchases in different ways and the theory of demand is concerned with only one of these decision-making processes. He who follows that procedure is deemed "rational."

Rationality in demand theory means only bundles of commodities preferred or indifferent to all other bundles in the available budget set are chosen. Write $h = (h^1, \ldots, h^n)$ for the rational man's demand function. Then

3.1-12. For every (p, m) in Γ, $x = h(p, m)$ if and only if $u(x) \geq u(x')$ for all x' in $B^{\leq}(p, m)$.

To tell whether observed demand functions are consistent with assumptions 3.1-1–3.1-4 and 3.1-12, it is necessary to know what the latter imply about h. Then if the former do not exhibit these properties, the theory does not apply to the consumer in question. The remainder of this section and the next are therefore concerned with the properties of h.

The first question raised by 3.1-12 is whether it is always possible to be rational; that is, does there exist a utility maximizing bundle for every positive (p, m)? If so, then h is defined everywhere on Γ by 3.1-12. The next theorem answers this in the affirmative and further asserts that every positive commodity bundle is demanded for some budget.

Theorem 3.1-13 h *is a* $1:1$ *correspondence mapping* Γ *onto* E.

PROOF:

Let (p, m) be in Γ and choose $x^0 > 0$ in $B^{\leq}(p, m)$. Then $D = B^{\leq}(p, m) \cap C^{\geq}_{x^0}$ is a nonempty, compact subset of E. Since u is continuous on D, the latter contains an x^* such that $u(x^*) \geq u(x)$ for any other x in D [1, p. 73]. It is now shown that x^* is the unique maximizer of u over $B^{\leq}(p, m)$. The argument may be followed in Figure 3.1.

If x' is in $[B^{\leq}(p, m) - D] \cap E$, then clearly $u(x') \leq u(x^*)$. From the continuity of u and assumption 3.1-4, a similar conclusion holds for x'' in $B^{\leq}(p, m)$ on the boundary of $\bar{E}$. Since u is increasing (assumption 3.1-2), x^* is in $B^{=}(p, m)$. Finally, suppose there is another point x''' in $B^{=}(p, m) \cap C^{\geq}_{x^0}$ such that $u(x''') = u(x^*)$. Then by 3.1-3, if θ is between 0 and 1, $u(\theta x''' + (1 - \theta)x^*) > u(x^*)$, which contradicts the maximality of x^*. Therefore, for each (p, m) in Γ there exists a unique x^* such that $u(x^*) > u(x)$ for any other x in $B^{\leq}(p, m)$.

Now suppose x^* is any point of E. With (3.1-8) in mind, set

(3.1-14)
$$p_j = \frac{u_j(x^*)}{u_n(x^*)}, \quad j = 1, \ldots, n - 1,$$

$$m = (p, 1) \cdot x^*.$$

Then (p, m) is in Γ by 3.1-2 and $B^{\leq}(p, m)$ is as it appears in Figure 3.1. By the first part of this theorem there is a unique y' maximizing u over $B^{\leq}(p, m)$. If $u(y') > u(x^*)$, then y' is in the interior of $C^{\geq}_{x^*}$ (above the dashed curve in Figure 3.1), so $(p, 1) \cdot y' > m$. But this is a contradiction, since y' must be in $B^{=}(p, m)$. It follows that $y' = x^*$. Hence for each x^* in E there exists a unique (p, m) in Γ such that $u(x^*) > u(x)$ for any other x in $B^{\leq}(p, m)$.

Q.E.D.

The geometric interpretation of (3.1-14) together with (3.1-8) is that an indifference surface and budget hyperplane are tangent at x^*. Since x^* is always in $B^{\leq}(p, m)$,

$$(p, 1) \cdot h(p, m) = m$$

on Γ. Note also that if x^* maximizes u over $B^{\leq}(p, m)$ and if T is an increasing transformation of u, then x^* clearly maximizes $T(u)$ over $B^{\leq}(p, m)$. Therefore,

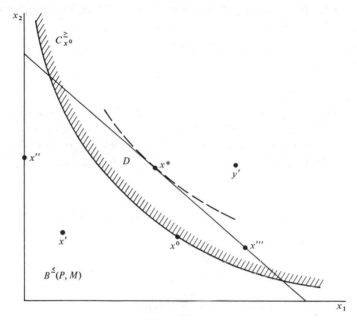

FIGURE 3.1

h is independent of the particular utility function representing the underlying preference ordering.

Demand functions may also be defined in terms of nonnormalized prices and income on Γ^*. Thus let

$$(3.1\text{-}15) \qquad h^*(P, M) = h\left(\frac{P_1}{P_n}, \ldots, \frac{P_{n-1}}{P_n}, \frac{M}{P_n}\right),$$

where h^* is again short for $(h^{*1}, \ldots, h^{*n})$. Theorem 3.1-13 implies that h^* is single valued and that $x = h^*(P, M)$ if and only if x maximizes u over $B^{\leq}(P, M)$. In addition, h^* is *homogeneous of degree zero*; i.e.,

$$h^*(\gamma P, \gamma M) = h^*(P, M)$$

for all $\gamma > 0$, and

$$P \cdot h^*(P, M) = M.$$

Commodity bundles which maximize utility subject to the budget constraint often are found by the well-known method of Lagrange. Its use is justified now under the assumptions of this chapter. The equations of (3.1-17) below are called *equilibrium conditions*.

Theorem 3.1-16   *There exists a positive function λ^* defined on Γ^* such that $x = h^*(P, M)$ if and only if*

(3.1-17)
$$u_i(x) = \lambda^*(P, M)P_i, \quad i = 1, \ldots, n,$$
$$P \cdot x = M.$$

PROOF:

If $x^0 = h^*(P, M)$, then x^0 maximizes u over $B^{\leq}(P, M)$, where $P \cdot x^0 = M$. Hence (3.1-17) follows from the well-known theorem of Lagrange [1, p. 153].

If (3.1-17) holds, then by an argument similar to the proof of the second part of Theorem 3.1-13, x maximizes u over $B^{\leq}(P, M)$, so $x = h^*(P, M)$.

Q.E.D.

Before discussing further properties of h and h^*, define $f = (f^1, \ldots, f^n)$ on E by

(3.1-18)
$$f^j(x) = \frac{u_j(x)}{u_n(x)}, \quad j = 1, \ldots, n - 1,$$
$$f^n(x) = x_n + \sum_{j=1}^{n-1} f^j(x)x_j.$$

Then from (3.1-14) or by taking ratios in (3.1-17),

$$(p, m) = f(x).$$

Thus f and h are inverses, the former being designated the *inverse demand function* of h. Now, f and h are really two ways of looking at the same thing. Nevertheless, as Pearce [7] has pointed out, the economic planner will find f more useful, since he is interested in the prices required to clear the market of planned outputs. In a free economy, on the other hand, a producer's concern is with quantities which can be sold at a given price. Hence the latter would be inclined to view the correspondence as h.

Because of the relationship between f and h, each property of one has a counterpart expressed in terms of the other. For example, f is continuous by 3.1-1 and therefore h (and h^*) is, too.[2] In addition, let

$$\Omega = \{(p, m): x = h(p, m) \text{ and } x \text{ is in } \Delta\}$$

be a subset of Γ. Then since Δ is at least a dense, open subset of E (Theorem 3.1-10), Ω is also at least a dense, open subset of Γ. Attention is now directed toward the differential properties of f, h, and h^*.

---

[2] If (p^0, m^0) is any point in Γ, write $(p^0, m^0) = f(x^0)$, with x^0 in E. Since there is a compact subset of E containing x^0 on which f is continuous, that h is continuous at (p^0, m^0) follows from a well-known theorem on the continuity of inverse functions. See Rudin [8, p. 166].

3.2 DIFFERENTIAL PROPERTIES OF DEMAND FUNCTIONS

Consider first the inverse demand function f. It is single valued and continuously differentiable on E. Denoting derivatives of the f^i by subscripts (e.g., f^i_j), for every x in E, define the functions

(3.2-1) $$a_{ij}(x) = f^i_j(x) - f^j(x)f^i_n(x), \quad i, j = 1, \ldots, n,$$

and matrix

$$A(x) = \begin{bmatrix} a_{11}(x) & \cdots & a_{1n-1}(x) \\ \vdots & & \vdots \\ a_{n-11}(x) & \cdots & a_{n-1n-1}(x) \end{bmatrix}.$$

These are called, respectively, *Antonelli functions* and *Antonelli matrix*, after the man who first introduced them.

Lemma 3.2-2 *For all x in E,*

$$a_{nj}(x) = \sum_{i=1}^{n} x_i a_{ij}(x), \qquad j = 1, \ldots, n,$$

$$a_{ij}(x) = -w^n_{ij}(x_{(n)}, \mu), \quad i, j = 1, \ldots, n-1,$$

where $u(x) = \mu$.

PROOF:

The first part of the lemma may be proved by computing the derivatives of f from (3.1-18) and combining them according to (3.2-1). To prove the second part, note that

$$-w^n_i(x_{(n)}, \mu) = f^i(x_{(n)}, w^n(x_{(n)}, \mu)), \quad i = 1, \ldots, n-1,$$

from (3.1-5), (3.1-8), and (3.1-18). Differentiation therefore yields

$$-w^n_{ij} = f^i_j - f^i_n w^n_j, \quad i, j = 1, \ldots, n-1,$$

whence, from (3.2-1) and the above,

$$-w^n_{ij} = a_{ij}, \quad i, j = 1, \ldots, n-1.$$

Q.E.D.

The next two theorems assert the important differential properties of f.

Theorem 3.2-3 (Symmetry) *For all x in E,*

$$a_{ij}(x) = a_{ji}(x), \quad i, j = 1, \ldots, n-1.$$

PROOF:

This follows immediately from Lemma 3.2-2 and the fact that $w^n_{ij}(x_{(n)}, \mu) \equiv w^n_{ji}(x_{(n)}, \mu)$ [1, p. 121].

Q.E.D.

Theorem 3.2-4 (Negative definiteness) $A(x)$ *is negative semidefinite on E and negative definite on* Δ.

PROOF:

These results are obvious consequences of Lemma 3.2-2 and Theorems B.5-1 and B.5-5.

Q.E.D.

Returning to demand functions themselves, recall that h is single-valued and continuous. Differentiation, however, may not be possible everywhere.

Theorem 3.2-5 h *is continuously differentiable at* (p, m) *if and only if* (p, m) *is in* Ω.

PROOF:

Using (3.1-18) it may be shown that for every x in E, the Jacobian determinant of f,

$$\begin{vmatrix} f_1^1 & \cdots & f_n^1 \\ \vdots & & \vdots \\ f_1^n & \cdots & f_n^n \end{vmatrix} = \left(\frac{1}{u_n}\right)^{n+1} |U|.$$

Hence if (p, m) is in Ω and $x = h(p, m)$, then by the inverse function theorem, h is continuously differentiable at (p, m). On the other hand, Theorem C-1 implies that if $|U| = 0$, h cannot be differentiable.

Q.E.D.

Remarks at the end of Section 3.1 therefore imply that h must have derivatives on at least a dense, open subset of Γ. But the example in Section 3.3 shows that h need not be differentiable everywhere. Where they exist, let h_j^i be the derivative of h^i with respect to p_j and h_m^i that with respect to m. Define the *Slutsky functions*

(3.2-6) $s_{ij}(p, m) = h_j^i(p, m) + h^j(p, m)h_m^i(p, m),$

for (p, m) in Ω, where $i = 1, \ldots, n$, and $j = 1, \ldots, n - 1$. Now let

$$\Omega^* = \{(P, M): x = h^*(P, M) \text{ and } x \text{ is in } \Delta\}.$$

Then in view of (3.1-15), h^* is differentiable on Ω^*. Let its derivatives also be denoted by subscripts as with h and define the corresponding Slutsky functions

(3.2-7) $s_{ij}^*(P, M) = h_j^{*i}(P, M) + h^{*j}(P, M)h_M^{*i}(P, M),$

on Ω^* for $i, j = 1, \ldots, n$. The following lemma is a trivial consequence of the chain rule [1, p. 113] and its proof is omitted.

Lemma 3.2-8   *For every $i = 1, \ldots, n$, and $j = 1, \ldots, n - 1$,*

$$h_j^{*i} = \frac{1}{P_n} h_j^i,$$

$$h_M^{*i} = \frac{1}{P_n} h_m^i,$$

$$s_{ij}^* = \frac{1}{P_n} s_{ij},$$

for all (P, M) in Ω^*.

Next write $U(P, M)$ for $U(x)$, where $x = h^*(P, M)$, and let $|U^{ij}|$ and $|U^{0j}|$ denote the cofactor of, respectively, u_{ij} and u_j in U, where u_j is in the first row. (These should not be confused with the symbol $|U^k|$.) It is now possible to establish a fundamental relationship between the Slutsky functions and the cofactors of U.

Lemma 3.2-9   *For all (P, M) in Ω^*,*

$$s_{ij}^*(P, M) = \frac{\lambda^*(P, M) |U^{ij}(P, M)|}{|U(P, M)|}, \quad i, j = 1, \ldots, n$$

PROOF:

Let (P, M) be in Ω^*. If $x = h^*(P, M)$, then from equilibrium conditions (3.1-17) and the budget constraint

$$-\lambda^*(P, M)P_i + u_i(h^*(P, M)) = 0, \quad i = 1, \ldots, n,$$

(3.2-10)

$$P \cdot h^*(P, M) = M.$$

Differentiating (3.2-10) with respect to M, substituting $u_i(h^*)/\lambda^*$ for P_i in accordance with (3.1-17), and using Cramer's rule [4, p. 99] to solve for h_M^{*i} yields

$$h_M^{*i} = \lambda^* \frac{|U^{0i}|}{|U|}, \quad i = 1, \ldots, n.$$

Similarly, differentiating (3.2-10) with respect to P_j, making the same substitution for P_i, and solving for h_j^{*i} gives

$$h_j^{*i} = \frac{-\lambda^* h^{*j} |U^{0i}| + \lambda^* |U^{ij}|}{|U|}, \quad i, j = 1, \ldots, n.$$

The conclusion now follows by combining these equations with (3.2-7).

Q.E.D.

As with f, the differential properties of h and h^* are expressed in terms of matrices whose elements, this time, are the Slutsky functions. Thus let

$$S(p, m) = \begin{bmatrix} s_{11}(p, m) & \cdots & s_{1n-1}(p, m) \\ \vdots & & \vdots \\ s_{n-11}(p, m) & \cdots & s_{n-1n-1}(p, m) \end{bmatrix},$$

$$S^*(P, M) = \begin{bmatrix} s_{11}^*(P, M) & \cdots & s_{1n-1}^*(P, M) \\ \vdots & & \vdots \\ s_{n-11}^*(P, M) & \cdots & s_{n-1n-1}^*(P, M) \end{bmatrix},$$

$$\mathbb{S}^*(P, M) = \begin{bmatrix} s_{11}^*(P, M) & \cdots & s_{1n}^*(P, M) \\ \vdots & & \vdots \\ s_{n1}^*(P, M) & \cdots & s_{nn}^*(P, M) \end{bmatrix},$$

on, respectively, Ω and Ω^*.

Theorem 3.2-11 (Symmetry)   *For all* (p, m) *in* Ω,

$$s_{ij}(p, m) = s_{ji}(p, m), \quad i, j = 1, \ldots, n - 1,$$

and for all (P, M) *in* Ω^*,

$$s_{ij}^*(P, M) = s_{ji}^*(P, M), \quad i, j = 1, \ldots, n.$$

PROOF:

Since $u_{ij} = u_{ji}$, Lemma 3.2-9 implies $s_{ij}^* = s_{ji}^*$ for $i, j = 1, \ldots, n$. The first part of the theorem now follows from Lemma 3.2-8.

Q.E.D.

Theorem 3.2-12 (Negative definiteness)   *For every* (P, M) *in* Ω^*, $S^*(P, M)$ *is negative definite and* $|\mathbb{S}^*(P, M)| = 0$. *Furthermore,* $S(p, m)$ *is negative definite on* Ω.

PROOF:

Consider the equations

$$\frac{(\lambda^*)^k}{|U|} \begin{vmatrix} 0 & u_{k+1} & \cdots & u_n \\ u_{k+1} & u_{k+1k+1} & \cdots & u_{k+1n} \\ \vdots & \vdots & & \vdots \\ u_n & u_{nk+1} & \cdots & u_{nn} \end{vmatrix} = \left(\frac{\lambda^*}{|U|}\right)^k \begin{vmatrix} |U^{11}| & \cdots & |U^{1k}| \\ \vdots & & \vdots \\ |U^{k1}| & \cdots & |U^{kk}| \end{vmatrix},$$

which hold for $k = 1, \ldots, n$, on Ω^* [4, p. 85]. (Note that when $k = n$ the left-hand side is zero.) By Lemma 3.2-9, the right-hand side is a principal minor of $\mathbb{S}^*$. But the determinant in the numerator on the other side is $|U^{n-k}|$ for an appropriate permutation of the rows and columns of U. Therefore applying Theorem 3.1-10, S^* is negative definite and $|\mathbb{S}^*| = 0$ [2, pp. 296, 298]. The second part of the theorem follows from Lemma 3.2-8.

Q.E.D.

It is interesting to note that the vanishing of $|S^*|$ on Ω^* may also be deduced from the fact that h^* is homogeneous of degree zero.

In view of the similarity of the properties of S and A and the fact that h and f are inverses, it is quite reasonable to conjecture that $S = A^{-1}$. This turns out to be true and its proof is due to Samuelson [10].

Theorem 3.2-13 *For all (p, m) in Ω,*

$$S(p, m) = [A(x)]^{-1},$$

where $x = h(p, m)$.

PROOF:

Since f and h are inverse functions, their respective Jacobians, J_f and J_h, are inverse matrices. Using (3.1-18), (3.2-1), and $p_j = f^j(x)$ for $j = 1, \ldots, n - 1$, it is not hard to verify that

$$J_f = \begin{bmatrix} I & 0' \\ x_{(n)} & 1 \end{bmatrix} \begin{bmatrix} A & \bar{f}' \\ 0 & 1 \end{bmatrix} \begin{bmatrix} I & 0' \\ p & 1 \end{bmatrix},$$

where I is the $n - 1$ by $n - 1$ identity matrix, $x_{(n)} = (x_1, \ldots, x_{n-1})$, 0 is an $n - 1$ vector of zeros, $\bar{f} = (f_n^1, \ldots, f_n^{n-1})$, and primes denote the transpose vectors. Hence for (p, m) in Ω, the inverse J_h exists and

$$J_h = \begin{bmatrix} I & 0' \\ -p & 1 \end{bmatrix} \begin{bmatrix} A^{-1} & \tau' \\ 0 & 1 \end{bmatrix} \begin{bmatrix} I & 0' \\ -x_{(n)} & 1 \end{bmatrix},$$

where τ is a vector whose elements do not have to be determined explicitly. On the other hand, from (3.2-6) and $x_i = h^i(p, m)$ for $i = 1, \ldots, n$,

$$\begin{bmatrix} & & & h_m^1 \\ & S & & \vdots \\ s_{1n} & \cdots & s_{nn-1} & h_m^n \end{bmatrix} = J_h \begin{bmatrix} I & 0' \\ x_{(n)} & 1 \end{bmatrix},$$

which, upon substitution,

$$= \begin{bmatrix} I & 0' \\ -p & 1 \end{bmatrix} \begin{bmatrix} A^{-1} & \tau' \\ 0 & 1 \end{bmatrix},$$

$$= \begin{bmatrix} A^{-1} & \tau^{2'} \\ \tau^1 & \tau^3 \end{bmatrix},$$

for some vectors τ^1 and τ^2 and scalar τ^3. Therefore, $S = A^{-1}$.

Q.E.D.

Thus the symmetry and negative definiteness of S may be deduced directly from that of A.

3.3 SUMMARY AND EXAMPLE

At this point it is worth pausing for a moment to take stock of what has been accomplished. There are now a substantial number of properties which observed demand functions must exhibit in order not to reject the Slutsky theory. These are summarized in Table 3.1. It does not matter if one chooses to express them in terms of, say, f rather than h, since each group of properties implies the other. The equivalent set of restrictions in terms of h^* are those listed in Table 3.1 together with the fact that h [defined in this case by setting

$$h(p, m) = h^*\left(\frac{P_1}{P_n}, \ldots, \frac{P_{n-1}}{P_n}, 1, \frac{M}{P_n}\right)$$

on Γ] is a 1:1 correspondence mapping Γ into E.

The importance of assumptions 3.1-1–3.1-4 in deducing these properties should not be underestimated. The precise role of each is apparent from the argument of Sections 3.1 and 3.2. In general, their contributions may be summarized as follows:

(1) Smoothness (assumption 3.1-1) prevents indifference surfaces from having kinks which, in turn, would make f a multivalued function. It also implies differentiability of f, h, and h^* and provides a relatively easy way of demonstrating symmetry and negative definiteness (although, as is shown in Chapter 6, the latter may be proved without it).

(2) Increasingness (assumption 3.1-2) implies that utility maximizing bundles, and hence f, h, and h^* satisfy the appropriate budget constraint. It rules out possible maxima in the interior of the budget set.

(3) Strict quasi-concavity (assumption 3.1-3) prevents indifference surfaces from containing linear segments or being tangent to a budget surface at more than one point. Otherwise, the uniqueness of utility maximizing bundles and the single-valuedness of h (and h^*) would be destroyed. It also implies all the negative definiteness conditions.

(4) Assumption 3.1-4 implies that indifference surfaces do not intersect the boundary of E. Hence all utility maximizers lie in E and not on its boundary. If this were not the case, f could be defined outside of E and would be multivalued there.

The difficulties arising without these hypotheses are illustrated, respectively, in Figure 3.2, where x^0 and x' denote chosen points and p and p' alternative price ratios.

The fact that h and h^* need not be differentiable everywhere may at first seem somewhat surprising. But it occurs for the same reason that the well-known calculus "second-order" condition[3] for a function to be maximized

---

[3] For functions of one variable, the second-order condition requires that the second derivative be negative in a neighborhood of the maximum.

TABLE 3.1

Summary of Observable Properties of Demand Functions

PROPERTY	FUNCTION AND AUXILIARY SET		
	f, Δ	h, Ω	h^*, Ω^*
1. Type of mapping	$E \to \Gamma$, 1:1, onto	$\Gamma \to E$, 1:1, onto	$\Gamma^* \to E$, single-valued, onto
2. Continuity	everywhere	everywhere	everywhere
3. Differentiability and domain of definition of a_{ij}, s_{ij}, or s_{ij}^*	everywhere	on Ω	on Ω^*
4. Budget constraint	$x_n + \sum_{i=1}^{n-1} f^i(x)x_i = f^n(x)$	$(p, 1) \cdot h(p, m) = m$	$P \cdot h^*(P, M) = M$
5. Homogeneity	—	—	of degree zero
6. Symmetry	$a_{ij} = a_{ji}$	$s_{ij} = s_{ji}$	$s_{ij}^* = s_{ji}^*$
7. Negative definiteness (a)	A negative semi-definite everywhere	—	S^* negative semi-definite and $|S^*| = 0$ on Ω^*
(b)	A negative definite on Δ	S negative definite on Ω	S^* negative definite on Ω^*
8. Inverse matrices	$A^{-1} = S$		—
9. Auxiliary sets (a)	x is in $\Delta \leftrightarrow (p, m)$ is in Ω, where $x = h(p, m)$ $\leftrightarrow (P, M)$ is in Ω^*, where $x = h(P, M)$		
(b)	Δ, Ω, Ω^* are at least dense, open subsets of, respectively, E, Γ, and Γ^*.		

is sufficient but not necessary. [Example: The function $r(z) = -z^4$, where z is a scalar, has a maximum at $z = 0$ but its second derivative $r''(0) = 0$.] From Theorem 3.1-10, the strict quasi-concavity of u implies, if x is in E, $yU^{00}(x)y' \leq 0$ for all vectors y (here the prime again denotes transpose) such that

$$(3.3\text{-}1) \qquad\qquad \sum_{i=1}^{n} y_i u_i(x) = 0,$$

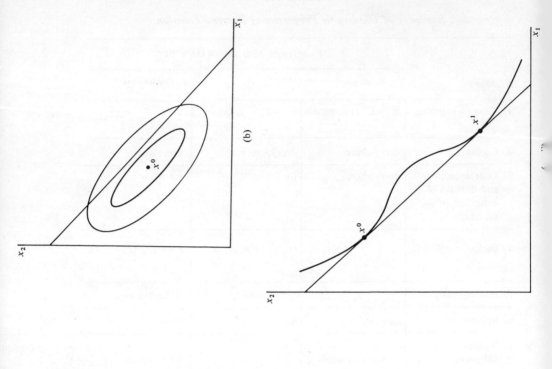

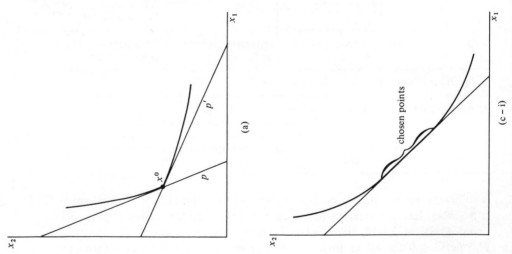

(a)

(b)

(c – i)

chosen points

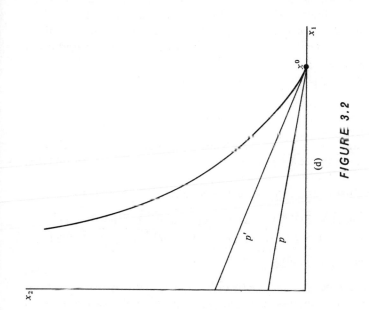

(d)

FIGURE 3.2

where U^{00} is U without its first row and column [2, p. 299]. The latter is also necessary for the maximization of u subject to the budget constraint at all (p, m) in Γ. But the corresponding and stronger sufficient condition, which is frequently assumed in place of 3.1-3, is that $yU^{00}(x)y' < 0$ for nonzero y satisfying (3.3-1). The latter, not the former, implies $|U(x)| \neq 0$ on E and hence demand functions which are differentiable everywhere.

As an illustration, let $n = 2$ and consider

$$(3.3\text{-}2) \qquad u(x) = x_1^3 x_2 + x_1 x_2^3.$$

Then 3.1-1–3.1-4 are satisfied and the preference ordering generated by u is seen to be homothetic.

Now $|U(x)| = 0$ whenever $x_1 = x_2$. This property is invariant under rotations of the coordinate axes of E. In particular a rotation of $+135°$ transforms the indifference curves into the form $y_2 = -y_1^4 + \alpha$. This is precisely the example mentioned in the above discussion of second-order conditions [in fact, (3.3-2) was originally constructed by using the reverse rotation]. Letting $p = p_1$, the inverse demand function f^1 is

$$(3.3\text{-}3) \qquad p = \frac{3x_1^2 x_2 + x_2^3}{3x_2^2 x_1 + x_1^3},$$

so $x_1 = x_2$ if and only if $p = 1$. Thus $\Delta = \{x : x_1 \neq x_2\}$ and $\Omega = \{(p, m) : p \neq 1\}$. It is interesting to note that for the very similar function $u(x) = x_1^2 x_2 + x_1 x_2^2$, $\Delta = E$.

Inverting (3.3-3) and using the budget constraint,

$$h^1(p, m) = \frac{m[(1 - q^2)^{1/3}(1 - q)^{1/3} - (1 - q^2)^{1/3}(1 + q)^{1/3} + q]}{1 + p[(1 - q^2)^{1/3}(1 - q)^{1/3} - (1 - q^2)^{1/3}(1 + q)^{1/3} + q]},$$

$$h^2(p, m) = m - ph^1(p, m),$$

where $q = 1/p$. It can be verified directly or by appeal to the theory of Sections 3.1 and 3.2 that h is continuous on Γ and has continuous derivatives only on Ω.

3.4 THE SLUTSKY EQUATION AND SUBSTITUTION

Aside from observables, there are also important interpretations of demand functions and their derivatives in terms of the utility function which generates them. This section is concerned with the derivatives, the section that follows with the functions themselves.

It has already been shown in Lemma 3.2-2 that

$$(3.4\text{-}1) \qquad a_{ij}(x) = -w_{ij}^n(x_{(n)}, u(x)),$$

for all $i, j \neq n$ and x in E. In order to give an analogous interpretation to the derivatives of h and h^*, it is convenient to define a new kind of demand function based on expenditure minimization rather than utility maximization. Thus let $\Pi = \{(p, \mu): p > 0$ and $\mu = u(x)$ for some x in $E\}$ and write $\bar{x} = g(p, \mu)$ whenever $\bar{x}$ minimizes $(p, 1) \cdot x$ over $C_{x^0}^{\geq}$, where $u(x^0) = \mu$. Many of the properties of g and their proofs are analogous to those of h. Several are stated below without proof.

Theorem 3.4-2 *g is a $1:1$ correspondence mapping Π onto E.*

Theorems 3.1-13 and 3.4-2 imply the existence of a $1:1$ correspondence between Π and Γ. The inverse of g is defined by the equations

$$p_j = \frac{u_j(x)}{u_n(x)}, \quad j = 1, \ldots, n - 1,$$

$$\mu = u(x).$$

As before, the Jacobian of this system is nonzero on Δ. Hence g is differentiable on at least a dense, open subset, Θ, of Π.

Let $\Pi^* = \{(P, \mu): P > 0, \mu = u(x)$ for some x in $E\}$ and define

$$g^*(P, \mu) = g\left(\frac{P_1}{P_n}, \ldots, \frac{P_{n-1}}{P_n}, \mu\right),$$

on Π^*. Then g^* is differentiable on at least a dense, open subset, Θ^*, of Π^*. Denote its partial derivatives with respect to prices by subscripts (e.g., g_j^{*i}). Now there also exists a function η^* defined on Π^* such that

$$-\eta^*(P, \mu)P_i + u_i(g^*(P, \mu)) = 0, \quad i = 1, \ldots, n,$$

$$u(g^*(P, \mu)) = \mu.$$

By differentiating this system with respect to P_j and applying the technique used in the proof of Lemma 3.2-9, it is not hard to show that

$$g_j^{*i}(P, \mu) = \frac{\eta^*(P, \mu) |U^{0j}(P, \mu)|}{|U(P, \mu)|}, \quad i, j = 1, \ldots, n,$$

for all (P, μ) in Θ^*. In view of the aforementioned correspondence between Γ and Π and the fact that $\eta^*(P, \mu) = \lambda^*(P, M)$ whenever $x = h^*(P, M)$ and $u(x) = \mu$, the proof of the next result is obvious.

Theorem 3.4-3 *For all (P, μ) in Θ^*,*

$$g_j^{*i}(P, \mu) = s_{ij}^*(P, M), \quad i, j = 1, \ldots, n,$$

where $x = h^*(P, M)$ and $u(x) = \mu$.

Thus, except for its domain of definition, the matrix consisting of the elements g_j^{*i} is identical to S^* and consequently has similar properties. In particular, $g_j^{*i}(P, \mu) < 0$ on Θ^*.

Combining (3.2-7) and Theorem 3.4-3 gives the famous equation of Slutsky:

$$(3.4\text{-}4) \qquad h_j^{*i}(P, M) = g_j^{*i}(P, \mu) - h^{*j}(P, M)h_M^{*i}(P, M)$$

for $i, j = 1, \ldots, n$. Thus h_j^{*i} may be decomposed into the rate of change in x_i as P_j changes while the consumer remains on the same indifference surface and a term involving the rate of change in x_i as M changes with prices held constant. The former is called the *substitution effect* and the latter the *income effect*. At least two geometric interpretations of these effects in terms of small price and quantity changes may be given. They are associated with the names of Slutsky and Hicks and in the limit turn out to be identical. To simplify notation only the case $n = 2$ is considered; the extension to more than two commodities is trivial.

Consider Figure 3.3. Let the coordinates of x^0, x', and x'' be

$$x^0 = (x_1^0, x_2^0),$$

$$x' = (x_1^0 + \Delta x_1, x_2^0 + \Delta x_2),$$

$$x'' = (x_1^0 + \overline{\Delta x_1}, x_2^0 + \overline{\Delta x_2}),$$

the symbol Δ denoting appropriate increments. Suppose $x^0 = h^*(P^0, M^0)$, $u(x^0) = \mu^0$, $x' = h^*(P^0 + \Delta P, M')$, $x'' = h^*(P^0 + \Delta P, M'')$, and $x''' = h^*(P^0 + \Delta P, M^0)$, where $\Delta P = (\Delta P_1, 0)$, $\Delta P_1 < 0$, and $M'' = (P^0 + \Delta P) \cdot x^0$. Thus the lower two indifference curves are tangent at x' and x'' to budget lines parallel to the one through x'''. Also x^0 lies on the budget line through x''. The Slutsky and Hicks decompositions of the movement between x^0 and x''' are listed in Table 3.2. The substitution effects with respect to commodity 1 may be measured, respectively, by the ratios $\overline{\Delta x_1}/\Delta P_1$ and $\Delta x_1/\Delta P_1$. Assume that (P^0, M^0) is in Ω^*. Then it will be shown that as ΔP_1 goes to zero, both ratios approach $g_1^{*1}(P^0, \mu^0)$. A similar result holds for substitution effects in terms of commodity 2. Since the Slutsky and Hicks decompositions are two

TABLE 3.2

Income and Substitution Effects

AUTHOR	SUBSTITUTION EFFECT	INCOME EFFECT
Slutsky	x^0 to x''	x'' to x'''
Hicks	x^0 to x'	x' to x'''

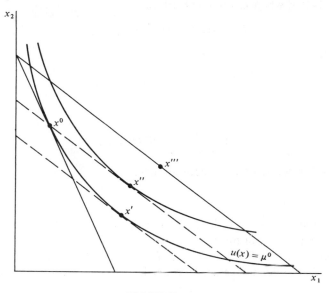

FIGURE 3.3

ways of breaking up the same thing, the corresponding income ratios for each commodity must also, in the limit, be identical. Hence as ΔP_1 becomes small, the difference between the two interpretations becomes negligible. This result was originally proved by Wald.[4]

Theorem 3.4-5 *If (P^0, M^0) is in Ω^*, then*

$$\lim_{\Delta P_1 \to 0} \frac{\Delta x_1}{\Delta P_1} = \varlimsup_{\Delta P_1 \to 0} \frac{\Delta x_1}{\Delta P_1} = g_1^{*1}(P^0, \mu^0).$$

PROOF:

Let (P^0, M^0) be in Ω^* and set $\Delta M = M^0 - M''$. Then by the construction of x^0 and x'',

$$\Delta M = h^{*1}(P^0, M^0)\Delta P_1.$$

Let $\epsilon > 0$ be an arbitrary real number and

$$\delta = \frac{\epsilon}{\sqrt{1 + [h^{*1}(P^0, M^0)]^2}}.$$

By the differentiability of h^* there is a neighborhood of (P^0, M^0) in which

$$|\overline{\Delta x_1} - h_1^{*1}(P^0, M^0)\Delta P_1 - h_M^{*1}(P^0, M^0)\Delta M| \leq \delta |(\Delta P_1, \Delta M)|,$$

[4] See Mosak [6, p. 73, n. 5].

[1, pp. 107–109] whence, upon substitution,

$$\overline{|\Delta x_1 - s_{11}^*(P^0, M^0)\Delta P_1|} \le \epsilon|\Delta P_1|.$$

Therefore,

$$\lim_{\Delta P_1 \to 0} \frac{\overline{\Delta x_1}}{\Delta P_1} = s_{11}^*(P^0, M^0).$$

But since

$$\lim_{\Delta P_1 \to 0} \frac{\Delta x_1}{\Delta P_1} = g_1^{*1}(P^0, \mu^0),$$

the conclusion follows from Theorem 3.4-3.

Q.E.D.

One of the reasons for decomposing h_j^{*i} into income and substitution effects is for the special insight it gives into the case $i = j$. The *Marshallian demand function* is defined as $h^{*i}(P, M)$, where only P_i and M are allowed to vary and all other prices are held fixed. Under stronger assumptions than

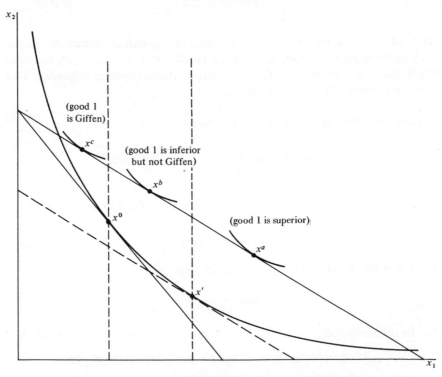

FIGURE 3.4

those made here, Marshall deduced the so-called "law of demand," that the slope of his demand curve with respect to price, i.e., h_i^{*i}, is always negative (see Chapter 5). But it is now clear from the Slutsky equation (3.4-4) that more than hypotheses 3.1-1–3.1-4 and 3.1-12 are required if this law is to remain valid. For although g_i^{*i} is negative on Ω^*, nothing guarantees that h_M^{*i} will always be positive. There are three cases:

(1) If $h_M^{*i}(P, M) > 0$, then commodity i is called a *superior good* at (P, M). Hence $h_i^{*i}(P, M) < 0$, and this is enough to ensure that the Marshallian demand curve is downward sloping in some neighborhood of (P, M). It follows from the budget constraint that at least one good must be superior at every (P, M).
(2) Commodity i is an *inferior good* at (P, M) if $h_M^{*i}(P, M) < 0$. Even for inferior goods, the substitution effect may still outweigh the income effect, so that $h_i^{*i} < 0$.
(3) The case in which i is inferior and the income effect overpowers the substitution effect, so $h_i^{*i} > 0$ is called the *Giffen paradox*. The most common example of this is that of a poor family spending such a large percentage of its income on rice that a rise in price reduces their purchasing power to a degree where they can no longer afford to consume other foods. Hence their consumption of rice increases.

These three cases are illustrated in Figure 3.4. A formal example appears in Exercise 3.6. Note that under the assumptions made here the only demand function which is always downward sloping with respect to its own price is g^i.

3.5 INDIRECT UTILITY FUNCTIONS

The indirect utility function has become an important tool of demand analysis. Apart from its applications to welfare problems (Chapter 7) and its use in generating additional properties of demand functions (Chapter 5), it also provides a simple technique for computing demand functions which may not otherwise be available.

The indirect utility function l is defined on Γ^* by

$$(3.5\text{-}1) \qquad l(P, M) = u(h^*(P, M)).$$

From 3.1-1 and Theorem 3.2-5, l is continuously differentiable on Ω^*. It is also homogeneous of degree zero. Denote its derivatives with respect to P_i by l_i and with respect to income by l_M.

Theorem 3.5-2 *For all (P, M) in Ω^*,*

$$l_M(P, M) = \lambda^*(P, M).$$

PROOF:

Differentiating $P \cdot h(P, M) = M$ with respect to M and using (3.5-1) and equilibrium conditions (3.1-17),

$$l_M = \sum_{i=1}^{n} u_i h_M^{*i} = \lambda^* \sum_{i=1}^{n} P_i h_M^i = \lambda^*$$

on Ω^*.

Q.E.D.

Since l_M is the rate of change of utility with respect to changes in M, it is not surprising that λ^* is frequently referred to as the *marginal utility of income*. Note that the latter is not invariant under increasing transformations of u. For if T is a differentiable transformation whose derivative, T', is positive, then $T(l) = T(u)$ and hence the new marginal utility of income is $T'l_M = T'\lambda^*$. Since $\lambda^* > 0$, Theorem 3.5-2 also implies that for each P, as a function of M alone l is increasing. Further discussion of λ^* is presented in Chapter 5.

The next result provides an interesting interpretation of demand functions and the means for computing them when l rather than u is known.

Theorem 3.5-3   *For all* (P, M) *in* Ω^*,

$$h^{*i}(P, M) = - \frac{l_i(P, M)}{l_M(P, M)}, \quad i = 1, \ldots, n.$$

PROOF:

Differentiating $P \cdot h^*(P, M) = M$ with respect to P_i and using (3 1-17), (3.5-1), and Theorem 3.5-2,

$$-\frac{l_i}{l_M} = - \frac{\sum_{j=1}^{n} u_j h_i^{*j}}{\lambda^*} = - \sum_{j=1}^{n} P_j h_i^{*j} = h^{*i}$$

for $i = 1, \ldots, n$ on Ω^*.

Q.E.D.

A basic mathematical aspect of Slutsky's theory is concerned with maximizing u subject to the linear constraint $P \cdot x = M$, where P and M are fixed parameters. A *dual problem* is to minimize l subject to $P \cdot x = M$, where x is now the parameter. One of the consequences of Theorem 3.5-3 is that on Ω^* solutions to these problems correspond: if x^0 solves the former given (P^0, M^0), then (P^0, M^0) solves the latter given x^0, and conversely. Proof is left to Exercise 3.7.

Returning to the indirect utility function itself, Samuelson [11] has pointed out that l has properties analogous to 3.1-2 and 3.1-3.

Theorem 3.5-4   *For all* (P, M) *in* Γ^*, $-l(P, M)$ *is increasing in P and strictly quasi-concave. Furthermore, l is increasing in M.*

PROOF:

Let $x' = h^*(P', M')$ and $x'' = h^*(P'', M'')$. If $P' > P''$ and $M' = M''$, then

$$P'' \cdot x'' = P' \cdot x' > P'' \cdot x',$$

so x' is in the interior of $B^{\leq}(P'', M'')$. Hence $u(x') < u(x'')$ and $-l(P', M') > -l(P'', M'')$. Similarly, l is increasing in M.

Now suppose $l(P', M') = l(P'', M'')$ and consider $(\bar{P}, \bar{M}) = \theta(P', M') + [1 - \theta](P'', M'')$ for any θ between 0 and 1. Let $\bar{x} = h^* (\bar{P}, \bar{M})$. Note that x', x'', and $\bar{x}$ are all distinct points. If either $P' \cdot \bar{x} \leq P' \cdot x'$ or $P'' \cdot \bar{x} \leq P'' \cdot x''$, an argument similar to the above shows that, respectively, $-l(\bar{P}, \bar{M}) > -l(P', M')$ or $-l(\bar{P}, \bar{M}) > -l(P'', M'')$. To complete the proof, then, it is only necessary to demonstrate that at least one of these cases must hold. But if this were not so, then $P' \cdot \bar{x} > M'$ and $P'' \cdot \bar{x} > M''$. Hence

$$\bar{P} \cdot \bar{x} = \theta P' \cdot \bar{x} + (1 - \theta)P'' \cdot \bar{x} > \bar{M},$$

which is a contradiction.

Q.E.D.

Using the formula for h^* in Theorem 3.5-3, it is possible to derive the symmetry and negative definiteness of S^* directly from the differentiability and quasi-concavity of $-l$, provided l has continuous partial derivatives of the second order. The argument is identical to that proving the corresponding restrictions on A. This suggests that neither preferences nor their utility representations are needed to derive the observable properties of h^* and that a theory of demand may be constructed by making assumptions on l instead of on u. (See Exercises 3.9 and 3.10.) Such a conclusion is not surprising in view of the fact that a utility function (and hence preference ordering) generating h^* may be obtained from l by first normalizing its arguments as in (3.1-11) and then replacing them by the inverse demand function $f(x)$.

EXERCISES

3.1   Prove Lemma 3.1-9 for $n = 2$ and $k = 1$; that is,

$$|U(x)| = (u_2(x))^3 w_{11}^2(x_1, \mu)$$

for all x in E.

3.2   Show by differentiation that demand functions are invariant under positively differentiable transformations of their utility generators.

3.3   From the homogeneity of h^* deduce that $|S^*| = 0$ on Ω^*.

3.4   Consider $u(x) = x_1^2 x_2 + x_1 x_2^2$ defined on $\bar{E}$. Show that hypotheses 3.1-1–3.1-4 are satisfied and derive h. Prove in two different ways that the latter is differentiable everywhere on Γ.

3.5   Show that at each point of Ω there always must be at least one superior good.

3.6   Suppose $u(x) = (x_1 - 1)(x_2 - 2)^{-2}$ is defined on $D = \{x : x_1 \geq 1,$ $0 \leq x_2 < 2\}$. Prove that u satisfies 3.1-1–3.1-3 on D and derive h^* for its interior points. Show that good 2 is superior and $h_2^{*2} < 0$ everywhere on the domain of h^*. Find subsets of the latter on which good 1 is (a) Giffen, and (b) not Giffen.[5]

3.7   Under the assumptions of this chapter prove that x^0 maximizes $u(x)$ subject to $P^0 \cdot x = M^0$ if and only if (P^0, M^0) minimizes $l(P, M)$ subject to $P \cdot x^0 = M$.

3.8   Verify that $u(x) = \sqrt{x_1} + \sqrt{x_2}$ satisfies hypotheses 3.1-1–3.1-3 on $\bar{E}$. Obtain expressions for $l(P, M)$ and $\lambda^*(P, M)$.

3.9   Let l be any function which is homogeneous of degree zero. Show that if h^{*i} is defined by the equation of Theorem 3.5-3 for $i = 1, \ldots, n$, then h^* satisfies the budget constraint. Show further that if $-l_i > 0$ for $i = 1, \ldots, n$, then $\lambda^* > 0$ on Ω^*.

3.10   Derive symmetry and negative definiteness of S^* from the differentiability and quasi-concavity of $-l$.

3.11   Define $\epsilon_{ij} = h_j^{*i}[P_i/h^{*i}]$ for $i, j = 1, \ldots, n$, and $\epsilon_{iM} = h_M^{*i}[M/h^{*i}]$, where $i = 1, \ldots, n$, to be, respectively, *price* and *income elasticities of demand*. Prove the following:

a. $\displaystyle\sum_{j=1}^{n} \epsilon_{ij} = -\epsilon_{iM}, \quad i = 1, \ldots, n.$

b. $\displaystyle\sum_{i=1}^{n} h^{*i}\epsilon_{ij} = -h_j^{*i}, \quad j = 1, \ldots, n.$

c. $\displaystyle\sum_{i=1}^{n} \theta_i \epsilon_{iM} = 1$, where θ_i is the ratio of expenditure on commodity i to total income.

REFERENCES

[1]   Apostol, T. M., *Mathematical Analysis* (Reading, Mass.: Addison-Wesley, 1957).

[2]   Debreu, G., "Definite and Semidefinite Quadratic Forms," *Econometrica* (1952), pp. 295–300.

---

[5] This example is due to Wold and Juréen [13, p. 102].

[3] Hicks, J. R., *Value and Capital* (London: Oxford University Press, 1939).

[4] Hohn, F. E., *Elementary Matrix Algebra*, 2nd ed. (New York: Macmillan, 1964).

[5] Katzner, D. W., "A Note on the Differentiability of Consumer Demand Functions," *Econometrica* (1968), pp. 415–418.

[6] Mosak, J. L., "On the Interpretation of the Fundamental Equation of Value Theory," in O. Lange, F. McIntyre, and T. O. Yntema (eds.), *Studies in Mathematical Economics and Econometrics* (Chicago: University of Chicago Press, 1942).

[7] Pearce, I. F., *A Contribution to Demand Analysis* (London: Oxford University Press, 1964).

[8] Rudin, W., *Principles of Mathematical Analysis* (New York: McGraw-Hill, 1953).

[9] Samuelson, P. A., "The Empirical Implications of Utility Analysis," *Econometrica* (1938), pp. 344–356.

[10] Samuelson, P. A., "The Problem of Integrability in Utility Theory," *Econometrica* (1950), pp. 376–385.

[11] Samuelson, P. A., "Using Full Duality to Show that Simultaneously Additive Direct and Indirect Utilities Implies Unitary Price Elasticity of Demand," *Econometrica* (1965), pp. 781–796.

[12] Slutsky, E. E., "On the Theory of the Budget of the Consumer," *Giornale degli economisti* (1915), pp. 1–26. English translation in G. Stigler and K. Boulding (eds.), *A.E.A. Readings in Price Theory*, v. IV (Homewood, Ill.: Irwin, 1952), pp. 27–56.

[13] Wold, H., and L. Juréen, *Demand Analysis* (New York: Wiley, 1953).

4

Integrability

In a very real sense, the Slutsky theory as presented in the last chapter is incomplete. Utility maximization implies an array of restrictions on the consumer's demand functions which, if not exhibited, invalidate the theory as an explanation of his behavior. But what if these properties are observed? Is he then necessarily a utility maximizer? This question, frequently referred to as the problem of integrability, is as important from an empirical point of view as the implications of utility maximization themselves.

Generally speaking, the answer to the integrability question is rather subtle. For under no conditions will it ever be possible to assert by observing a consumer's behavior that he maximizes a utility function to determine his purchases. But the results of this chapter demonstrate that there may exist a utility function which, when maximized, yields the observed demand functions. Regardless of whether the consumer actually is a utility maximizer, then, his behavior still may be explained as if he were.

To solve the integrability problem requires establishing two facts: (1) that there exists a utility function generating the observed demand functions, and (2) that this utility function satisfies the assumptions of Chapter 3. The given data consist of demand functions and their properties as listed in Table 3.1. Recall that it makes no difference whether the latter are expressed in terms of f, h, or h^*, since the three sets of properties are equivalent. The approach taken here will be to use f. In addition, it is necessary to insist that f have further (relatively unimportant) properties not implied by utility maximization. Reasons for this will become clear below.

4.1 PRELIMINARY CONSIDERATIONS

The term "integrability" is derived from the fact that to establish the existence of Slutsky-type utility functions, it must be possible to perform the

mathematical operation of integration. To see what is involved consider a
two-commodity case. When a utility function is known to exist, the inverse
demand function f^1 is defined at each x in E as the slope of an indifference
curve at x:

$$f^1(x_1, x_2) = -w_1^2(x_1, u(x_1, x_2)).$$

The budget constraint together with f^1 serve as a basis for defining f^2 [recall
(3.1-18)] and inversion then leads to the demand function h. If, on the other
hand, h is given and a utility function is to be found, a natural way of proceeding is by reversing these steps. Inverting h and obtaining, in particular,
f^1 thus provides information on the slopes of possible indifference curves at
each point of E. This is illustrated by Figure 4.1, in which straight-line segments reflect such slopes at selected points. The mathematical issue is whether,
through integration, appropriate slopes can be fitted together to form indifference curves. If so, a utility function may be constructed from them.

Formally, interest centers about the differential equation

$$(4.1\text{-}1) \qquad \frac{dx_2}{dx_1} = -f^1(x_1, x_2),$$

with initial condition x^0. To say that (4.1-1) has a solution through x^0
means that there exists a continuous function w such that

$$\frac{dw(x_1, x^0)}{dx_1} = -f^1(x_1, w(x_1, x^0)),$$

$$x_2^0 = w(x_1^0, x^0).$$

With x^0 interpreted as a parameter, $x_2 = w(x_1, x^0)$ is the equation of an
indifference curve, the first of the above conditions asserting that its slope
is $-f^1$, and the second that it goes through the point x^0. Varying x^0 changes
the curve. But if solutions are unique, one and only one curve may pass
through each point of E. Furthermore, the domain of w (i.e., the set over
which x_1 varies) can range from a local neighborhood about x_1^0 to the entire
space $\{x_1 : x_1 > 0\}$. In the former case utility functions are defined only
locally around x^0, in the latter they are defined globally throughout E.
Because it is possible to have a local solution of (4.1-1) in some neighborhood of each $x_1^0 > 0$ without the existence of a global one, it should not be
surprising that global constructions necessitate more stringent assumptions
than their local counterparts.

Continuing, for expositional purposes, in the local context, (4.1-1) has a
solution under very weak circumstances. The only requirement is that f be
continuous.[1] For uniqueness f must in addition satisfy a *Lipschitz condition*;[2]

[1] See Theorem 6 in Hurewicz [3, p. 10].
[2] See Theorem 3 in Hurewicz [3, pp. 7–8].

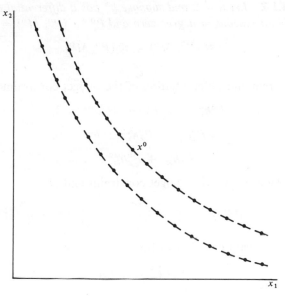

FIGURE 4.1

specifically there should exist a constant $\alpha > 0$ such that for every (x_1, x_2') and (x_1, x_2'') sufficiently close to x^0,

$$|f^1(x_1, x_2') - f^1(x_1, x_2'')| \leq \alpha |x_2' - x_2''|.$$

Of course, to obtain appropriate properties of indifference curves and utility functions, still further restrictions are needed. But the question of integration now is resolved.

The matter would rest here were it not for the fact that a two-commodity world is of little practical interest and that an increase in dimensionality complicates the mathematics considerably. For to obtain integral solutions when there are more than two commodities, it is necessary that a special *integrability condition* also be satisfied. The latter may be stated in any of three equivalent (see Theorem 3.2-13) ways: symmetry of the Antonelli matrix A or of either Slutsky matrices S or S^*. Thus differentiability is an implicit part of the integrability requirement. Note that when $n = 2$ both A and S consist of single elements a_{11} and s_{11}, respectively; hence they are trivially symmetric. On the other hand, S^* is a 2 by 2 matrix and so from the definitional properties of h^* (homogeneity and the budget equality) it should be possible to prove $s_{12}^* = s_{21}^*$. The following theorem shows that this is indeed the case.

Theorem 4.1-2   *Let $n = 2$ and suppose h^* has a differential at (P^0, M^0) in Γ^*. If h^* is homogeneous of degree zero and $P^0 \cdot h^*(P^0, M^0) = M^0$, then*

$$s_{12}^*(P^0, M^0) = s_{21}^*(P^0, M^0).$$

PROOF:

Euler's theorem and differentiation of the budget constraint give

(4.1-3) $P_1^0 h_1^{*1} + P_2^0 h_2^{*1} + M^0 h_M^{*1} = 0,$

(4.1-4) $P_1^0 h_1^{*1} + P_2^0 h_1^{*2} + h^{*1} = 0,$

(4.1-5) $P_1^0 h_M^{*1} + P_2^0 h_M^{*2} - 1 = 0,$

at (P^0, M^0). Hence from the budget constraint and (4.1-5),

$$h_2^{*1} + h^{*2} h_M^{*1} = h_2^{*1} + \frac{M^0}{P_2^0} h_M^{*1} - \frac{1}{P_2^0} h^{*1} + h^{*1} h_M^{*2},$$

which, upon application of first (4.1-3) and then (4.1-4),

$$= h_1^{*2} + h^{*1} h_M^{*2}.$$

Q.E.D.

In what follows both local and global arguments take the approach described above for the two-commodity world. Assumptions are imposed on inverse demand functions, integration is based on f, and the resulting indifference map is used to construct a utility function with the desired properties. An alternative route has been suggested by Hurwicz and Uzawa [4]: impose restrictions on and integrate h. This yields the support or expenditure function (see Section 6.2), from which a utility representation then can be derived. The latter method and its relation to the former are not explored here. Suffice it to note that in many situations either technique may be employed, although there are circumstances which permit use of only one. These procedures, then, apply to overlapping but different classes of demand functions.

4.2 LOCAL INTEGRATION

Let x^0 be a fixed point of E and $(p^0, m^0) = f(x^0)$. Suppose f is defined in some neighborhood, N, of x^0 and $f(N)$ is a subset of Γ. Let the matrix $A(x)$ be as in Chapter 3 and f_{nn}^j denote the second partial derivative of f^j with respect to the last commodity. Assume

4.2-1. f is $1:1$ and continuously differentiable on N.

4.2-2. f_{nn}^j exists continuously on N for $j = 1, \ldots, n$.

4.2-3. For all x in N,

$$f^n(x) = x_n + \sum_{j=1}^{n-1} f^j(x)x_j.$$

4.2-4. $A(x)$ is symmetric and negative definite on N.

These assumptions are stronger than the implications of utility maximization (relative to N) in two respects. First, 4.2-2 is added to deduce the second-order differentiability of u. Second, in view of the discussion of Section B.5, more then negative definiteness of $A(x)$ on at least a dense, open subset of N is required to prove the strict convexity of indifference surfaces. For convenience it is assumed that $A(x)$ is negative definite on N, although this could be weakened slightly by using Theorem B.5-9 or B.5-10. Note that f satisfies the appropriate Lipschitz condition on any compact subset of N.

The integration theorem needed here is due to Nikliborc. Using the continuous differentiability of f and the integrability condition, its proof is based on Piccard's method of successive approximations and may be found in [5].

Theorem 4.2-5   *For each* $x^* = (x_{(n)}^*, x_n^*)$ *in N there is an* $(n-1)$*-dimensional neighborhood* N^* *of* $x_{(n)}^*$ *and a unique function* $w(x_{(n)}, x^*)$ *defined on* N^* *such that*

$$w(x_{(n)}^*, x_n^*) = x_n^*,$$

and the derivatives[3]

$$w_j(x_{(n)}, x^*) = -f^j(x_{(n)}, w(x_{(n)}, x^*)), \quad j = 1, \ldots, n-1,$$

for all $x_{(n)}$ *in* N^*.

Of course, w is the indifference surface w^n through x^* of Chapter 3. The next two results assert properties of w formerly derived from the utility function.

Theorem 4.2-6   *Let* x^* *be any point of N. Then as a function of* $x_{(n)}$, w *is strictly convex on* N^* *and* $w_j(x_{(n)}, x^*) < 0$ *for* $j = 1, \ldots, n-1$.

PROOF:

That the w_j are negative follows immediately from Theorem 4.2-5 and the definition of f. Also from Theorem 4.2-5, $w_{ij} = -a_{ij}$ (recall the proof of Lemma 3.2-2). The negative definiteness of $A(x_{(n)}, w(x_{(n)}, x^*))$ and Theorem B.5-2 now imply that w is strictly convex.

Q.E.D.

---

[3] These derivatives are with respect to the first $n-1$ arguments of w only.

In addition to thinking of w as a function of $x_{(n)}$ for fixed x^*, it may also be considered a function of $x_{(n)}$ and x_n^* for fixed $x_{(n)}^*$. Under the latter interpretation, it follows without using assumption 4.2-2 that w is continuous[4] in $(x_{(n)}, x_n^*)$ on N. Thus a preference ordering can be constructed which is increasing, total, strictly convex, and continuous in a neighborhood of x^0. By the argument of Chapter 2, a continuous, increasing, strictly quasi-concave utility representation exists locally around x^0. But 4.2-2 is needed to obtain second-order differentiability of the utility function. To this end denote the first and second-order derivatives of w with respect to x_n^* by w_n and w_{nn}.

Lemma 4.2-7   *For any x^* in N, $w_n(x_{(n)}, x^*) > 0$ and w_{nn} exists and is continuous at $(x_{(n)}, x^*)$.*

PROOF:

By a straightforward generalization of a well-known result from the theory of ordinary differential equations [3, pp. 13–14], it may be verified that

$$(4.2\text{-}8) \qquad w_n(x_{(n)}, x^*) = \exp \sum_{k=1}^{n} \int_{x_k^\ast}^{x_k} f_n^k(x_{(n)}, w(x_{(n)}, x^*)) dx_k,$$

for $x_{(n)}$ in N^*. Therefore, $w_n > 0$. The rest of the conclusion follows from 4.2-2 by differentiating (4.2-8).[5]

Q.E.D.

A utility function may now be constructed on N. Let $L = \{x : x \text{ is in } N \text{ and } x = (x_{(n)}^0, x_n)\}$ be a line segment through the original x^0. Suppose that for each x^* the surface $w(x_{(n)}, x^*)$ and L have exactly one point in common. Then for any x in N define u by

$$u(x) = \bar{x}_n,$$

where

$$\bar{x}_n = w(x_{(n)}^0, x).$$

This is illustrated in Figure 4.2. (If not all indifference surfaces intersect L, u can be extended to the remainder of N, as in Theorem 2.3-3. The following argument is modified accordingly.) Since each integral surface, $w(x_{(n)}, x^*)$, is unique, the above definition is equivalent to

$$(4.2\text{-}9) \qquad\qquad u(x) = \bar{x}_n,$$

where $\bar{x}_n$ is the (unique) solution of the equation

$$x_n = w(x_{(n)}, x_{(n)}^0, \bar{x}_n).$$

---

[4] This may be verified by appropriately generalizing Theorem 8 in Hurewicz [3, pp. 12–13].

[5] Differentiation under the integral sign is justified by Theorem 9-37 in Apostol [2, p. 219].

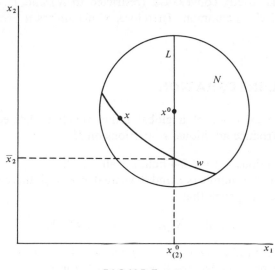

$$FIGURE\ 4.2$$

Theorem 4.2-10   *For all x in N, u is twice continuously differentiable,*
$u_i(x) > 0$, *where* $i = 1, \ldots, n$, *and u is strictly quasi-concave.*

PROOF:
Applying the implicit function theorem to the function w of definition
(4.2-9) at each point of N, it follows from Lemma 4.2-7 that u is twice continuously differentiable on N and $u_n(x) > 0$. Furthermore,

$$u_j(x) = -w_j(x_{(n)}, x_{(n)}^0, \bar{x}_n)u_n(x), \quad j = 1, \ldots, n - 1.$$

The rest of the conclusion is now a consequence of Theorem 4.2-6.

Q.E.D.

Thus the local integrability problem is almost solved: a utility function
exists on N which satisfies the appropriate requirements. It remains to show
that u generates the original inverse demand function f.

Theorem 4.2-11   *Let x' be in N and* $(p', m') = f(x')$. *Then x' maximizes u*
(locally) over $B^{\leq}(p', m')$.

PROOF:
From 4.2-3, $(p', 1) \cdot x' = m'$ and hence x' is in $B^{=}(p', m')$. Also, by Theorem
4.2-5,

$$w_j(x'_{(n)}, x') = -p'_j, \quad j = 1, \ldots, n - 1.$$

Thus, since w is strictly convex, $C_{x'}^{\geq}$ (restricted to N) and $B^=(p', m')$ have only one point, x', in common. Therefore, x' maximizes u over $B^{\leq}(p', m')$.

Q.E.D.

4.3 GLOBAL INTEGRATION

To prove the existence of a global utility function defined on $\bar{E}$ it is necessary to introduce additional restrictions on f:

4.3-1. Assumptions 4.2-1–4.2-4 hold for all x in E.

4.3-2. For any real numbers α and β where $0 < \alpha < \beta$, there exists a finite number $K_{\alpha,\beta}$ such that

$$|f_n^j(x)| \leq K_{\alpha,\beta}, \quad j = 1, \ldots, n - 1,$$

for all x in E where $\alpha < x_j < \beta$ and $j = 1, \ldots, n - 1$.

4.3-3. f may be extended to $D = \{x : x_j > 0 \text{ for } j = 1, \ldots, n - 1, \text{ and } x_n = 0\}$ such that

(a) $f(x) = 0$ on D,

(b) f is continuously differentiable on $E \cup D$.

Note that from the point of view of Chapter 3, assumptions 3.1-2 and 3.1-4 imply

$$\lim_{x_n \to 0} f^j(x) = 0, \quad j = 1, \ldots, n,$$

for all x in E. Hence 4.3-3 is a relatively minor strengthening of this property.

The purpose of 4.3-2 and 4.3-3 is to permit application of a global integration theorem due to Hurwicz and Uzawa [4]. Their proof is similar to that of Theorem 4.2-5 and is not presented here.

Theorem 4.3-4 *For every x^0 in $E \cup D$ there exists a unique function $w(x_{(n)}, x^0)$ mapping $E^{(n)}$ into the nonnegative real line such that*

(a) *$w(x_{(n)}^0, x^0) = x_n^0$, where $x^0 = (x_{(n)}^0, x_n)$.*

(b) *For all $x_{(n)}$ in $E^{(n)}$,*

$$w(x_{(n)}, x^0) \begin{cases} > 0, & \text{if } x^0 \text{ is in } E, \\ = 0, & \text{if } x^0 \text{ is in } D. \end{cases}$$

(c) *For all $x_{(n)}$ in $E^{(n)}$ and any $j = 1, \ldots, n - 1$,*

$$w_j(x_{(n)}, x^0) = \begin{cases} -f^j(x_{(n)}, w(x_{(n)}, x^0)), & \text{if } x^0 \text{ is in } E, \\ 0, & \text{if } x^0 \text{ is in } D. \end{cases}$$

The argument is now almost identical to that of the previous section. The proofs of Theorems 4.2-6 and 4.2-10 need only trivial adjustments. Thus w is strictly convex and $w_j < 0$ on E. A global utility function, u, may be defined as in Figure 4.2 and equation (4.2-9). It is twice continuously differentiable, strictly quasi-concave, and has positive partial derivatives on E. Extend u to the boundary of E by setting

$$u(x) = \lim_{k \to \infty} u(x^k)$$

for x in $\bar{E} - E$, where $\{x^k\}$ is any sequence in E converging to x as k approaches ∞. Then u is continuous on $\bar{E}$ and

(4.3-5) $$u(x) = 0$$

for all x in $\bar{E} - E$. [Note that the existence of a utility representation satisfying (4.3-5) is implied by the hypotheses of Chapter 3.] Furthermore, since f is everywhere 1:1, the indifference surfaces of u cannot intersect the boundary of E. Finally, Theorem 4.2-11 also carries over to this case. The following solution to the global integrability problem has therefore been established.

Theorem 4.3-6 *Assumptions 4.3-1–4.3-3 imply that there exists a utility function satisfying 3.1-1–3.1-4 which, through the process of constrained maximization, generates the given inverse demand function f.*

EXERCISES

4.1 Consider the demand functions

$$h^{*i}(P, M) = \frac{M}{3P_i}, \quad i = 1, 2, 3.$$

Compute f and show that assumptions 4.3-1–4.3-3 are satisfied. Find a utility generator and verify 3.1-1–3.1-4 along with the property $u(x) = 0$ on the boundary of E.

4.2 Repeat Exercise 4.1 for

$$h^{*i}(P, M) = \frac{1}{\sqrt{P_i}} \left(\frac{M}{\sqrt{P_1} + \sqrt{P_2} + \sqrt{P_3}} \right), \quad i = 1, 2, 3.$$

Note that in this case all assumptions except 4.3-2 are met. Nevertheless, global integration still can be performed and a utility function found having the properties of Exercise 4.1. Thus the hypotheses of Theorem 4.3-6 are sufficient but not necessary to solve the integrability problem. What does Theorem 4.3-4 imply about indifference surfaces in general which is not satisfied here?

REFERENCES

[1] Antonelli, G. B., *Teoria mathematica della economica politica* (Pisa, 1886); English translation, "On the Mathematical Theory of Political Economy," in J. S. Chipman et al. (eds.), *Studies in the Mathematical Foundations of Utility and Demand Theory* (New York: Harcourt, Brace & World, forthcoming).

[2] Apostol, T. M., *Mathematical Analysis* (Reading Mass.: Addison-Wesley, 1957).

[3] Hurewicz, W., *Lectures on Ordinary Differential Equations* (New York: Wiley, 1958).

[4] Hurwicz, L., and H. Uzawa, "On the Integrability of Demand Functions," in J. S. Chipman et al. (eds.), *Studies in the Mathematical Foundations of Utility and Demand Theory* (New York: Harcourt, Brace & World, forthcoming).

[5] Nikliborc, W., "Sur les équations linéaires aux différentielles totales," *Studia Mathematica* (1929), pp. 41–49.

[6] Pareto, V., "Economie mathématique," *Encyclopédie des Sciences Mathématiques*, tome 1, 4, fasc. 4 (Paris, 1911), pp. 591–640; English translation, "Mathematical Economics," *International Economic Papers*, no. 5 (1955), pp. 58–102.

[7] Samuelson, P. A., "The Problem of Integrability in Utility Theory," *Economica* (1950), pp. 335–385.

5

Special Kinds
of Utility Functions

$\mathbf{F}$or a wide variety of theoretical and empirical reasons, it is often useful to study special classes of utility functions which satisfy restrictions additional to 3.1-1–3.1-4. Extra assumptions, in particular, may permit considerable analytical simplification, the application of specific empirical techniques, or may provide a basis for exploring independent economic problems such as the theory of index numbers. In this chapter the more popular of these are characterized in terms of their implications for market behavior. Many have already been discussed with respect to preference orderings in Chapter 2.

As a pedagogical device it is convenient to refer to the properties of demand functions listed in Table 3.1 as *necessary properties*. These follow necessarily from the assumptions of utility maximization. Similarly, the hypotheses of Theorem 4.3-6 are called *sufficient properties* because they are sufficient to ensure the existence of an appropriate utility generator. Most questions raised in this chapter, then, are of two kinds: what are the additional necessary properties implied by the particular utility functions considered, and what are the additional sufficient properties needed to guarantee the existence of such a special utility generator? Loosely speaking, the additional necessary properties turn out to be additionally sufficient.

Similar problems arise when 3.1-1–3.1-4 are not entirely met. Thus, for example, all quasi-linear and quadratic (see Exercise 5.9) utility functions violate 3.1-4, and in the latter case 3.1-2 does not hold everywhere. Nevertheless, both types of representations satisfy 3.1-1–3.1-3 on an appropriate subset of $\bar{E}$. The consequences of these weaker restrictions in general are studied in Chapter 6. But it is still important to know the additional implications of certain utility functions occurring only under such circumstances. Some attention will be devoted to them below.

Before proceeding, however, one word of caution: frequent use is made of phrases such as "assume that a utility function has a certain additional property." This is not intended to imply that all utility representations of the underlying preference ordering have that property. Rather it should be interpreted to mean only that there exists at least one representation with the required property and this representation is under consideration at the moment.

5.1 HOMOGENEITY

A function $u(x)$ is said to be *homogeneous of* degree k whenever $u(\alpha x) = \alpha^k u(x)$ for any x and all real $\alpha > 0$. Recall the cases $k = 1$ (linear homogeneity) and $k = 0$ which have appeared earlier. Only $k > 0$ is considered here. It is clear that if u is homogeneous of degree $k > 0$, then applying the transformation $T(\mu) = \mu^{1/k}$ yields a linearly homogeneous function. But if u is a utility representation, this transformation can have no effect on either the consumer's underlying preferences or his market behavior. There is no loss in generality, then, in confining attention to the implications for demand functions of assuming only the existence of a linearly homogeneous representation.

Theorem 5.1-1 *If, in addition to 3.1-1–3.1-4, u is homogeneous of degree one, then for all (p, m) in Γ,*

$$(5.1\text{-}2) \qquad\qquad h(p, m) = m\varphi(p),$$

where φ has a single-valued inverse and $\varphi(p) = h(p, 1)$ for every $p > 0$.

PROOF:

Since u is homogeneous of degree one, its derivatives, u_i, are homogeneous of degree 0. Hence the inverse demand functions may be written in either of two equivalent forms:

$$f(x) = (p, m),$$

or

$$f\left(\frac{1}{m} x\right) = (p, 1).$$

But regardless of how it is written, f still has an inverse (Theorem 3.1-13). In the former case it is $h(p, m)$ defined on Γ, in the latter denote it by $\varphi(p)$ defined for all $p > 0$. Therefore,

$$h(p, m) = m\varphi(p).$$

Setting $m = 1$,

$$\varphi(p) = h(p, 1)$$

for all $p > 0$.

Q.E.D.

Further properties of φ may be deduced from those of h and are not considered here. Note that the expenditure proportionality exhibited in (5.1-2) implies that all income elasticities of demand (see Exercise 3.11) are unity on Γ. Furthermore, $h_m^i(p, m) = \varphi^i(p) > 0$ for $i = 1, \ldots, n$, and all (p, m) in Γ. Thus from Slutsky's equation, $h_i^i < 0$; i.e., the Marshallian demand curves are downward sloping.

Linear homogeneity of u also implies

$$w_j^n(\alpha x_{(n)}, u(\alpha x)) = w_j^n(x_{(n)}, u(x)), \quad j = 1, \ldots, n - 1,$$

for all positive α and x. Thus no partial derivative of w^n can vary along any ray from the origin in E. This is illustrated in Figure 5.1, where the slope of indifference curve 1 at x' is identical to that of 2 at x''. Now the *Engel curve given p^0* is defined to be the set of points in E satisfying

$$f^j(x) = p_j^0, \quad j = 1, \ldots, n - 1.$$

Clearly, then, if the budget line in Figure 5.1 has slope $-p^0$ (here p^0 is a scalar), then γ is the corresponding Engel curve. In general, linear homogeneity guarantees that all Engel curves are linear and, if extended, would intersect the origin.

The integrability problem in this context is as follows; given demand functions of the form (5.1-2), does there exist a linearly homogeneous utility function generating them? In other words, is it possible to derive (5.1-2)

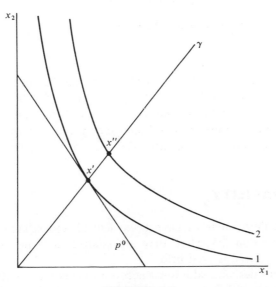

FIGURE 5.1

from a preference ordering which is not homothetic? An answer is provided by the next result.

Theorem 5.1-3 *Let u satisfy 3.1-1–3.1-4 and generate h. If for some φ, $h(p, m) = m\varphi(p)$ on Γ, then there exists a linearly homogeneous generator of h.*

PROOF:

Let $p^0 > 0$ be fixed and consider

$$\mu = u(m\varphi(p^0)).$$

Then as a function of the single variable m, the derivative of u is always positive. By the inverse function theorem there exists a function T defined on the range of u such that $m = T(\mu)$ or

$$m = T(u(x)).$$

Now $T(u)$ is an increasing transformation of u and therefore generates h. Furthermore, for any i,

$$x_i = T(u(x))\varphi^i(p^0),$$

from (5.1-2). Thus for all real numbers $\alpha > 0$,

$$\alpha x_i = T(u(\alpha x))\varphi^i(p^0).$$

The last two equations imply

$$T(u(\alpha x)) = \alpha T(u(x)),$$

thus completing the proof of the theorem.

Q.E.D.

Note the hypothesis of the above theorem may be stated completely in terms of h by assuming 4.3-1–4.3-3 together with (5.1-2). But in view of Theorem 4.3-6, the conclusion and its proof remain unchanged.

It turns out that the property of homogeneity and its implications appear frequently throughout the remainder of this chapter.

5.2 SEPARABILITY

Separable utility functions have been defined and related to preference orderings in Section 2.4. Here they are studied in terms of h. Notation previously introduced is used below.

The argument deriving additional necessary properties implied by various kinds of separability has an interesting structure. It is essentially based on

Theorem 5.2-2, which permits use of the ordinary theory of utility maximization to analyze weak separability. The implications of strong separability may then be deduced by repeated application of the results for weak separability. Similarly, those of additivity are derived by applying the conclusions from strong separability. The argument concerned with additional sufficiency properties is structured analogously.

Given the partition $\{N_1, \ldots, N_\pi\}$, where $N_i = \{k_{i-1} + 1, \ldots, k_i\}$, recall that weak separability requires

$$u(x) = V(v^1(x_{\bar{1}}), \ldots, v^\pi(x_{\bar{\pi}})),$$

where V and the $v^1, \ldots, v^\pi$ are continuous. Assume $\pi > 1$,

5.2-1. $V, v^1, \ldots, v^\pi$ are twice continuously differentiable in the interior of their respective domains and all the first-order partial derivatives of V are everywhere positive,

and, for convenience only, that each N_i contains more than one element.

Theorem 5.2-2 *If, in addition to 3.1-1–3.1-4, u is weakly separable under 5.2-1, then each v^i also satisfies 3.1-1–3.1-4 on $\bar{E}^i$.*

PROOF:

Properties 3.1-1, 3.1-2, and 3.1-4 are trivial. To prove that v^i is strictly quasi-concave, suppose $v^i(x'_{\bar{i}}) = v^i(x''_{\bar{i}})$ for distinct $x'_{\bar{i}}$ and $x''_{\bar{i}}$ in E^i. Choose $x'_{(\bar{i})} = x''_{(\bar{i})}$. Then

$$u(x') = u(x''),$$

where $x' = (x'_{\bar{i}}, x'_{(\bar{i})})$ and $x'' = (x''_{\bar{i}}, x''_{(\bar{i})})$. By the strict quasi-concavity of u, for any θ between 0 and 1,

$$V(\ldots, v^i(\theta x'_{\bar{i}} + [1 - \theta]x''_{\bar{i}}), \ldots) > V(\ldots, v^i(x'_{\bar{i}}), \ldots),$$

where "$\ldots$" replaces appropriate $v^j(x'_{\bar{j}})$ identical on both sides of the inequality. Since the derivative $V_i > 0$, the conclusion is now immediate.

Q.E.D.

Note from the relationship between derivatives of indifference surfaces and utility functions in (3.1-8) that if j and r are in N_i, the slopes, w^r_j, of the former depend only on the commodities in N_i. In particular,

$$w^r_j(x_{(r)}, \mu) = -\frac{v^i_j(x_{\bar{i}})}{v^i_r(x_{\bar{i}})},$$

where subscripts on the v^i, as usual, denote derivatives and, recall, $x_{(r)} = (x_1, \ldots, x_{r-1}, x_{r+1}, \ldots, x_n)$. This suggests an analogous property of demand functions to be derived next.

From the theory of Chapter 3, a utility function u generates demand functions $h(p, m)$ which satisfy various restrictions on Γ. In accordance with the underlying partition of commodities, let

$$p_{\bar{\imath}} = \left(\frac{P_{k_{i-1}+1}}{P_{k_i}}, \ldots, \frac{P_{k_i-1}}{P_{k_i}}\right),$$

$$h^{\bar{\imath}} = (h^{k_{i-1}+1}, \ldots, h^{k_i}),$$

(5.2-3) $m_{\bar{\imath}} = (p_{\bar{\imath}}, 1) \cdot h^{\bar{\imath}}(p, m),$

and $\Gamma^i = \{(p_{\bar{\imath}}, m_{\bar{\imath}}): p_{\bar{\imath}} > 0, m_{\bar{\imath}} > 0\}$ for $i = 1, \ldots, \pi$. Now for each i, think of the consumer as choosing $x_{\bar{\imath}}$ so as to maximize v^i subject to (5.2-3) and apply the theory of Chapter 3 (this approach is justified by Theorem 5.2-2). It is clear from (5.2-3) that any point of Γ^i may appear by suitably choosing (p, m). Hence there exists a vector of functions $g^{\bar{\imath}} = (g^{k_{i-1}+1}, \ldots, g^{k_i})$ defined on Γ^i having all the properties listed in Table 3.1. These may be called *conditional demand functions*, since they depend on expenditure allocated to other commodities; i.e.,

$$m_{\bar{\imath}} = m - \sum_{j \neq i} m_{\bar{\jmath}}.$$

Furthermore, $g^{\bar{\imath}}$ has been defined so that

(5.2-4) $h^{\bar{\imath}}(p, m) = g^{\bar{\imath}}(p_{\bar{\imath}}, m_{\bar{\imath}}), \quad i = 1, \ldots, \pi,$

on Γ. Therefore if the consumer knows v^i, $p_{\bar{\imath}}$, and $m_{\bar{\imath}}$, he can determine all his purchases of commodities in group i without knowing the remainder of his utility function. He need only order by preference the points of E^i to be able to behave rationally.

These conclusions have special importance in empirical analysis. For by assuming weak separability many price variables in the equations $x_i = h^i(p, m)$ can be eliminated. Demand for a particular commodity within a group depends only on the prices of goods in that group and expenditure on the group as a whole. Hence the computational and data-gathering problems associated with estimating h in general for extremely large values of n can be substantially reduced. The reader interested in an example of the use of this technique is referred to Pearce [8]. An illustration of theoretical applications of weak separability appears in Chapter 7 (Theorem 7.3-8).

The differential properties implied by weak separability may be expressed in terms of the Slutsky functions s_{jr} defined on Ω with respect to h. The proof below is due to Pollak [9].

Theorem 5.2-5   *Let $i' \neq i''$ and suppose $\partial m_{\bar{\imath}'}/\partial m$, $\partial m_{\bar{\imath}''}/\partial m$, and h_m^j for all j in $N_{i'} \cup N_{i''}$, do not vanish on Ω. Then there exists a function $\sigma^{i'i''}$ defined on Ω such that for all j in $N_{i'}$ and r in $N_{i''}$,*

$$s_{jr}(p, m) = \sigma^{i'i''}(p, m)h_m^j(p, m)h_m^r(p, m).$$

PROOF:

Let j be in $N_{i'}$ and r in $N_{i''}$. Differentiating (5.2-4),

$$h_r^j = \tau^{i'i''r} h_m^j,$$

where

$$\tau^{i'i''r} = \frac{\partial m_{i'}/\partial p_r}{\partial m_{i'}/\partial m}.$$

Since $h_m^r \neq 0$ on Ω, this and the definition of s_{jr} in (3.2-6) imply that

$$s_{jr} = \sigma^{i'i''r} h_m^j h_m^r,$$

where

$$\sigma^{i'i''r} = \frac{\tau^{i'i''r} + h_m^r}{h_m^r}.$$

Similarly,

$$s_{rj} = \sigma^{i''i'j} h_m^r h_m^j.$$

But $s_{jr} = s_{rj}$ (Theorem 3.2-11) and hence $\sigma^{i'i''r}$ and $\sigma^{i''i'j}$ depend neither on r and j nor on the order of i' and i''. Writing $\sigma^{i'i''}$ for $\sigma^{i'i''r}$ and $\sigma^{i''i'j}$ completes the proof.

Q.E.D.

The additional necessary properties implied by weak separability, then, are (5.2-4), Theorem 5.2-5, and all the properties of each set of functions $g^{\bar{\imath}}$. To obtain additional sufficient properties, it is only required to add to the restrictions on each $g^{\bar{\imath}}$ in the same fashion that restrictions were added to h in Section 4.3 to obtain a utility generator of the latter.

Theorem 5.2-6 *Let u satisfy 3.1-1–3.1-4 and generate h. For each $i = 1, \ldots, \pi$, assume $g^{\bar{\imath}}$ (i.e., its inverse) satisfies 4.3-1–4.3-3 on Γ^i. If h and the $g^{\bar{\imath}}$ are related by (5.2-4), then u is weakly separable.*

PROOF:

By Theorem 4.3-6 there exist utility generators v^i satisfying 3.1-1–3.1-4 for each $g^{\bar{\imath}}$. A continuous V could now be defined as in the proof of Theorem 2.4-1. But to obtain the differentiability of 5.2-1 requires an argument from the theory of functional dependence.

Write $z_i = v^i(x_{\bar{\imath}})$ and let the indifference surfaces of each v^i be

$$x_{k_i} = \psi^i(y_i, z_i), \quad i = 1, \ldots, \pi,$$

where $y_i = (x_{k_{i-1}+1}, \ldots, x_{k_i-1})$. Then ψ^i is twice continuously differentiable on its domain (recall Section 3.1). Let $y = (y_1, \ldots, y_\pi)$, $z = (z_1, \ldots, z_\pi)$, and $\psi = (\psi^1, \ldots, \psi^\pi)$. Define V by

$$V(y, z) = u(y, \psi(y, z)),$$

where the arguments of u have been rearranged so that $\mu = u(y, x_{k_1}, \ldots, x_{k_n})$. Note that V is twice continuously differentiable and its first-order partial derivatives with respect to each z_i are positive. The theorem will therefore be proved upon showing that the derivatives of V with respect to the elements of y are identically zero. But if x_j is one of these elements, then the derivative with respect to it is

$$V_{x_j} = u_j + u_r \psi_j^r,$$

for some r where $1 \le r \le \pi$ and ψ_j^r is the derivative of ψ^r, also with respect to x_j. On the other hand, by virtue of (5.2-4) and (3.1-8),

$$\psi_j^r = -\frac{u_j}{u_r},$$

whence $V_{x_j} \equiv 0$.

Q.E.D.

The concept of strong separability is defined in terms of utility functions for partitions containing three or more sets. For simplicity, the trivial case in which the N_i may contain only one element is again avoided. Thus

$$u(x) = V\left(\sum_{i=1}^{\pi} v^i(x_{\overline{i}})\right),$$

where, as in 5.2-1, it is now assumed that

5.2-7. The derivative V' exists and is positive on the interior of its domain.

In this case the slopes of indifference surfaces, say w_j^r, do not depend on commodities outside of the N_i which contain r and j. Recall that for weak separability this was true only if r and j were in the same N_i.

As has been previously pointed out, strong separability with respect to $\{N_1, \ldots, N_\pi\}$ implies weak separability with respect to $\{N_1, \ldots, N_\pi\}$ and to each of the partitions consisting of all possible unions of $N_1, \ldots, N_\pi$ except $\{1, \ldots, n\}$. Let each such partition be represented by a number ϵ and set

$$g^\epsilon(p, m) = (g^{\epsilon \overline{1}}(p_{\overline{1}}, m_{\overline{1}}), \ldots, g^{\epsilon \overline{\pi}_\epsilon}(p_{\overline{\pi}_\epsilon}, m_{\overline{\pi}_\epsilon})),$$

where π_ϵ is the number of sets in the partition ϵ and the $g^{\epsilon \tau}$ are defined as in (5.2-4) with respect to ϵ. The previous discussion of weak separability now implies the following result.

Theorem 5.2-8 *If, in addition to 3.1-1–3.1-4, u is strongly separable with respect to $\{N_1, \ldots, N_\pi\}$, then there exist distinct functions g^ϵ such that each $g^{\epsilon \tau}$ has all the properties implied by utility maximization and for all (p, m) in Γ,*

$$h(p, m) = g^\epsilon(p, m),$$

for every ϵ.

Similarly, the differential properties derived from strong separability may be proved by repeated applications of Theorem 5.2-5.

Theorem 5.2-9 *If for all i and j, $\partial m_i/\partial m$ and h_m^j do not vanish on Ω, then there exists a function σ defined thereon such that*

$$s_{jr}(p, m) = \sigma(p, m)h_m^j(p, m)h_m^r(p, m),$$

for any j and r not in the same N_i.

On the sufficiency side, application is again made of the results from weak separability.

Theorem· 5.2-10 *Let u satisfy 3.1-1–3.1-4 and generate h. If each g^ϵ satisfies the hypothesis of Theorem 5.2-6, then u is strongly separable.*

PROOF:

By Theorem 5.2-6 there exist twice continuously differentiable functions V^ϵ and $v^{\epsilon i}$ such that

$$u(x) = V^\epsilon(v^{\epsilon 1}(x_{\bar{1}}), \ldots, v^{\epsilon \pi_\epsilon}(x_{\bar{\pi}_\epsilon})),$$

where the V^ϵ have positive, first order derivatives. As in Theorem 2.4-2, the conclusion now follows from a differential version of the theorem on functional equations used there [1, p. 329] and an induction argument on π.

Q.E.D.

The most stringent form of separability is, of course, additivity. Recall that u is additive if and only if it is strongly separable with respect to the pointwise partition $\{\{1\}, \ldots, \{n\}\}$ and V is the identity function. Thus

$$u(x) = \sum_{i=1}^{n} v^i(x_i),$$

for all x in E. For $n = 2$ Samuelson [11] gives one additional necessary and sufficient property. It may be stated in terms of the inverse demand function, f, provided the latter is twice differentiable:

$$f(x)f_{12}(x) = f_1(x)f_2(x),$$

or, equivalently,

$$\frac{\partial \log f(x)}{\partial x_1\, \partial x_2} = 0,$$

on E. To prove sufficiency, note that integration of the latter gives

$$f(x) = \frac{\xi^1(x_1)}{\xi^2(x_2)}$$

for appropriate functions ξ^1 and ξ^2. Hence the utility function

$$u(x) = \int \xi^1(x_1)dx_1 + \int \xi^2(x_2)dx_2$$

generates f. Necessity may be verified by differentiating

$$f(x) = \frac{v_1^1(x_1)}{v_2^2(x_2)}.$$

If $n > 2$ the theory of strong separability applies to every partition of $\{1, \ldots, n\}$ whose sets contain at least two elements. Note that if a set contains only, say, commodity 1, then clearly

$$h^1(p, m) = \frac{m_{\bar{1}}}{p_1}.$$

Therefore, in the additive case h may be written in the largest number of distinct ways. In addition, there exists a function σ defined on Ω such that

$$s_{ij}(p, m) = \sigma(p, m)h_m^i(p, m)h_m^j(p, m), \quad i \neq j,$$

whenever $h_m^r \neq 0$ on Γ for all r.

At this point in the discussion of separability of Section 2.4 the Bergson class of utility functions was introduced as a special case of both additivity and homogeneity. This class also provides a convenient illustration of the present analysis. Note, however, that Bergson utility functions do not satisfy 3.1-4 when $0 < b < 1$. The following properties of demand therefore apply only to that subset of Γ mapped by h into interior points of $\bar{E}$. General treatment of boundary maxima is deferred to Chapter 6. If u is Bergson with $b < 1$ [in addition to 3.1-1–3.1-3], then from (2.4.5),

$$(5.2\text{-}11) \quad h^i(p, m) = m \frac{(p_i/\alpha_i)^{1/(b-1)}}{(1/\alpha_n)^{1/(b-1)} + \sum\limits_{j=1}^{n-1} p_j(p_j/\alpha_j)^{1/(b-1)}}, \quad i = 1, \ldots, n-1,$$

and h^n is identical except that p_i in the numerator is replaced by 1. If $b = 0$, (5.2-11) reduces to

$$(5.2\text{-}12) \qquad h^i(p, m) = \delta_i \frac{m}{p_i}, \quad i = 1, \ldots, n-1,$$

where $h^n(p, m) = \delta_n m$ and $\sum_{i=1}^n \delta_i = 1$. The function φ of (5.1-2) and the various forms in which h, by dint of additivity, may appear are easily written down. Also, if $i \neq j$,

$$(5.2\text{-}13) \qquad \begin{aligned} h_j^i &= -\frac{b}{b-1} h^i h_m^j, \\[2mm] s_{ij} &= -\frac{m}{b-1} h_m^i h_m^j, \end{aligned}$$

and hence, since $h_m^r > 0$ for all r, the latter cross-substitution terms are positive. That (5.2-11) is sufficient for there to exist a Bergson generator of h may be deduced from the argument of the previous paragraph and Theorems 5.1-3 and 2.4-4. This is often called the *Bergson class of demand functions.*

5.3 INDIRECT SEPARABILITY

Assuming separability of the indirect utility function, l, provides another means of obtaining additional restrictions on demand functions; and in view of Theorem 5.3-4, properties analogous to (5.2-4) are not difficult to obtain. To avoid repetition, however, only two kinds of separability are considered. It will greatly simplify matters to assume that the indirect utility function is continuously differentiable everywhere; i.e., $\Gamma^* = \Omega^*$. This will be done throughout. Results are also stated in terms of h^* rather than h and the discussion begins with further analysis of the properties of l.

Recall from Section 3.5 that the indirect utility function is defined by

(5.3-1) $$l(P, M) = u(h^*(P, M)),$$

on Γ^*. Thus l is homogeneous of degree zero and l_M (the marginal utility of income) and the l_i are homogeneous of degree -1. Recall also that

(5.3-2) $$h^{*i}(P, M) = -\frac{l_i(P, M)}{l_M(P, M)}, \quad i = 1, \ldots, n,$$

for all (P, M) in Γ^* (Theorem 3.5-3). Now write

$$l(f(x)) = l(f^1(x), \ldots, f^{n-1}(x), 1, f^n(x)),$$

where f is the inverse demand function. Then a converse to Theorem 3.5-3 may be proved.

Theorem 5.3-3 *Let u satisfy 3.1-1–3.1-4 and generate h^*. If there is a function l satisfying (5.3-2) on Γ^*, then there exists an increasing transformation T such that*

$$l(P, M) = T(u(h^*(P, M))),$$

for all (P, M) in Γ^*.

PROOF:

Let $\zeta(x) = l(f(x))$. Then ζ is differentiable and, using (5.3-2), its derivatives

$$\zeta_i = l_M f^i, \quad i = 1, \ldots, n-1,$$

$$\zeta_n = l_M.$$

Thus

$$\frac{\zeta_i}{\zeta_n} = f^i, \quad i = 1, \ldots, n,$$

so ζ is an increasing, strictly quasi-concave utility function generating h^*. Hence there must be an increasing transformation T such that

$$\zeta(x) = T(u(x)).$$

The conclusion now follows by substituting $x = h^*(P, M)$ into this equation.

Q.E.D.

Thus, under the assumptions of Theorem 5.3-3, l is an indirect utility function if and only if it satisfies either (5.3-1) or (5.3-2).

Theorem 5.3-4   *For all (P, M) in Γ^*,*

$$h^{*i}(P, M) = M \frac{l_i(P, M)}{\sum\limits_{j=1}^{n} P_j l_j(P, M)}, \quad i = 1, \dots, n.$$

PROOF:
From (5.3-2) it follows that

$$h^{*i} = \frac{l_i}{l_j} h^{*j},$$

for all i and j. Hence

$$M = \sum_{j=1}^{n} P_j h^{*j} = h^i \frac{1}{l_i} \sum_{j=1}^{n} P_j l_j,$$

from which the conclusion is immediate.

Q.E.D.

Theorem 5.3-4 provides a different characterization of h^* in terms of l from that given in (5.3-2). It will be used as the basis for the discussion of separability which follows momentarily. But first it is necessary to relate homogeneity of u to that of l.

Theorem 5.3-5   *Let $u(x)$ and $l(P, M)$ be related by (5.3-1). Then u is homogeneous of degree $k > 0$ if and only if for each $M > 0$, as a function of P, $-l$ is also.*

PROOF:
From (5.3-2), the equilibrium conditions (3.1-17), and the fact $l_M = \lambda^*$ (Theorem 3.5-2), it follows that

$$\sum_{i=1}^{n} x_i u_i = -\sum_{i=1}^{n} P_i l_i.$$

Hence if u is homogeneous of degree $k > 0$,

$$\sum_{i=1}^{n} P_i(-l_i) = -ku = k(-l),$$

by Euler's theorem and (5.3-1). Again by Euler's theorem, $-l$ is now homogeneous of degree k. A similar argument proves the converse.

Q.E.D.

In view of this result, the implications for demand functions of homogeneity of l are established by applying the analysis of Section 5.1.

The first kind of indirect separability considered here originated with Houthakker [5]. The function l will be called $P_i - M$ *additive* whenever there exist n continuously differentiable functions l^i such that

$$(5.3\text{-}6) \qquad\qquad l(P, M) = \sum_{i=1}^{n} l^i(P_i, M)$$

on Γ^*. It is clear from Theorem 5.3-4 that if there is a $P_i - M$ additive, indirect utility function, then h^* may be written in terms of functions of (P_i, M), each of which is homogeneous of degree zero.

$$(5.3\text{-}7) \qquad h^{*i}(P, M) = M\,\dfrac{l_i^i(P_i, M)}{\displaystyle\sum_{j=1}^{n} P_j l_j^j(P_j, M)}, \qquad i = 1, \ldots, n.$$

The next result is an easy consequence of (5.3-7); its proof is omitted.

Theorem 5.3-8   *Let u satisfy 3.1-1–3.1-4 and generate h^*. If, in addition, there exists an indirect utility function which is $P_i - M$ additive, then*

$$\dfrac{h_j^{*i}(P, M)}{h^{*i}(P, M)} = \dfrac{h_j^{*r}(P, M)}{h^{*r}(P, M)}, \qquad i, r \neq j,$$

for all (P, M) in Γ^*.

On the other hand, if demand functions generated by utility maximization are given which may be written as in (5.3-7), then integration of each l_i^i gives l^i. Define l by (5.3-6). Then l clearly satisfies (5.3-2), so from Theorem 5.3-3, l is an indirect utility function. Therefore, (5.3-7) is sufficient (as well as necessary) for the existence of a $P_i - M$ additive indirect utility function.

A stronger form of indirect separability is additivity; i.e.,

$$(5.3\text{-}9) \qquad\qquad l(P, M) = \sum_{i=1}^{n} l^i(P_i) + l^M(M),$$

where l^M and the l^i are continuously differentiable. Since the derivatives of the latter are homogeneous of degree -1,

$$l_j^i(P) = -\frac{\alpha_j}{P_j}, \quad j = 1, \ldots, n,$$

for some constants α_j. Thus, by (5.3-7),

$$(5.3\text{-}10) \qquad\qquad h^{*i}(P, M) = \frac{\alpha_i}{\sum\limits_{j=1}^{n} \alpha_i P_i} \frac{M}{P_i}, \quad i = 1, \ldots, n,$$

so h^* is Bergson with $b = 0$ [recall (5.2-12)]. On the sufficiency side, if h^* is given as in (5.3-10), then

$$u(x) = \sum_{i=1}^{n} \alpha_i \log x_i$$

generates h^*. Furthermore, $u(h^*(P, M))$ satisfies (5.3-9). Thus (5.3-10) is necessary and sufficient for the existence of an additive indirect utility function.

The preceding argument also demonstrates the fact that if there exists an additive l, then there also exists an additive u. Thus indirect additivity implies direct additivity. The converse, however, is not true: $u(x) = -(1/x_1 + 1/x_2)$ is additive but its demand functions (Exercise 4.2) are not of the form (5.3-10). Hence there can not exist an additive l. Similarly, it is easy to find examples showing that $P_i - M$ additivity of l and additivity of u do not imply each other. But these latter properties are not simultaneously incompatible. Samuelson [12, 13] and Hicks [4] have proved under two separate interpretations that simultaneity occurs only for a slightly larger collection of demand functions than the Bergson class (5.2-11). Their propositions are presented below. The symbol Γ' denotes that subset of Γ^* mapped into E by h^*.

Theorem 5.3-11 *Let u satisfy 3.1-1–3.1-3 and generate h^*. Assume that none of the partial derivatives of h^{*i} vanish on Γ' for each i. Then h^* is Bergson with $b \neq 0$ and $b < 1$ if and only if there exist an increasing transformation T and an indirect utility function l such that $T(u)$ is additive and $l = u(h^*)$ is $P_i - M$ additive.*

PROOF:

If h^* is Bergson, then there is a Bergson utility function, ζ generating it. Hence there must exist an increasing transformation T such that $\zeta(x) = T(u(x))$. Now ζ must have the same form as (2.4-5), so, in particular, ζ is additive. But upon substitution of (5.2-11), with the latter expressed in terms of nonnormalized prices and incomes,

$$\zeta(h^*(P, M)) = -M \left[\sum_{j=1}^{n} \alpha_j^{-1/(b-1)} P_j^{b/(1-b)} + \gamma_j \right]^{1-b}.$$

Thus by choosing l so that

$$l(P, M) = [\zeta(h^*(P, M))]^{1/(1-b)}$$

it is evident that l is $P_i - M$ additive.

Alternatively, if $T(u)$ and l [not necessarily related by (5.3-1)] are, respectively, additive and $P_i - M$ additive, then from the discussion of Section 5.2,

$$h_j^{*i} = \tau^j h_M^{*i}, \quad i, j = 1, \ldots, n,$$

for some function τ^j. This, together with the nonvanishing of all h^{*i} and Theorem 5.3-8, imply

(5.3-12) $$\frac{h_M^{*i}}{h^{*i}} = \frac{h_M^{*r}}{h^{*r}}, \quad i, r = 1, \ldots, n.$$

Differentiation of the budget constraint and (5.3-12) thus yield the differential equations

$$Mh_M^{*i} = h^{*i}, \quad i = 1, \ldots, n,$$

whose unique solution is

$$h^*(P, M) = M\varphi(P),$$

for some function φ. By Theorem 5.1-3 there exists a linearly homogeneous generator of h^*, so the underlying preference ordering is both additive and homothetic. Applying Theorem 2.4-4 there is also a Bergson generator, and therefore h^* is Bergson. Finally, if $b = 0$, then $h_j^{*i}(P, M) = 0$ on Γ^* for every $i \neq j$. Since this is ruled out by hypothesis, $b \neq 0$.

Q.E.D.

The first part of the proof of Theorem 5.3-11 (but obviously not the second) remains valid for $b = 0$. Also the theorem does not require l to be obtainable from $T(u)$ upon substitution of h^* for x. The next interpretation, however, insists on such a relationship. Call u *quasi-Bergson* provided

(5.3-13) $$u(x) = u^j(x_j) + \sum_{i \neq j} \alpha_i (\log x_i) + \gamma_i,$$

on E where u^j is arbitrary and the $\alpha_i > 0$. If $u^j(x_j) = \alpha_j (\log x_j) + \gamma_j$, then (5.3-13) becomes Bergson with $b = 0$. Demand functions generated by (5.3.13) in general are referred to as *quasi-Bergson*. Note that quasi-Bergson utility functions also need not satisfy 3.1-4. Once again let Γ' consist of those points of Γ^* which are not mapped into the boundary of E by h^*.

Theorem 5.3-14   *Let u satisfy 3.1-1–3.1-3 and generate h^*. Assume that for any $i \neq j$, either h_j^{*i} is identically zero or vanishes nowhere on Γ'. Then* *h* is quasi-Bergson if and only if there exists an increasing transformation T such that $T(u(x))$ is additive and $l(P, M) = T(u(h^*(P, M)))$ is $P_i - M$ additive on Γ'.*

PROOF:

If h^* is quasi-Bergson, it is generated by (5.3-13), which is additive. For that u set $l(P, M) = u(h^*(P, M))$ on Γ'. Now from the equilibrium conditions (3.1-17),

$$\lambda^*(P, M) = \frac{\alpha_i}{P_i h^{*i}(P, M)}, \quad i \neq j,$$

whence, by (5.3-2), the derivatives

$$l_i(P, M) = -\frac{\alpha_i}{P_i}, \quad i \neq j.$$

Therefore, $l_{ir}(P, M) = l_{ri}(P, M) = 0$ on Γ' for all $i \neq r$, where $i, r = 1, \ldots, n$, so l is $P_i - M$ additive.

On the other hand, assume without loss of generality that $l(P, M) = u(h^*(P, M))$, where u is additive and l is $P_i - M$ additive. Write $u(x) = \sum_{i=1}^{n} u^i(x_i)$. Using (5.3-2) and the equilibrium conditions,

$$h^{*i}(P, M)u_i^i(h^{*i}(P, M)) = -P_i l_i^i(P_i, M), \quad i = 1, \ldots, n,$$

on Γ'. Differentiating with respect to P_j gives

(5.3-15) $h_j^{*i}[u_i^i + u_{ii}^i h^{*i}] \equiv 0, \quad i \neq j,$

for any i and j. There are three cases to consider.

(1) If $h_j^{*i} = 0$ on Γ' for all $j \neq i$, where $j = 1, \ldots, n$, then by Theorem 5.3-8, $h_j^{*i} = 0$ for $i \neq j$ and $i, j = 1, \ldots, n$. Upon differentiating the budget constraint with respect to any P_j,

$$P_j h_j^{*j} = -h^{*j}.$$

Integration now shows that h^* is Bergson with $b = 0$.

(2) If $h_j^{*i} \neq 0$ on Γ' for some i and exactly one $j = j^0$, then, again by Theorem 5.3-8, $h_{j^0}^{*i} \neq 0$ for all $i \neq j^0$. From (5.3-15),

(5.3-16) $u_i^i + u_{ii}^i h^{*i} \equiv 0, \quad i \neq j^0.$

Integrating these equations yields (5.3-13) with j replaced by j^0.

(3) If $h_j^{*i} \neq 0$ on Γ' for more than one j, then (5.3-16) holds for all i, and as in case (2), h^* is Bergson with $b = 0$. But this implies that all h^{*i} where $i \neq j$ vanish, contrary to assumption. Hence only cases (1) and (2) are applicable.

Q.E.D.

5.4 CLASSICAL UTILITY FUNCTIONS

The implications of three classical hypotheses described in Section 2.5 will be considered here: (1) simultaneous additivity and diminishing marginal utility, (2) constancy of the marginal utility of income with respect to all prices, and (3) constancy of the latter with respect to income and all prices except one. These assumptions turn out to have considerable relevance for the first three sections of this chapter. They are discussed in the order in which they are listed above.

Theorem 5.4-1   *Let u satisfy 3.1-1–3.1-4 and generate h. If, in addition,* $u(x) = \sum_{i=1}^{n} u^i(x_i)$ *and the second-order derivatives* $u_{ii}^i < 0$ *everywhere on E, then*

$$h_m^i(p, m) > 0, \quad i = 1, \ldots, n,$$

on Γ.

PROOF:

As in the proof of Lemma 3.2-9,

$$h_M^{*i} = \lambda^* \frac{|U^{0i}|}{|U|},$$

for each i. But from the additivity of u it follows that

$$|U^{0i}| = -u_i^i \prod_{j \neq i} u_{jj}^j.$$

Thus, since $u_{ii}^i < 0$ and $u_i^i > 0$,

$$|U^{0i}| \begin{cases} < 0, & \text{if } n \text{ is odd,} \\ > 0, & \text{if } n \text{ is even.} \end{cases}$$

Therefore, since $\lambda^* > 0$,

$$h_m^i = \frac{1}{P_n} h_M^{*i} > 0,$$

by Theorem 3.1-10 and Lemma 3.2-8.

Q.E.D.

The converse of Theorem 5.4-1, of course, is not true. All commodities may be superior goods without there existing an additive generator of h. The example $u(x) = x_1^2 x_2 + x_1 x_2^2$ of Exercise 3.4 illustrates this phenomenon. On the other hand, the result does give another sufficient condition for downward-sloping Marshallian demand curves since it ensures that $h_i^i < 0$ on Γ. But additivity and diminishing marginal utility imply still more.

Theorem 5.4-2   *Under the assumptions of Theorem 5.4-1, for all* (p, m) *in* Γ,

$$s_{ij}(p, m) > 0, \quad i \neq j.$$

PROOF:

From Lemma 3.2-9,

$$s_{ij}^* = \frac{\lambda |U^{ij}|}{|U|}.$$

By expanding $|U^{ij}|$ along its first row, additivity implies

$$|U^{ij}| = u_i u_j \prod_{r \neq i,j} u_{rr}^r,$$

and hence, from the diminishing marginal utility,

$$|U^{ij}| \begin{cases} < 0, & \text{if } n \text{ is odd,} \\ > 0, & \text{if } n \text{ is even.} \end{cases}$$

As in Theorem 5.4-1,

$$s_{ij} > 0$$

on Γ.

Q.E.D.

Note that these properties—$h_i^i < 0$ and $h_m^i > 0$ for all i, and $s_{ij} > 0$ for $i \neq j$—are also those of Bergson demand functions.

Both interpretations of constancy of the marginal utility of income mentioned above have been studied by Samuelson [10]. To assume that λ^* does not vary with price changes is to require, in view of its homogeneity, that

(5.4-3) $$\lambda^* = \frac{\beta}{M},$$

where β is a positive constant. It is now shown that (5.4-3) is equivalent to the case in which preferences may be represented by a homogeneous utility function.

Theorem 5.4-4   *Let u satisfy 3.1-1–3.1-4. Then* $\lambda^* = \beta/M$ *if and only if there exists an increasing transformation T such that*

(5.4-5) $$T(u(x)) = \beta \log q(x),$$

where q is linearly homogeneous.

PROOF:

Let d be defined by

$$d(x) = \beta \log \frac{q(x)}{x_1}.$$

Then d is homogeneous of degree zero and

(5.4-6) $$T(u(x)) = \beta \log x_1 + d(x).$$

Clearly (5.4-5) and (5.4-6) are equivalent ways of writing the same thing.

Now suppose $T(u(x))$ may be written as in (5.4-6). Upon differentiation and use of equilibrium conditions (3.1-17),

$$\frac{\beta}{x_1} + d_1(x) = \lambda^* P_1,$$

$$d_j(x) = \lambda^* P_j, \quad j = 2, \ldots, n,$$

where subscripts on d denote derivatives. Hence, from the budget constraint,

$$M = \frac{1}{\lambda^*} \left[\beta + \sum_{i=1}^{n} x_i d_i(x) \right],$$

whence (5.4-3) follows by Euler's theorem as applied to the homogeneous d.

On the other hand, if $\lambda^* = \beta/M$, then again by the equilibrium conditions,

(5.4-7) $$\sum_{i=1}^{n} x_i u_i(x) = \beta.$$

Setting $d(x) = u(x) - \beta \log x_1$, differentiating, and using (5.4-7) leaves

$$\sum_{i=1}^{n} x_i d_i(x) \equiv 0.$$

Making use of Euler's theorem once again, d is homogeneous of degree zero. Therefore u may be written in the required form.

Q.E.D.

Applying the transformation $\tilde{T}(\mu) = \exp[(1/\beta)\mu]$ to (5.4-5) yields a linearly homogeneous utility function. Thus constancy of λ^* with respect to all prices implies the necessary and sufficient restrictions on demand functions given in Section 5.1. The first two classical hypotheses, then, both require positive income effects for every good and hence downward-sloping Marshallian demand curves. The latter is also true of the third, but for a different reason: it eliminates income effects for all but one commodity.

The third classical hypothesis is equivalent, for example, to

(5.4-8) $$\lambda^* = \frac{\delta}{P_n},$$

where δ is a positive constant. As with the previous constancy assumption, (5.4-8) also requires the existence of a particular kind of utility function. Note the necessary absence of 3.1-4 in this context.

Theorem 5.4-9   *Let u satisfy 3.1-1–3.1-3. Then $\lambda^* = \delta/P_n$ if and only if there exists an increasing transformation T such that $T(u)$ is quasi-linear with respect to x_n; i.e.,*

(5.4-10) $$T(u(x)) = \eta(x_{(n)}) + \delta x_n,$$

where $x_{(n)} = (x_1, \ldots, x_{n-1})$ and η is an appropriate function.

PROOF:

If $T(u(x))$ has the form of (5.4-10), then application of equilibrium conditions (3.1-17) with $i = n$ proves that λ^* has the required form. If $\lambda^* = \delta/P_n$, then again from (3.1-17), $u_n \equiv \delta$. Integration now yields (5.4-10).

                                                                          Q.E.D.

Demand functions are easily derived from (5.4-10). They are

$$h^i(p, m) = \psi^i(p), \quad i = 1, \ldots, n-1,$$

(5.4-11)
$$h^n(p, m) = m - \sum_{j=1}^{n-1} p_j \psi^j(p),$$

for some functions $\psi^1, \ldots, \psi^{n-1}$. Note that h is not defined by (5.4-11) on all of Γ but only for (p, m) such that $h(p, m) \geq 0$. Furthermore,

$$h_m^i(p, m) \equiv 0, \quad i = 1, \ldots, n-1,$$

(5.4-12)
$$h_m^n(p, m) \equiv 1.$$

Now let (5.4-11) be given and suppose that u is any generator satisfying 3.1-1–3.1-3. Because of the special form of h, the inverse demand functions, f^i, for $i = 1, \ldots, n-1$, depend only on $x_{(n)}$. Hence, as in the proof of Lemma 3.2-2,

$$w_i^n(x_{(n)}, \mu) = -f^i(x_{(n)}), \quad i = 1, \ldots, n-1,$$

so in this case, the derivative of w_i^n with respect to μ is identically zero for all i. It follows that

$$x_n = w^n(x_{(n)}, \mu) = -\eta(x_{(n)}) + T(\mu)$$

for some functions η and T, where T is increasing. Hence the utility function

$$\tilde{u}(x) = \eta(x_{(n)}) + x_n$$

generates h. Therefore, (5.4-11) is both necessary and sufficient for the existence of a quasi-linear utility generator.

It is clear that any quasi-linear utility function has indifference surfaces which intersect the boundary of the commodity space and hence is incompatible with assumption 3.1-4. Furthermore, in view of (5.4-12), the differential implications of the separability hypotheses derived in Section 5.2 do not apply anywhere on Γ. This is in sharp contrast to the previously discussed classical assumptions, which provide sufficient conditions for them to be valid everywhere. Finally, note that combining hypotheses (1) and (2) listed at the beginning of this section places the demand functions into the Bergson class.

EXERCISES

5.1 If u is linearly homogeneous, show that

$$w_j^n(\alpha x_{(n)}, u(\alpha x)) = w_j^n(x_{(n)}, u(x)), \quad j = 1, \ldots, n - 1,$$

for all positive α and x.

5.2 Show that all utility functions are weakly separable with respect to $\{\{1\}, \ldots, \{n\}\}$. Does this fact have any implications for market behavior?

5.3 Let $u(x) = x_1 x_2 x_3 x_4$. List all the different ways of writing h permitted by the theory of separability.

5.4 Derive the market implications of Pearce separability as defined in Exercise 2.5.

5.5 Where does the proof of Theorem 5.3-11 break down if (a) some $h_M^{*i} = 0$, or (b) $b = 0$ and $h_M^{*i} \neq 0$ for all i on Γ'?

5.6 Is simultaneous $P_i - M$ additivity of l and additivity of u (as in Theorem 5.3-14) equivalent to additivity of l?

5.7 As an illustration of the quasi-Bergson class consider $u(x) = x_1 + \log x_2$. Show that u satisfies 3.1-1–3.1-3 on E. Compute l and note that it is $P_i - M$ additive but not additive (see Exercise 5.6).

5.8 Derive the demand functions h^* generated by

$$u(x) = \sum_{i=1}^{n} \alpha_i \log (x_i + \delta_i),$$

where $\delta_i > 0$ and $\sum_{i=1}^{n} \alpha_i = 1$. Note that they are linear in appropriate price and income–price ratios (see Klein and Rubin [7] and Geary [2]). Show that the associated Engel curves are linear and compare with the Bergson class.

5.9 The *quadratic* utility function is defined by

$$u(x) = \sum_{i=1}^{n} \alpha_i x_i + \tfrac{1}{2} \sum_{i,j=1}^{n} \theta_{ij} x_i x_j,$$

where $\alpha_i > 0$ for $i = 1, \ldots, n$, and the matrix of constants θ_{ij} is symmetric and negative definite. For the case $n = 2$ find that subset of E on which 3.1-1–3.1-3 are satisfied and derive h^*. Show that the associated Engel curves are linear.

REFERENCES

[1] Aczél, J., *Lectures on Functional Equations and Their Applications* (New York: Academic Press, 1966).

[2] Geary, R. C., "A Note on 'A Constant-Utility Index of the Cost of Living'," *Review of Economic Studies*, v. 18 (1950–51), pp. 65–66.

[3] Goldman, S. M., and H. Uzawa, "A Note on Separability in Demand Analysis," *Econometrica* (1964), pp. 387–398.

[4] Hicks, J. R., "Direct and Indirect Additivity," *Econometrica* (1969), pp. 353–354.

[5] Houthakker, H. S., "Additive Preferences," *Econometrica* (1960), pp. 244–257.

[6] Katzner, D. W., "A Note on the Constancy of the Marginal Utility of Income," *International Economic Review* (1967), pp. 128–130.

[7] Klein, L. R., and H. Rubin, "A Constant-Utility Index of the Cost of Living," *Review of Economic Studies*, v. 15 (1947–48), pp. 84–87.

[8] Pearce, I. F., *A Contribution to Demand Analysis* (London: Oxford University Press, 1964).

[9] Pollak, R. A., "The Implications of Separability," Discussion Paper no. 31, Department of Economics, University of Pennsylvania, Philadelphia, 1966.

[10] Samuelson, P. A., "Constancy of the Marginal Utility of Income," in O. Lange, F. McIntyre, and T. O. Yntema (eds.), *Studies in Mathematical Economics and Econometrics* (Chicago: University of Chicago Press, 1942), pp. 75–91.

[11] Samuelson, P. A., *Foundations of Economic Analysis* (Cambridge, Mass.: Harvard University Press, 1947).

[12] Samuelson, P. A., "Using Full Duality to Show that Simultaneous Additive Direct and Indirect Utilities Implies Unitary Price Elasticity of Demand," *Econometrica* (1965), pp. 781–796.

[13] Samuelson, P. A., "Corrected Formulation of Direct and Indirect Additivity," *Econometrica* (1969), pp. 355–359.

6

Occam's Razor

William of Occam was a fourteenth-century English philosopher, continually harassed but never condemned by the Church. Although not originating with him, the dictum, "Things ought not to be multiplied except out of necessity," has become known as Occam's razor. This principle has stimulated economists to search for ways of explaining market behavior with fewer restrictions on utility functions. Weaker hypotheses, of course, expand the variety of preferences admissible for analysis, thereby enlarging the class of persons whose behavior can be described. Thus a measure of flexibility and increased applicability are added to the theory of demand. However, greater generality does not come free of charge. The weaker the assumptions, the more situations that are capable of inclusion but the less that can be said about each. The magnitude of such losses will become clear below.

Use of the razor may also be justified on empirical grounds. For there is not much evidence currently available suggesting that utility maximization provides an adequate description of consumer behavior. Future data may resolve the issue, but narrowness of hypotheses and resulting strictness of demand implications can only make rejection all the more likely. Thus it is worth considering increasingly general points of view which, by virtue of their broader scope, have a better chance of receiving empirical support.

The process of applying Occam's razor is exactly opposite to that studied in the last chapter. Recall, however, that the discussions there of additional restrictions on utility functions usually were based on the model of Chapters 3 and 4. But there is no reason why the same additional restrictions could not be analyzed when the assumptions of those chapters are weakened. The ensuing results, although not pursued here, are easily derived.

Several cases in which 3.1-4 does not hold have already been encountered. Elimination of this restriction in general constitutes the first stroke of

Occam's razor presented here. Thereafter assumptions are sliced away little by little until neither the utility function nor the property of integrability remain. More precisely, Sections 6.1 and 6.2 explore the implications for demand of gradually weakening the hypotheses of Chapter 3 until a continuous, increasing, and strictly quasi-concave utility function is obtained. Section 6.3 is concerned with integrability under similar circumstances. The last section goes much further by permitting consumer preferences to be non-transitive and to vary over the commodity space. A larger bundle of commodities no longer is required to be preferred to a smaller one, and disposal is allowed with the introduction of negative prices. At this point the reader may wonder if the razor has left anything upon which to build an explanation of consumer behavior. The answer, perhaps surprisingly, turns out to be yes.

6.1 BOUNDARY MAXIMA; LINEAR AND KINKED INDIFFERENCE SURFACES

By way of introduction, it is worth studying the effects of relatively small changes in the assumptions of Chapter 3. In this section several examples are considered. Since a general model covering such cases and many others is presented in Section 6.2, not much attention will be paid here to details. Discussion will be somewhat informal and examples will be used to make as well as illustrate points.

Perhaps the least desirable assumption of Chapter 3 is 3.1-4, which prevents indifference surfaces from touching the boundary of E. For, in addition to the implications already discussed, it also requires the consumer to purchase some amount of every commodity; and in all but specially contrived cases, observed demand functions cannot be expected to have this property. Thus consider a utility function such that

6.1-1. u has continuous, second-order partial derivatives on E and is continuous where finite on $\bar{E}$.

6.1-2. $u_i(x) > 0$ for $i = 1, \ldots, n$, and all x in E.

6.1-3. u is strictly quasi-concave.

These requirements are identical to 3.1-1–3.1-3. But since utility-maximizing bundles of commodities may now lie on the boundary of E, important complications arise. For interior maxima, however, nothing is changed. At such points, defining h by utility maximization as in 3.1-12, leaves the argument of Chapter 3 valid.

Theorem 6.1-4 *h is a* 1:1 *correspondence which maps an open subset* Γ' *of* Γ *onto* E *and has all the properties listed in Table 3.1 on* Γ'.

To define h on $\Gamma - \Gamma'$ when $\Gamma' \neq \Gamma$, let $\bar{D}^k$ be a hyperplane of maximal dimension in the boundary of E which contains points of $C_x^{\geq}$ in its relative interior, D^k, for some $x > 0$. There can be at most n of these hyperplanes, so k varies from 1 to n. Consider any k and suppose that $\bar{D}^k$ has dimension $n - 1$, consisting of vectors of the form $x_{(1)} = (x_2, \ldots, x_n)$. Now on $\bar{D}^k$ the utility function u is continuous, increasing, and strictly quasi-concave. If, in addition, u satisfies 6.1-1 on $\bar{D}^k$, a second application of the theory of Chapter 3 shows that there is a $1:1$ correspondence between D^k and an open set, G, of vectors $(p_2, \ldots, p_{n-1}, m) > 0$, now defined by utility maximization over $\bar{D}^k$. Let $\xi = (\xi^2, \ldots, \xi^n)$ denote this map going from G to D^k and set $\Gamma^k = \{(p, m): (p, m)$ is in $\Gamma - \Gamma'$ and $(p_2, \ldots, p_{n-1}, m)$ is in $G\}$. Then Γ^k will not be empty provided the indifference surfaces of u do not intersect $\bar{D}^k$ tangentially. (If they did, no extension of h would be possible here except to the boundary of Γ.) Extend h to Γ^k by

$$h^1(p, m) \equiv 0,$$

$$h^j(p, m) = \xi^j(p_2, \ldots, p_{n-1}, m), \quad j = 2, \ldots, n.$$

Note that for $j \neq 1$, the ξ^j and hence h^j must exhibit all properties of Table 3.1 relative to the interior of Γ^k. In particular, the Slutsky functions (3.2-6) behave as usual although

$$s_{1j} = s_{j1} = 0, \quad j = 1, \ldots, n.$$

By an argument similar to that of Theorem 6.2-5, h is continuous on $\Gamma' \cup \Gamma^k$. If u does not satisfy 6.1-1 on $\bar{D}^k$, then properties of h on Γ^k are deduced as in Section 6.2.

It is clear that if indifference surfaces in $\bar{D}^k$ also intersect its boundary, then a similar analysis may be applied to an appropriate hyperplane of smaller dimension. This process will continue, if necessary, until one-dimensional bounding hyperplanes are obtained and demand functions reduced to

$$h^i(p, m) = \frac{m}{p_i},$$

$$h^j(p, m) = 0, \quad j \neq i,$$

for some i, at appropriate points of Γ. If $\bar{D}^k$ has smaller dimension than the originally assumed $n - 1$, the same argument adjusted for dimensionality change may be used. Applying this technique to every D^k, therefore, will extend the definition of h continuously to Γ in such a manner that the usual implications of utility maximization appear, if somewhat modified, everywhere. Corresponding conclusions may be drawn for the inverse demand function, f, although at least one f^i must be multivalued off of E.

An example will help to clarify matters. The utility function

$$u(x) = (x_1 + 1)(x_2 + 1)x_3,$$

has indifference surfaces which intersect the x_1–x_3 and x_2–x_3 planes (Figure 6.1a). Let D^1 denote the former, D^2 the latter, and D^3 the x_3-axis.[1] The corresponding partitions of Γ are

$$\Gamma' = \{(p, m): m - 2p_1 + p_2 > 0, m - 2p_2 + p_1 > 0\},$$

$$\Gamma^1 = \{(p, m): m - 2p_2 + p_1 \leq 0, m > p_1\},$$

$$\Gamma^2 = \{(p, m): m - 2p_1 + p_2 \leq 0, m > p_2\},$$

$$\Gamma^3 = \{(p, m): m \leq p_1, m \leq p_2\},$$

which appear for a fixed value of m in Figure 6.1b. From utility maximization,

$$h^1(p, m) = \begin{cases} \dfrac{m - 2p_1 + p_2}{3p_1}, & \text{on } \Gamma', \\[2ex] \dfrac{m - p_1}{2p_1}, & \text{on } \Gamma^1, \\[2ex] 0, & \text{on } \Gamma^2 \cup \Gamma^3, \end{cases}$$

$$h^2(p, m) = \begin{cases} \dfrac{m - 2p_2 + p_1}{3p_2}, & \text{on } \Gamma', \\[2ex] \dfrac{m - p_2}{2p_2}, & \text{on } \Gamma^2, \\[2ex] 0, & \text{on } \Gamma^1 \cup \Gamma^3, \end{cases}$$

$$h^3(p, m) = \begin{cases} \frac{1}{3}(m + p_1 + p_2), & \text{on } \Gamma', \\[1ex] \frac{1}{2}(m + p_1), & \text{on } \Gamma^1, \\[1ex] \frac{1}{2}(m + p_2), & \text{on } \Gamma^2, \\[1ex] m, & \text{on } \Gamma^3. \end{cases}$$

It is easy to verify that h is everywhere continuous and the Slutsky functions have the appropriate properties on the interiors of Γ', Γ^1, Γ^2, and Γ^3.

Thus the elimination of 3.1-4 results in possibly multivalued inverse demand functions and corresponding subregions of Γ, where one or more of the h^i have constant values. On the other hand, weakening strict quasiconcavity to permit linear segments in indifference surfaces provides similar conclusions, but with the roles of f and h interchanged. To analyze this case,

---

[1] The use of D^3 to denote the x_3-axis takes a slight but inconsequential liberty with the notation introduced above since D^3 is not of maximal dimension. It is done to simplify matters here.

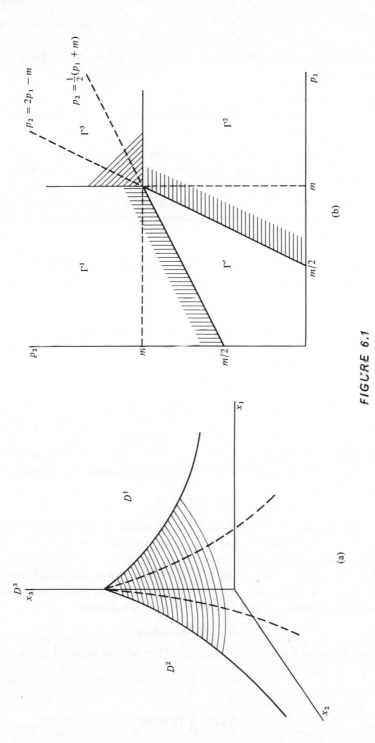

$$p_2 = 2p_1 - m$$

$$p_2 = \frac{1}{2}(p_1 + m)$$

Γ^3

Γ^2

Γ^1

Γ'

p_2

m

$m/2$

p_1

m

$m/2$

(b)

D^1

D^3

x_3

x_1

D^2

x_2

(a)

FIGURE 6.1

first consider the model of Chapter 3 with only 3.1-3 modified. Thus assume 6.1-1, 6.1-2, and

6.1-5. u is quasi-concave.
6.1-6. For any distinct x' and x'' in $\bar{E}$ such that $u(x') = u(x'')$, if $x' > 0$, then $x'' > 0$.

For x^0 in E let $Q_{x^0} = \{x: u(x) = u(x^0)$ implies $u(\theta x + (1 - \theta)x^0) = u(x^0)$ for all $0 \leq \theta \leq 1\}$. Then Q_{x^0} is a closed and bounded subset of E which contains x^0. If $Q_{x^0} \neq \{x^0\}$, it is a part of a hyperplane. Letting $Q = \{x^0: Q_{x^0} \neq \{x^0\}\}$, the latter is the set of points of E through which linear segments on indifference surfaces pass. As with the previous model, off of Q the argument of Chapter 3 applies.

Theorem 6.1-7 *There exists a $1:1$ correspondence (defined by utility maximization) between $E - Q$ and a subset Γ'' of Γ having all the properties listed in Table 3.1.*

Now the inverse demand function f may be extended continuously to E by defining $f(x)$ to be an appropriate (p, m) vector on Q. Thus if x^0 is in Q and $(p^0, m^0) = f(x^0)$, then

$$(6.1-8) \qquad\qquad f(x) = (p^0, m^0)$$

for all x in Q_{x^0}. Note that the a_{ij} are defined and continuous everywhere on E because f is still related to the derivatives of the utility function by (3.1-18). However the matrix A will be only semidefinite and not definite on Q. Furthermore, although h has all the usual properties on Γ'', it must be multivalued on $\Gamma - \Gamma''$. Indeed, if x^0 and (p^0, m^0) are related by f as indicated in (6.1-8), then

$$h(p^0, m^0) = Q_{x^0}.$$

The two models discussed thus far may easily be combined to permit simultaneously boundary maxima and linear regions on indifference surfaces. Restrictions 6.1-1, 6.1-2, and 6.1-5 would be assumed and the results obtained would involve appropriate partitions of $\bar{E}$ and Γ. This will not be pursued further except to point out that any linear utility function illustrates the simultaneous violation of 6.1-3 and 6.1-6. If, for example,

$$u(x) = \alpha x_1 + \beta x_2,$$

where α and β are positive constants, then the inverse demand functions

$$f^1(x) = \frac{\alpha}{\beta},$$

$$f^2(x) = \frac{\alpha}{\beta} x_1 + x_2,$$

are defined on E but multivalued on its boundary. Letting D^1 be the x_1-axis and D^2 the x_2-axis, the corresponding partition of Γ consists of $\Gamma^1 = \{(p, m): p_1 \geq \alpha/\beta\}$ and $\Gamma^2 = \{(p, m): p_1 \leq \alpha/\beta\}$. Thus h is multivalued on $\Gamma^1 \cap \Gamma^2$ and single valued elsewhere:

$$h^1(p, m) = \begin{cases} \dfrac{m}{p_1}, & \text{on the interior of } \Gamma^1, \\ 0, & \text{on the interior of } \Gamma^2, \end{cases}$$

$$h^2(p, m) = \begin{cases} m, & \text{on the interior of } \Gamma^2, \\ 0, & \text{on the interior of } \Gamma^1. \end{cases}$$

Permitting indifference surfaces to have kinks brings discussion back to the first model considered above: once again h may become constant over regions and f assume multiple values. Furthermore, h often extends to Γ in much the same way as in the boundary maxima case. But since there are many ways to introduce individual kinks, application of the method of this section does not produce analysis of much generality. Thus it will suffice here to illustrate the problem with an example. The general theory is postponed to Section 6.2.

Consider, then, the function

$$u(x) = \begin{cases} x_1\sqrt{x_2 x_3}, & \text{if } x_2 \geq x_1, \\ \sqrt{x_1 x_2 x_3}, & \text{if } x_1 \geq x_2, \end{cases}$$

which is continuous on $\bar{E}$ and whose indifference surfaces are kinked in the plane $K = \{x: x \text{ is in } E \text{ and } x_1 = x_2\}$. Let $\Gamma^1 = \{(p, m): p_2 < \tfrac{1}{2}p_1\}$ and $\Gamma^2 = \{(p, m): p_2 > 2p_1\}$. Then there is a 1:1 correspondence between $E - K$ and $\Gamma^1 \cup \Gamma^2$ defined by utility maximization where

$$h^1(p, m) = \begin{cases} \dfrac{2m}{5p_1}, & \text{on } \Gamma^1, \\[2ex] \dfrac{m}{5p_1}, & \text{on } \Gamma^2, \end{cases}$$

$$h^2(p, m) = \begin{cases} \dfrac{m}{5p_2}, & \text{on } \Gamma^1, \\[2ex] \dfrac{2m}{5p_2}, & \text{on } \Gamma^2, \end{cases}$$

and

$$h^3(p, m) = \tfrac{2}{5}m,$$

on $\Gamma^1 \cup \Gamma^2$. Now h may be extended to $\Gamma - (\Gamma^1 \cup \Gamma^2)$ by setting $x_1 = x_2$ in both the utility function and the budget constraint. This yields a two-dimensional setting in which the Slutsky theory may be applied again. Hence

$$h^1(p, m) = h^2(p, m) = \frac{3m}{5(p_1 + p_2)},$$

$$h^3(p, m) = \tfrac{2}{5}m,$$

on $\Gamma - (\Gamma^1 \cup \Gamma^2)$. It is easily verified that h is continuous on Γ.

The above partitions of Γ for any fixed m are pictured in Figure 6.2. Note that h satisfies all the properties derived from utility maximization on $\Gamma^1 \cup \Gamma^2$. Along lines in $\Gamma - (\Gamma^1 \cup \Gamma^2)$ such that $p_1 + p_2$ is constant, h is constant. But if $p_2 = \gamma p_1$ is any ray from the origin into $\Gamma - (\Gamma^1 \cup \Gamma^2)$, then

$$(1 + \gamma)h^1(p, m) = (1 + \gamma)h^2(p, m) = \frac{3m}{5p_1},$$

$$h^3(p, m) = \tfrac{2}{5}m,$$

which, as functions of p_1 and m have all the properties implied by two-dimensional utility maximization over K. Hence the extension of h to $\Gamma - (\Gamma^1 \cup \Gamma^2)$ is quite similar to that of the first model studied above.

A further example in which indifference curves have kinks and are also not strictly convex is

$$u(x) = \min\,(\alpha x_1, \beta x_2),$$

where α and β are positive constants. Here commodities are always consumed in the ratio $x_1/x_2 = \beta/\alpha$ and

$$h^{*1}(P, M) = \frac{\beta M}{\beta P_1 + \alpha P_2},$$

$$h^{*2}(P, M) = \frac{\alpha M}{\beta P_1 + \alpha P_2}$$

on Γ^*.

Consider next a case in which u satisfies 6.1-1, is strictly concave, and has a global maximum at, say, x^0 in $\bar{E}$. Then on the set $\{x : u_i(x) > 0, \text{ for each } i\}$, 6.1-2 and 6.1-3 are also satisfied. Applying the results derived in the beginning of this section, h^* may be defined on some partitioned subset Λ^* of Γ^* and has appropriate properties there. Of course, h^* may be continuously extended to Γ^* by setting

$$x^0 = h^*(P, M),$$

on $\Gamma^* - \Lambda^*$, but at these points the consumer may not spend all his income.

Finally, note that any utility function with strictly concave rather than strictly convex indifference surfaces and which also satisfies 6.1-1 and 6.1-2 will still generate, through maximization, demand functions on Γ^*. But these

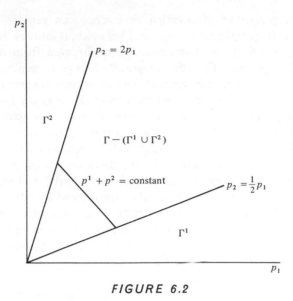

FIGURE 6.2

will differ from those produced by the linear utility function on such a small subset of Γ^* that it is usually unreasonable to expect empirical observation to be able to distinguish between them.

6.2 NONDIFFERENTIABLE UTILITY FUNCTIONS

Section 6.1 provides useful insight into the kinds of things that can happen when the original assumptions of Chapter 3 do not hold. Given a utility function violating them in specific ways, both the commodity and price–income spaces may be partitioned accordingly and appropriate functions defined on each partitioning set. In this section a more general point of view is taken by simultaneously eliminating 3.1-4 and doing away with differentiability entirely.

Under these circumstances the restrictions imposed on market activity are of essentially two types. In the process of purchasing commodity bundles consumers reveal their preferences relative to various price–income configurations they face. Thus their behavior defines a "revealed preference" relation on $\bar{E}$. The translation of properties of preferences (i.e., utility functions) into those of revealed preferences yields the first type of observable restrictions mentioned above. For special cases in which 3.1-1–3.1-4 are satisfied, the latter may be regarded as additions to Table 3.1. But because they are stated in terms of a binary relation rather than derivatives, different if not more fruitful methods of empirical verification become possible. Of course, before properties of revealed preference can replace the Slutsky properties as a characterization of rational behavior, it must be demonstrated that appropriate utility functions may be constructed from demand and revealed preference data. This, the integrability issue, is resolved in Section 6.3. Properties of revealed preferences turn out to be more general necessary and sufficient restrictions on demand than those of Chapters 3 and 4.

The second category of restrictions imposed on market activity are symmetry and negative definiteness of the Slutsky matrix where the latter is defined (recall that if 3.1-1–3.1-4 hold, it will be defined on Ω or Ω^*). Since utility need no longer be differentiable, the derivation of these requirements by manipulation of the derivatives of u is hardly valid and an alternative procedure must be found. One possibility introduced by McKenzie [16] is to use properties of expenditure functions. Because this approach also provides a third independent point of departure (in addition to utility and indirect utility functions) for arriving at the market conditions of Table 3.1, some attention will be devoted to it below.

To avoid inconvenience, results are stated in terms of h^*, a procedure adopted for the remainder of Chapter 6. In addition, properties of inverse demand functions are not considered.

The following restrictions on utility functions are required:

6.2-1. u is continuous on $\bar{E}$.

6.2-2. u is increasing on $\bar{E}$.

6.2-3. u is strictly quasi-concave on $\bar{E}$.

Note that in the absence of differentiability, all properties of u now may be stated equivalently in terms of preference orderings as indicated in Chapter 2. Furthermore, most of the arguments of Chapter 3 must be abandoned. One exception, however, is the first part of Theorem 3.1-13, which, with minor modifications, remains valid here. It is restated below in terms of non-normalized prices and income.

Theorem 6.2-4   *For every (P, M) in Γ^* there exists a unique vector $\bar{x}$ in $\bar{E}$ which maximizes u over $B^{\leq}(P, M)$.*

Thus single-valued demand functions, h^*, are defined on Γ^*. Continuity of h^* also does not depend on differentiability of u. Its proof is due to Uzawa [21].

Theorem 6.2-5   *h^* is continuous on Γ^*.*

PROOF:

Let (P^0, M^0) be in Γ^* and suppose $\{P^r, M^r\}$ is a sequence converging to it. Write $x^r = h^*(P^r, M^r)$. Then x^r is contained in $\bigcup_{r=1}^{\infty} B^{\leq}(P^r, M^r)$ for every r. Since the latter is bounded, $\{x^r\}$ has a limit point [4, p. 49], say x^0. It is now shown that $x^0 = h^*(P^0, M^0)$.

First note that

$$P^0 \cdot x^0 = \lim_{r \to \infty} P^r \cdot x^r = \lim_{r \to \infty} M^r = M^0,$$

so x^0 is in $B^=(P^0, M^0)$. Furthermore, for any x in the interior of $B^\leq(P^0, M^0)$ there is an r' such that

$$P^r \cdot x < M^r,$$

for all $r > r'$ (for otherwise, passing to the limit, $P^0 \cdot x \geq M^0$, contradicting the choice of x). Therefore, $u(x^r) > u(x)$ by Theorem 6.2-4, and applying the continuity of u,

$$u(x^0) = \lim_{r \to \infty} u(x^r) \geq u(x).$$

Finally, if x is in $B^=(P^0, M^0)$, let $\{x^\epsilon\}$ be a sequence in $B^<(P^0, M^0)$ converging to it. Then from the above $u(x^0) \geq u(x^\epsilon)$ for all ϵ. Again by the continuity of u, $u(x^0) \geq u(x)$. Therefore, x^0 maximizes u over $B^\leq(P^0, M^0)$.

Q.E.D.

Turning to revealed preference properties of h^*, define the *direct* and *indirect revealed preference relations*, $\tilde{R}$ and R, on $\bar{E}$ as follows. Write $x' \, \tilde{R} \, x''$ whenever

(1) $x' \neq x''$.
(2) There exist vectors (P', M') and (P'', M'') in Γ^* such that $x' = h^*(P', M')$ and $x'' = h^*(P'', M'')$.
(3) $P' \cdot x' \geq P' \cdot x''$.

Let $x' \, R \, x''$ if and only if either $x' \, \tilde{R} \, x''$ or there is a finite collection of vectors $x^1, \ldots, x^k$ in $\bar{E}$ such that $x' \, \tilde{R} \, x^1, x^1 \, \tilde{R} \, x^2, \ldots, x^k \, \tilde{R} \, x''$. The aim of the next few paragraphs is to establish equivalence of the statements $x' \, R \, x''$ and $u(x') > u(x'')$. Utility maximization will then imply the same restrictions on R as implicitly assumed on the underlying ordering $\oslash$. Initial concern, however, is with two preliminary lemmas.

Lemma 6.2-6 *For all x' and x'' in $\bar{E}$, if $x' \, \tilde{R} \, x''$, then $u(x') > u(x'')$.*

PROOF:
Let x' and x'' be in $\bar{E}$ and suppose $x' \, \tilde{R} \, x''$. Then there exist (P', M') and (P'', M'') in Γ^* such that $x' = h^*(P', M')$, $x'' = h^*(P'', M'')$, and $P' \cdot x' \geq P' \cdot x''$. But this implies x'' is in $B^\leq(P', x')$, so by Theorem 6.2-4, $u(x') > u(x'')$.

Q.E.D.

Lemma 6.2-7 *Let x' and x'' be in $\bar{E}$ and suppose that $u(x') > u(x'')$. If $u(x') > u(x) > u(x'')$ for all x on the line segment between x' and x'', then $x' \, \tilde{R} \, x''$.*

PROOF:

Clearly from the definition of $\tilde{R}$, if $x' \geq x''$, then $x'\,\tilde{R}\,x''$. Similarly, in view of Lemma 6.2-6, it is impossible for $x'' \geq x'$. In the remaining case these exists a (P^0, M^0) in Γ^* such that

$$P^0 \cdot x' = P^0 \cdot x'' = M^0.$$

Let $x^0 = h^*(P^0, M^0)$. Now if $x^0 = x'$, then $x'\,\tilde{R}\,x''$. Otherwise by hypothesis and Lemma 6.2-6, $x^0\,\tilde{R}\,x'$, $u(x^0) > u(x')$, and $x^0 = \theta x' + (1 - \theta)x''$ for some $\theta > 1$. Hence using Lemma 6.2-6 again, $x'\,\bar{\tilde{R}}\,x^0$, where the bar over $\tilde{R}$ denotes its complement. Thus $P' \cdot x' < P' \cdot x^0$, whence, upon substitution for x^0,

$$(1 - \theta)P' \cdot x' < (1 - \theta)P' \cdot x''.$$

But since $\theta > 1$, this implies that $P' \cdot x' > P' \cdot x''$. Therefore, $x'\,\tilde{R}\,x''$.

Q.E.D.

Theorem 6.2-8   *For all x' and x'' in $\bar{E}$, $x'\,R\,x''$ if and only if $u(x') > u(x'')$.*

PROOF:

If $x'\,R\,x''$, then there exists a finite sequence of vectors $x^1, \ldots, x^k$, such that $x'\,\tilde{R}\,x^1$, $x^1\,\tilde{R}\,x^2, \ldots, x^k\,\tilde{R}\,x''$. Repeated applications of Lemma 6.2-6 shows that $u(x') > u(x'')$.

On the other hand, suppose that $u(x') > u(x'')$. If $u(x') > u(x) > u(x'')$ for all x on the line segment between x' and x'', then $x'\,\tilde{R}\,x''$ by Lemma 6.2-7. Hence $x'\,R\,x''$. Otherwise, since u is continuous, there exists an $\hat{x} = \theta x' + (1 - \theta)x''$, where $0 < \theta < 1$, such that $u(x') > u(\hat{x}) > u(x'')$ and $u(\hat{x}) > u(x) > u(x'')$ for all x on the line connecting $\hat{x}$ and x''. As before, $\hat{x}\,\tilde{R}\,x''$. To complete the proof, a finite sequence of points $x^1, \ldots, x^k$, will be constructed such that $x'\,\tilde{R}\,x^1$, $x^1\,\tilde{R}\,x^2, \ldots, x^k\,\tilde{R}\,\hat{x}$. This being accomplished, it follows that $x'\,R\,x''$. The argument is illustrated in Figure 6.3.

Write $x' = h^*(P', M')$ and let $B^=(P^0, M^0)$ be the budget hyperplane containing x' and x'' such that $x^0 = h^*(P^0, M^0)$ is on the line between x' and x''. Let $\bar{x}^1$ be the unique point in $B^\leq(P^0, M^0)$ satisfying both $P' \cdot \bar{x}^1 = M'$ and $u(\bar{x}^1) = u(\hat{x})$, and set

$$x^1 = \tfrac{1}{2}x' + \tfrac{1}{2}\bar{x}^1.$$

Then $x'\,\tilde{R}\,x^1$ and $u(x') > u(x^1) > u(\hat{x})$. Denote the line segment connecting $\bar{x}^1$ and $\hat{x}$ by L. Again, write $x^1 = h^*(P^1, M^1)$ and let $\bar{x}^2$ be the unique point in L such that $P^1 \cdot \bar{x}^2 = M^1$. Then, with

$$x^2 = \tfrac{1}{2}x^1 + \tfrac{1}{2}\bar{x}^2,$$

it follows that $x^1\,\tilde{R}\,x^2$ and $u(x^1) > u(x^2) > u(\hat{x})$. Set $x^2 = h^*(P^2, M^2)$. If $\hat{x}$ is in $B^\leq(P^2, M^2)$, then $x^2\,\tilde{R}\,\hat{x}$ and there is nothing more to do. Otherwise,

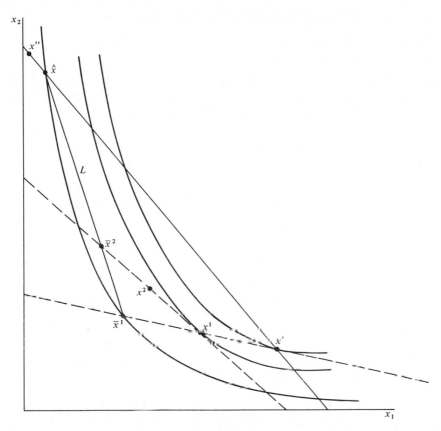

FIGURE 6.3

continue in this manner, requiring each $\bar{x}^k$ to be in L, until $\hat{x}$ is in $B^{\le}(P^{k^0}, M^{k^0})$ for some k^0. When this happens, $x^{k^0} \tilde{R} \hat{x}$ and hence $x^1, \ldots, x^{k^0}$ is the desired sequence.

If $\hat{x}$ is not in $B^{\le}(P^k, M^k)$ for any k, then the infinite sequence $\{\bar{x}^k\}$ must have a limit point in L, since the latter is bounded. Hence $\{x^k\}$ also has a limit, x^*, such that $u(x^*) \ge u(\hat{x})$. There are two cases to consider. First, if $u(x^*) > u(\hat{x})$, then $u(x^*) > u(x) > u(\hat{x})$ for all x on the line segment between x^* and $\hat{x}$, for otherwise x^* could not be a limit point of $\{x^k\}$. Furthermore, since u is continuous, there must also be an x^{k^0} such that $u(x^{k^0}) > u(x) > u(\hat{x})$ for all x on the line connecting x^{k^0} and $\hat{x}$. By Lemma 6.2-7, $x^{k^0} \tilde{R} \hat{x}$, so using $x^1, \ldots, x^{k^0}$ again shows that $x' R x''$. Finally, if $u(x^*) = u(\hat{x})$, then it is clear, since $x^k \tilde{R} \bar{x}^k$ and hence $u(x^k) > u(\bar{x}^k)$ for every k, that $x^* = \hat{x}$. Therefore, as in case 1, there is an x^{k^0} such that $x^{k^0} \tilde{R} x''$ and the proof is complete.

Q.E.D.

Now for any x' and x'' in $\bar{E}$ define $x' \rho x''$ provided

(1) either $x' R x''$, or

(2) both $x' \bar{R} x''$ and $x'' \bar{R} x'$,

where $\bar{R}$ denotes the complement of R. Note that (1) and (2) cannot hold simultaneously. Furthermore, it is a trivial consequence of Theorem 6.2-8 that ρ and the underlying preference ordering, $\gtreqless$, represented by u are identical; i.e., for all x' and x'' in $\bar{E}$, $x' \gtreqless x''$ if and only if $x' \rho x''$. Therefore, ρ and $\gtreqless$ have the same properties. Market implications of utility maximization under assumptions 6.2-1–6.2-3, then, are as follows:

6.2-9. h^* is continuous.

6.2-10. ρ is reflexive, transitive, total, continuous, and strictly convex.

6.2-11. R is increasing and asymmetric.

In addition, the second part of 6.2-11 also implies that $\tilde{R}$ is asymmetric. This property and the asymmetry of R are frequently referred to as, respectively, the *weak* and *strong axiom of revealed preference*. For reasons which will become apparent in Section 6.3, the latter is also considered to be the "integrability condition" in the present context.

As indicated earlier, even without assuming differentiability of u, it is still possible to demonstrate symmetry and negative semidefiniteness of the n by n matrix of Slutsky functions wherever h^* is differentiable. Proof of the latter is based on a lemma of Samuelson's below.[2]

Lemma 6.2-12 *$\tilde{R}$ is asymmetric if and only if for all (P', M') and (P'', M'') in Γ^* such that $h^*(P', M') \neq h^*(P'', M'')$, if $P' \cdot [h^*(P'', M'') - h^*(P', M')] \leq 0$, then $P'' \cdot [h^*(P'', M'') - h^*(P', M')] < 0$.*

PROOF:

Write $x' = h^*(P', M')$, $x'' = h^*(P'', M'')$, and $\Delta x = x'' - x'$. Now asymmetry of $\tilde{R}$ means $x' \tilde{R} x''$ implies $x'' \bar{\tilde{R}} x'$. From the definition of $\tilde{R}$, however, $x' \tilde{R} x''$ is equivalent to $P' \cdot \Delta x \leq 0$ and $x'' \bar{\tilde{R}} x'$ is equivalent to $P'' \cdot x'' < P'' \cdot x'$ or $P'' \cdot \Delta x < 0$. Hence asymmetry of $\tilde{R}$ is equivalent to the statement that $P' \cdot \Delta x \leq 0$ implies $P'' \cdot \Delta x < 0$.

Q.E.D.

Theorem 6.2-13 *If h^* has a differential[3] at (P^0, M^0) in Γ^*, then*

$$\sum_{i,j=1}^{n} s^*_{ij}(P^0, M^0) y_i y_j \leq 0$$

for all vectors $y = (y_1, \ldots, y_n)$.

[2] See Samuelson [18, pp. 110–111].
[3] See Apostol [4, p. 107]. The proof of this theorem is due to Professor Hurwicz.

PROOF:

Consider any y and let (ξ, η) map the closed interval $[0, 1]$ into Γ^* such that

(1) $\xi(0) = P^0$, $\eta(0) = M^0$.

(2) $\xi(0) \cdot h^*(\xi(t), \eta(t)) = M^0$, for all t in $[0, 1]$.

(3) $\dfrac{d\xi(0)}{dt} = y$.

For convenience write $h^*(t)$ for $h^*(\xi(t), \eta(t))$. Now, from (2),

$$\xi(0) \cdot [h^*(t) - h^*(0)] = 0$$

for all t. Applying Lemma 6.2-12 and using this expression,

$$[\xi(t) - \xi(0)] \cdot [h^*(t) - h^*(0)] < 0,$$

whence division by t and passing to the limit gives

$$\frac{dh^*(0)}{dt} \cdot y \leq 0.$$

But from (3), differentiating (2), and the chain rule it may be shown that

$$\frac{dh^*(0)}{dt} \cdot y = \sum_{i,j=1}^{n} s_{ij}^*(P^0, M^0) y_i y_j,$$

which completes the proof of the theorem.

Q.E.D.

To obtain symmetry, the McKenzie approach [16] now will be introduced. Let $\Pi^* = \{(P, \mu): P > 0 \text{ and } u(x) = \mu \text{ for some } x \text{ in } E\}$ and set

(6.2-14) $$H(P, \mu) = \min \{P \cdot x: u(x) = \mu\}.$$

By 6.2-1–6.2-3, H is well defined and single valued on Π^*. It is referred to either as the *expenditure function* or, given μ, as the *support function* of $C_x^{\geq}$, where $u(x) = \mu$. Note the results of Section B.6 apply to H for fixed μ even though it is defined slightly differently here than in the Appendix.

Lemma 6.2-15 *If* $H(P^0, \mu^0) = P^0 \cdot x^0$ *for some* P^0, μ^0, *and* x^0, *then* $x^0 = h^*(P^0, H(P^0, \mu^0))$.

PROOF:

If $x^0 \neq h^*(P^0, H(P^0, \mu^0))$, it is still true from the budget constraint that

$$H(P^0, \mu^0) = P^0 \cdot h^*(P^0, H(P^0, \mu^0)).$$

Thus $u(x^0) < u(h^*(P^0, H(P^0, \mu^0)))$ by Theorem 6.2-4. But since u is continuous, there must exist a vector $\bar{x}$ such that

$$u(x^0) < u(\bar{x}) < u(h^*(P^0, H(P^0, \mu^0))),$$

where $P^0 \cdot \bar{x} < P^0 \cdot x^0$. Then from (6.2-14), $H(P^0, \mu^0) \neq P^0 \cdot x^0$, which is a contradiction.

Q.E.D.

It is clear that $h^*(P, H(P, \mu)) = g^*(P, \mu)$, where g^* is the "price–utility demand function" of Section 3.4. Note the lemma could also be proved by appeal to Theorem 3.4-2.

Lemma 6.2-15 also states that if $H(P^0, \mu^0) = P^0 \cdot x^0$, then x^0 maximizes $u(x)$ subject to $P^0 \cdot x = M^0$, where $M^0 = H(P^0, \mu^0)$. Conversely, if x^0 maximizes $u(x)$ subject to $P^0 \cdot x = M^0$, then $H(P^0, \mu^0) = P^0 \cdot x^0$, where $\mu^0 = u(x^0)$. Hence duality exists between u and H in the same sense as that between u and the indirect utility function, l, established in Exercise 3.7. Furthermore, for each $P^0 > 0$ and any μ,

$$\mu = l(P^0, H(P^0, \mu)),$$

whence l and H may be obtained from each other by inversion.

Continuing in this vein, for fixed μ, H may be regarded as the infimum over a collection of concave (i.e., linear) functions. Since a function is concave if and only if its negative is convex, Lemma B.1-6 implies that H is concave in P. As a function of P for fixed μ, H is also linearly homogeneous and increasing, the latter, moreover, remaining true for given P and variable μ. Further properties of H appear in the argument of Theorem 6.2-16, which proves at last the symmetry of S^*.

Theorem 6.2-16   *If h^* has a differential at (P^0, M^0) in Γ^*, then*

$$s_{ij}^*(P^0, M^0) = s_{ji}^*(P^0, M^0), \quad i, j = 1, \ldots, n.$$

PROOF:

Denoting the derivatives of H with respect to prices by subscripts, Lemma 6.2-15 and Theorem B.6-12 imply that

(6.2-17) $H_i(P, \mu) = h^{*i}(P, H(P, \mu)), \quad i = 1, \ldots, n,$

on Γ^*. Let $\mu^0 = u(h^*(P^0, M^0))$ so $M^0 = H(P^0, \mu^0)$. Now if h^* has a differential at (P^0, M^0), then H_i must also at (P^0, μ^0). By Theorem C.2, $H_{ij}(P^0, \mu^0) = H_{ji}(P^0, \mu^0)$ for $i, j = 1, \ldots, n$. But from the chain rule,

(6.2-18) $H_{ij} = h_j^{*i} + h_M^{*i} H_j = s_{ij}^*, \quad i, j = 1, \ldots, n,$

thus proving the theorem.

Q.E.D.

The preceding proof provides a demonstration of $s_{ij}^* = g_j^{*i}$ on Ω^* alternative to that of Theorem 3.4-3. Note that (6.2-17) does the same thing for expenditure functions as Theorem 3.5-3 does for indirect utility functions: it establishes a link between a form of utility and demand. Thus, as is the case with indirect utility functions, demand theory may begin by placing restrictions on H, and then proceed by deriving h^* and its properties via (6.2-17) and (6.2-18) [see Exercise 6.3]. Taking this point of view, a utility function generating h^* may be obtained by inverting H to find l and substituting inverse demand functions for prices and income as suggested at the end of Chapter 3.

6.3 INTEGRATION AND REVEALED PREFERENCE

Occam's razor is as important on the sufficiency side of utility maximization as it is from the viewpoint of necessity. To begin with, by applying the theory of Chapter 4 to appropriate partitioning sets of Γ or $\bar{E}$, utility functions corresponding to those of Section 6.1 may be obtained by assuming the properties derived in that section. An alternative method of arriving at the same results is to perform one integration of f, when it is single valued and h multivalued, or of h in the opposite case. Integrating f will yield possibly linear segmented indifference surfaces, but a utility function still may be constructed as in Chapter 4. On the other hand, integration of h gives level contours of the expenditure function (6.2-14), which may then be used to define a utility representation whose indifference surfaces could have kinks or intersect the boundary of E. Since all the above are special cases of revealed preference theory, none will be pursued here. Readers interested in the specific integration of h are referred to Hurwicz and Uzawa [14].

The theory of revealed preference is concerned with existence of a utility generator of given demand functions under the conditions derived in the previous section. It shows that the latter are sufficient for existence of the former and hence that 6.2-1–6.2-3 constitute a minimal collection of assumptions on preferences (or utility functions) required to explain rational behavior. Originally posed by Samuelson [18], the problem was first solved by Houthakker [11] and considerably refined by Uzawa [21] and Richter [17]. The argument below follows Richter's in that it relies on the results of Sections 2.1 and 2.2 rather than on integration of differential equations as in Chapter 4. By avoiding the complexities of integration theory entirely, it presents a remarkably simple and transparent counterpart to the model of Section 6.2.

The argument begins with possibly multivalued demand functions h^* defined on Γ^* such that

$$(6.3-1) \qquad\qquad P \cdot h^*(P, M) = M.$$

The range of h^*, called E^*, determines the set on which a utility function, u, eventually will be proved to exist. Assume that

6.3-2. E^* is a convex subset of $\bar{E}$.

Next define the direct and indirect revealed preference relations, $\tilde{R}$ and R, on E^* as in Section 6.2. Then R is clearly transitive and increasing. Lemma 6.3-3 establishes a property of $\tilde{R}$ which turns out to be responsible for the strict quasi-concavity of u. It depends only on the way in which the concept of direct revealed preference (i.e., $\tilde{R}$) is defined and not on the weak or strong axioms to be introduced later on.

Lemma 6.3-3   *For any distinct x' and x'' in E^* and all θ between 0 and 1, either $[\theta x' + (1 - \theta)x''] \tilde{R} x'$ or $[\theta x' + (1 - \theta)x''] \tilde{R} x''$.*

PROOF:

Suppose for some $x' \neq x''$ and θ the conclusion is false. By 6.3-2 there is a (P^0, M^0) in Γ^* such that $\theta x' + (1 - \theta)x'' = h^*(P^0, M^0)$. Now $[\theta x' + (1 - \theta)x''] \bar{\tilde{R}}$ x' implies that $\theta P^0 \cdot x' + (1 - \theta)P^0 \cdot x'' < P^0 \cdot x'$ or

$$P^0 \cdot x'' < P^0 \cdot x'.$$

Similarly, $[\theta x' + (1 - \theta)x''] \bar{\tilde{R}} x''$ leads to

$$P^0 \cdot x' < P^0 \cdot x''.$$

Since these inequalities cannot hold simultaneously, the lemma is proved.

Q.E.D.

To proceed, it is necessary to introduce further assumptions. Implications of the weak axiom are explored first.

Theorem 6.3-4   *If $\tilde{R}$ is asymmetric, then h^* is single-valued and homogeneous of degree zero.*

PROOF:

Suppose $x^0 = h^*(P^0, M^0)$ and $x' = h^*(P^0, M^0)$, where $x^0 \neq x'$. Then clearly $x^0 \tilde{R} x'$ and $x' \tilde{R} x^0$, contrary to the asymmetry of $\tilde{R}$. Furthermore, if $x^0 = h^*(P^0, M^0)$ and $x' = h^*(tP^0, tM^0)$ for any $t > 0$, then a similar argument shows that $x' = x^0$.

Q.E.D.

Earlier remarks have already indicated that the strong axiom implies the weak. As is illustrated by the example at the end of Section 6.4, however, the converse is not true. Since the latter is insufficient to guarantee existence of a utility generator of h^*, the former is introduced as an assumption:

6.3-5. R is asymmetric on E^*.

Now let $X = \{\langle x, x \rangle : x \text{ is in } E^*\}$, where the symbol, $\langle x', x'' \rangle$ denotes an ordered pair and define $\rho = R \cup X$. (Note the difference between the definition of ρ given here and that of Section 6.2.) Since R is asymmetric, it is also irreflexive. Furthermore, ρ is reflexive and transitive. By Theorem 2.1-1 (applied to E^*) ρ is weakly representable, and hence there exists a function u defined on E^* such that $x' \rho x''$ implies $u(x') \geq u(x'')$ and the inequality is strict for at least one pair x' and x'' for which $x' R x''$. In general, of course, u need not be continuous nor will the underlying preference relation even be unique. This is illustrated by the example of Figure 2.2. Suppose there that the utility value of curve 2 is 15 while that of 3 is 17. Then assigning values $15 < \mu < 16$ to points above x^0 between 2 and 3 and values $16 < \mu < 17$ to points in the corresponding area below x^0 generates the same demand functions as assigning values between 16 and 17 to the first set and between 15 and 16 to the second. But these functions correspond to two distinct preference orderings neither of which is continuously representable. Thus continuity and uniqueness can be established only with the aid of additional hypotheses. Consider uniqueness first. Let $D_{x^0}^{<} = \{x : x^0 R x\}$ be a subset of E^*. Uzawa [21] has proved that $D_{x^0}^{<}$ is open.

Theorem 6.3-6 *For all x^0 in E^*, $D_{x^0}^{<}$ is open.*

PROOF:

If $x' R x''$, then either $x' \tilde{R} x''$ or there is a finite sequence of points $x^1, \ldots, x^k$ in E^* such that $x' \tilde{R} x^1, x^1 \tilde{R} x^2, \ldots, x^k \tilde{R} x''$. It thus suffices to show that $x' \tilde{R} x''$ implies there exists an open neighborhood N of x'' such that $x' R x$ for all x in N.

To this end write $x' = h^*(P', M')$ and $x'' = h^*(P'', M'')$. For any θ between 0 and 1 let $\bar{x} = \theta x' + (1 - \theta)x''$ and $\bar{\bar{x}} = h^*(\bar{P}, \bar{M})$. Since $x' \tilde{R} x''$ by assumption, it is clear that $x' \tilde{R} \bar{x}$. The asymmetry of $\tilde{R}$ now implies $\bar{P} \cdot \bar{x} < \bar{P} \cdot x'$, whence, upon substitution,

$$\theta \bar{P} \cdot x' + (1 - \theta)\bar{P} \cdot x'' < \bar{P} \cdot x',$$

or $\bar{P} \cdot x'' < \bar{P} \cdot x'$. Substituting for $\bar{x}$ again in $\bar{P} \cdot \bar{x}$ and using this last result,

$$\bar{P} \cdot \bar{x} > \bar{P} \cdot x''.$$

Therefore, there exists an open neighborhood N of x'' such that $\bar{P} \cdot \bar{x} > \bar{P} \cdot x$ and hence $\bar{x} \tilde{R} x$ for all x in N. Since $x' \tilde{R} \bar{x}$ the proof is complete.

Q.E.D.

By Theorem A-4, R can be extended to an irreflexive, transitive, and total relation, R', on E^*. Define ρ' as $R' \cup X$ and let $L_{x^0}^< = \{x: x^0 \, \rho' \, x$ and $x \, \bar{\rho}' \, x^0\}$ be a subset of E^*. Then $D_{x^0}^<$ is contained in $L_{x^0}^<$, but although the former is open, the same need not be true of the latter. Instead this will be assumed:

6.3-7. $L_{x^0}^<$ is open for every x^0 in E^*.

Now ρ' is reflexive, transitive, and total and R' is increasing on E^*. By Theorem 2.1-2 (applied to E^*), ρ' is representable. Thus there exists a function u such that for all x' and x'' in E^*, $x' \, \rho' \, x''$ if and only if $u(x') \geq u(x'')$. Since R' is increasing, u must be, too. Also, if x' and x'' are any distinct points such that $u(x')=u(x'')$, then for all θ between 0 and 1, either $[\theta x'+(1-\theta)x''] \, \tilde{R} \, x'$ or $[\theta x' + (1 - \theta)x''] \, \tilde{R} \, x''$ by Lemma 6.3-3. It follows that $u(\theta x' + (1 - \theta)x'')$ $> u(x')$ for all θ, so u is strictly quasi-concave. Finally, if $x^0 = h^*(P^0, M^0)$, then from (6.3-1), x^0 is in $B^\leq(P^0, M^0)$ and $x^0 \, \tilde{R} \, x$ for any other x contained therein. Hence $u(x^0) > u(x)$ for all x in $B^\leq(P^0, M^0)$ different from x^0. Theorem 6.3-8 has therefore been established.

Theorem 6.3-8. *There exists an increasing, strictly quasi-concave utility generator of h^* defined on E^*.*

But 6.3-7 is still not enough to ensure existence of a continuous generator. Nor is adding the requirement that demand functions be continuous sufficient either. For demand functions derived from the example of Figure 2.3 are continuous in spite of the fact that the underlying preference ordering is not continuously representable and all other hypotheses up to this point are satisfied. Thus it is necessary to assume something more:

6.3-9. ρ' is continuous on E^*.

Now applying Theorem 2.2-2, ρ' is continuously representable. Hence h^* is continuous by Theorem 6.2-5. Furthermore, as in Section 6.2, $R = \oslash$, and so $D_{x^0}^< = L_{x^0}^<$. And if E^* contains E, then u may be extended continuously to $\bar{E}$. In this case, then, (6.3-1), 6.3-2, 6.3-5, and 6.3-9 imply the existence of a utility function satisfying 6.2-1–6.2-3 which generates h^*. The results of Sections 6.2 and 6.3 may therefore be summarized as follows.

Theorem 6.3-9 *Restrictions (6.3-1), 6.3-2, 6.3-5, and 6.3-9, together with the requirement that E^* contains E, are both necessary and sufficient for there to exist a utility generator of h^* satisfying 6.2-1–6.2-3 on $\bar{E}$. Under either set of assumptions h^* is single-valued, homogeneous of degree zero, and continuous on Γ^*.*

Note that since differentiability of u and h^* no longer is of any concern, the discrepancies in Chapters 3 and 4 between necessary and sufficient conditions have disappeared.

6.4 NONINTEGRABILITY

All descriptions of consumer behavior considered thus far have been based on representable preference orderings and a postulate of rationality which has meaning only in terms of that ordering. Properties of behavior are derived from those of orderings through the postulate of rationality. Of the former, the integrability condition (i.e., symmetry of S^* or asymmetry of R) is perhaps the most difficult to justify intuitively and the least likely to receive empirical support. What, in fact, happens if a consumer is discovered whose observed market activity is incompatible with the integrability condition? Must demand theory be abandoned entirely or is there a way of defining rational behavior in such a context? In what follows an answer will be given to this question.

Consider for a moment the role of integrability conditions in demand theory. Cursory observation suggests a correspondence between each assumption of the hypothesis and an appropriate property of demand:

form of the budget constraint $\leftrightarrow$ homogeneity of h^*,

increasingness of $u \leftrightarrow$ satisfaction of the budget constraint by h^*,

convexity of indifference surfaces $\leftrightarrow$ negative definiteness of S^*,

convexity of indifference surfaces $\leftrightarrow$ nature of the revealed preference relation and the weak axiom of revealed preference.

Eliminating any particular hypothetical part would seem to exclude the corresponding property of demand and conversely. Since there is only one remaining element in each of the totalities of utility hypotheses and properties of demand, they should also correspond:

existence of a preference ordering or utility function $\leftrightarrow$ integrability condition.

Thus if the first group of assumptions could somehow be stated without relying on the existence of a utility function and if the postulate of rationality could similarly be reinterpreted, then applying Occam's razor to the integrability condition or existence of u should leave all other properties of demand in tact. Roughly speaking, this view is confirmed by the analysis below.

To free the hypotheses of demand theory from dependence on preference orderings as specified in Chapter 2, individual preferences are defined only locally about each point in the commodity space. Furthermore, any comparative feelings the consumer may have for two points could change depending on his frame of reference (i.e., on a third point of $\bar{E}$). The preferences themselves are permitted to be nontransitive. To obtain still greater generality, assumptions other than the existence of a utility function will be dispensed with: it is not required even locally that larger bundles of commodities be preferred to smaller ones, nor are prices and income restricted to be positive.

Since the consumer no longer can choose a point from his budget set having maximum utility, a new concept of "best point" relative to that set must be defined. However, such a consumer in general would be rather myopic. Placed at any x in the budget set, he only may be aware of his preferences for points near x, and so, if the best point lies beyond his vision, he has no way of knowing of its existence. A second aspect of the theory, then, is concerned with a procedure for looking outside his immediate vicinity. In fact, the new version of the postulate of rationality will require him to purchase that bundle at the end of this search. When a best point exists and when rational search leads him to it, demand functions can be defined. Thus a link is established between local preference and demand, permitting properties of the former to be translated into those of the latter. The empirical implications of nonintegrable demand theory are thereby deduced. Once again the analysis of Chapter 3 applies in the special case in which a utility function satisfying 3.1-1–3.1-4 exists.

Authors who have directly or indirectly contributed to the study of nonintegrability include Allen [1, 2, 3], Evans [6], Fisher [7], Georgescu-Roegen [9, 10], Samuelson [19], and Sonnenschein [20]. The analysis of this section relies heavily on their work. Unfortunately, but not surprisingly, it also requires a considerable number of new concepts and corresponding notation.

As usual the starting point is with consumer preferences. A *local quasi-preference ordering* at x^0 is a binary relation defined in a neighborhood containing x^0 which is asymmetric. Such an ordering will be denoted by $\ominus_{x^0}$ and the symbol $x' \ominus_{x^0} x''$ may be read, "x' is preferred to x'' at x^0." This should not be confused with the notion of conditional ordering discussed in Section 2.4.

For any distinct x^0 and x' in $\bar{E}$, let $\gamma_{x^0 x'}$ be the ray from x^0 through x'. Thus

$$\gamma_{x^0 x'} = \{tx' + (1 - t)x^0 : t \geq 0\}.$$

By $\overrightarrow{x^0 x'}$ will be meant the *direction from x^0 to x'* defined as

$$\overrightarrow{x^0 x'} = \{\langle x^0, x \rangle : x \text{ is in } \gamma_{x^0 x'} \text{ and } x \neq x^0\}.$$

Now $\overrightarrow{x^0 x'}$ will be called a *direction of preference* provided there exists a $\delta > 0$ such that if x is in $\gamma_{x^0 x'}$, $x \neq x^0$ and $|x - x^0| < \delta$, then $x \ominus_{x^0} x^0$. Similarly,

$\overrightarrow{x^0 x'}$ is a *direction of antipreference* whenever there exists a $\delta > 0$ such that for any x in $\gamma_{x^0 x'}$ different from x^0, $|x - x^0| < \delta$ implies $x^0 \ominus_{x^0} x$. If $\overrightarrow{x^0 x'}$ is neither a preference nor antipreference direction, then it will be called a *direction of indifference*. The phrase *direction of nonpreference* will refer to a direction which is either one of antipreference or indifference.

Let

$$Pd_{x^0} = \{x : \overrightarrow{x^0 x} \text{ is a direction of preference}\},$$

$$Nd_{x^0} = \{x : \overrightarrow{x^0 x} \text{ is a direction of nonpreference}\}$$

be subsets of $\bar{E}$. Denote their closures by $\overline{Pd}_{x^0}$ and $\overline{Nd}_{x^0}$, respectively, and set

$$\Phi_{x^0} = \overline{Pd}_{x^0} \cap \overline{Nd}_{x^0}.$$

The basic assumptions may now be stated: For each x^0 in $\bar{E}$ let there exist a local quasi-preference ordering such that

6.4-1. For all distinct x^0 and x' in $\bar{E}$ there exists a $\delta > 0$ such that for any x in $\gamma_{x^0 x'}$, where $x \neq x^0$ and $|x - x^0| < \delta$, $x \ominus_{x^0} x^0$ implies $x \ominus_x x^0$.

6.4-2. For all distinct x^0 and x' in $\bar{E}$, $\overrightarrow{x^0 x'}$ is either a preference, antipreference, or indifference direction.

6.4-3. For every x^0 in $\bar{E}$, if Φ_{x^0} is nonempty, then Pd_{x^0} is an open half-space in $\bar{E}$ and Φ_{x^0} is a hyperplane in $\bar{E}$ such that for any x in $Nd_{x^0} - \Phi_{x^0}$, $\overrightarrow{x^0 x}$ is a direction of antipreference.

Essentially all 6.4-1–6.4-3 require is that in some neighborhood of each point of $\bar{E}$, the consumer knows in which directions small changes will increase his satisfaction and in which directions they will not. This knowledge is based on local preferences exhibiting a certain degree of consistency and admitting to a kind of "separation." No transitivity of any type is assumed, nor is a direction in which quantities of all commodities increase necessarily one of preference.

If Φ_{x^0} is a hyperplane, then there exists a vector $\varphi(x^0)$ where $\varphi = (\varphi^1, \ldots, \varphi^n)$ such that

$$\varphi(x^0) \cdot (x - x^0) = 0$$

for all x in Φ_{x^0}. Using the convention $\varphi(x^0) = 0$ whenever Φ_{x^0} is empty, φ may be thought of as a function defined on $\bar{E}$ which contains almost all important information about the consumer's preferences. Without loss of generality, $\overrightarrow{x^0 x}$ may be regarded as a direction of preference or antipreference according as $\varphi(x^0) \cdot (x - x^0)$ is, respectively, positive or negative. Thus as long as $\varphi(x^0) \neq 0$, $\overrightarrow{x^0x}$ is a direction of nonpreference if and only if $\varphi(x^0) \cdot (x - x^0) \leq 0$. In general, if $\overrightarrow{x^0x}$ is a direction of indifference, then $\varphi(x^0) \cdot (x - x^0) = 0$ but not conversely.

Let x^0 be in $\bar{E}$ and $\varphi(x^0) \neq 0$. Then the vector $\varphi(x^0)$ is orthogonal to the hyperplane Φ_{x^0}. If x' in $\bar{E}$ satisfies the conditions

(1) $\varphi(x^0) \cdot (x' - x^0) > 0$,

(2) $\gamma_{x^0x'}$ is orthogonal to Φ_{x^0},

then $\overrightarrow{x^0x'}$ is called the *orthogonal preference direction* at x^0. When it exists, this direction is unique. Note that the orthogonal preference direction exists for all x^0 in E such that $\varphi(x^0) \neq 0$. An example is illustrated in Figure 6.4. Similarly, if K is a subset of $\bar{E}$ containing x^0 and x', then $\overrightarrow{x^0x'}$ is the *orthogonal preference direction relative to K* if and only if $\varphi(x^0) \cdot (x' - x^0) > 0$ and $\gamma_{x^0x'} \cap K$ is orthogonal to $\Phi_{x^0} \cap K$. A point with no orthogonal preference direction in general may still have one relative to a subset of $\bar{E}$.

A commodity bundle x^0 is called a *(local) saturation point* provided for all x in $\bar{E}$ different from x^0, $\overrightarrow{x^0x}$ is a direction of nonpreference. It is a *saturation point relative to K* if the same property holds for every x in K.

Finally, it is necessary to introduce an auxiliary function for reasons which will become clear momentarily. Let x^0 be fixed in $\bar{E}$ and suppose $\varphi^n \neq 0$ on Φ_{x^0}. Write $x = (x_{(n)}, x_n)$, where $x_{(n)} = (x_1, \ldots, x_{n-1})$ and define $\sigma = (\sigma^1, \ldots, \sigma^{n-1})$ by

$$(6.4\text{-}4) \quad \sigma^j(x_{(n)}) = \frac{\varphi^j\left(x_{(n)}, x_n^0 - \sum_{i=1}^{n-1} [\varphi^i(x^0)/\varphi^n(x^0)](x_i - x_i^0)\right)}{\varphi^n\left(x_{(n)}, x_n^0 - \sum_{i=1}^{n} [\varphi^i(x^0)/\varphi^n(x^0)](x_i - x_i^0)\right)}, \quad j = 1, \ldots, n-1,$$

for all $x_{(n)}$ such that $(x_{(n)}, x_n)$ is in Φ_{x^0}. Let $z = x_{(n)} - x_{(n)}^0$ and set

$$(6.4\text{-}5) \quad \psi_{x^0}^j(z) = \sigma^j(z + x_{(n)}^0) - \sigma^j(x_{(n)}^0), \quad j = 1, \ldots, n-1.$$

Thus $\psi_{x^0} = (\psi_{x^0}^1, \ldots, \psi_{x^0}^{n-1})$ is defined on Φ_{x^0} in terms of an $(n-1)$-dimensional coordinate system with x^0 as the origin. Where confusion cannot arise, ψ is written for ψ_{x^0}.

The concepts presented thus far can be placed in better perspective by considering a situation in which utility representations exist. The term *integrable case* will be used when there is a function u defined on $\bar{E}$ such that

(1) For all x^0, x', and x'' in $\bar{E}$, $u(x') > u(x'')$ if and only if $x' \ominus_{x^0} x''$.

(2) u is continuously differentiable on E and continuous where finite on $\bar{E}$.

(3) There exists a continuous, nonzero function λ such that for all x in E, $u_i(x) = \lambda(x)\varphi^i(x)$, where $i = 1, \ldots, n$.

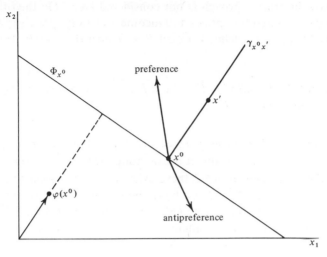

FIGURE 6.4

In the integrable case, then, $\bigotimes_{x^0}$ is independent of x^0 and becomes a part of the preference ordering discussed in Chapter 2, Φ_{x^0} is the hyperplane tangent at x^0 to the indifference surface through x^0, and the ratios φ^j/φ^n where defined are slopes of indifference surfaces comprising the inverse demand function generated by u. In addition, ψ_{x^0} is the inverse demand function translated and restricted to Φ_{x^0}; thus the $\psi^i_{x^0}$ are slopes of indifference surfaces defined relative to the hyperplane Φ_{x^0}. Moving a small distance in any preference direction increases utility and in the orthogonal preference direction utility increases at the fastest possible rate.

The purpose of introducing φ and ψ is to enable saturation points in general and those in $B^-(P, M)$ relative to $B^\leq(P, M)$ to be characterized in terms of their respective zeros so that in the integrable case the former will correspond to maxima of u and the latter to maxima constrained by the budget set. Since only the analogue of first-order maximization conditions have been assumed, it is not surprising that a second-order or convexity requirement must be added to achieve this characterization:

6.4-6. For all distinct x^0 in E and x' in $\bar{E}$, if $\varphi(x^0) \cdot (x' - x^0) \leq 0$, then
$\varphi(x') \cdot (x^0 - x') > 0$.

In the integrable case, 6.4-6 is nothing more than the weak axiom of revealed preference (Lemma 6.2-12). The reason x^0 is not allowed to be on the boundary of E is that again in the integrable case, utility functions whose indifference curves satisfy 3.1-4 would then be ruled out. It is possible to weaken 6.4-6 somewhat and still retain modified versions of many of the results which follow but this approach is not considered here.[4] On the other hand, it is no longer required that prices and income are always positive; $B^{\leq}(P, M)$ and $B^{=}(P, M)$ are now defined for all $P \neq 0$ such that $B^{\leq}(P, M)$ contains points of E.

Theorem 6.4-7   *For all x^0 in E and x in $\bar{E}$, $\overrightarrow{x^0 x}$ is a direction of nonpreference if and only if $\varphi(x^0) \cdot (x - x^0) \leq 0$.*

PROOF:

According to the definitions given earlier, it is only necessary to prove that if $\varphi(x^0) = 0$, then $\overrightarrow{x^0 x}$ is a direction of nonpreference for every x. If this were not the case, then by 6.4-2 there exists an x' in E such that $\overrightarrow{x^0 x'}$ is a direction of preference. Now from 6.4-1 there is an x'' in $\gamma_{x^0 x'}$ such that for all x in $\gamma_{x^0 x''}$, $x \ominus_x x^0$. But $\varphi(x^0) \cdot (x'' - x^0) = 0$, so by 6.4-6 $\overrightarrow{x'' x^0}$ must also be a direction of preference. Applying 6.4-1 again, there exists an x^* in $\gamma_{x^0 x''}$ such that $x^0 \ominus_{x^*} x^*$, contradicting the asymmetry of $\ominus_x$.

Q.E.D.

A similar assertion for preference directions was derived from its definition earlier. The theorem implies that 6.4-6 may be restated in terms of directions: if $\overrightarrow{x^0 x'}$ is a direction of nonpreference, then $\overrightarrow{x' x^0}$ is a direction of preference. Seen in this light, 6.4-6 does not seem to be an overly severe restriction at all. Its consequences, however, are far-reaching.

Theorem 6.4-8   *Let x^0 be in E. Then $\varphi(x^0) = 0$ if and only if x^0 is the unique saturation point of $\bar{E}$.*

PROOF:

That $\varphi(x^0) = 0$ if and only if x^0 is a saturation point follows immediately from Theorem 6.4-7. But if $\varphi(x^0) = 0$, then for all other x in E, $\overrightarrow{x x^0}$ is a direction of preference by 6.4-6. Therefore, no $x \neq x^0$ can be a saturation point, so x^0 is unique.

Q.E.D.

Theorem 6.4-9   *Let x^0 be in E and $\varphi^n \neq 0$ on Φ_{x^0}. Then there exists $P \neq 0$ and M such that $B^{=}(P, M) = \Phi_{x^0}$. Moreover, x^0 is the unique relative saturation point of $B^{\leq}(P, M)$ and $z = 0$ [which corresponds to x^0 in the $(n-1)$-dimensional coordinate system of Φ_{x^0}] is the only point where ψ_{x^0} vanishes.*

PROOF:

Setting $P = \varphi(x^0)$ and $M = \varphi(x^0) \cdot x^0$ gives $\Phi_{x^0} = B^{=}(P, M)$ and, by 6.4-3, x^0 is a relative saturation point of $B^{\leq}(P, M)$. As in Theorem 6.4-8, uniqueness follows from 6.4-6.

[4] See Katzner [15].

To prove the last part of the theorem, it is clear that $\psi_{x^0}(0) = 0$. By direct computation it also may be verified that for any distinct $x = (x_{(n)}, x_n)$ and $x' = (x'_{(n)}, x'_n)$ in Φ_{x^0},

(6.4-10) $\qquad \varphi(x') \cdot (x - x') = \varphi^n(x')[\psi_{x^0}(z') \cdot (z - z')],$

where $z = x_{(n)} - x_{(n)}^0$. Hence $\psi_{x^0}(z') = 0$ if and only if $\varphi(x') \cdot (x - x') = 0$. Using 6.4-6 again, the latter cannot hold unless $x^0 = x'$. Therefore, $\psi_{x^0}(z') = 0$ implies $z' = 0$.

Q.E.D.

In the integrable case the following results are easily verified: Saturation points in E correspond to global maxima of u, while those in $B^=(P, M)$ relative to $B^{\leq}(P, M)$ are constrained maxima over the budget set. If $\overrightarrow{x^0 x}$ is a direction of nonpreference, then $u(x^0) > u(x)$ but not conversely. There can be no indifference directions in E and, finally, indifference surfaces are strictly convex.

Returning to the general analysis, denote partial derivatives of φ and ψ when they exist by subscripts and let J_φ and J_ψ be their respective Jacobians. Thus, for example,

$$J_\psi(z) = \begin{bmatrix} \psi_1^1(z) & \cdots & \psi_{n-1}^1(z) \\ \vdots & & \vdots \\ \psi_1^{n-1}(z) & \cdots & \psi_{n-1}^{n-1}(z) \end{bmatrix}.$$

Recall that ψ is used for the appropriate ψ_{x^0}.

Theorem 6.4-11 *Let x^0 be in E, $\varphi^n \neq 0$ on Φ_{x^0}, and suppose that φ and ψ_{x^0} are differentiable there. If the integrability condition is satisfied in a neighborhood of x^0, then*

$$\psi_j^i(0) = \psi_i^j(0), \quad i, j = 1, \ldots, n - 1.$$

PROOF:

If the integrability condition is satisfied, then, as in Chapter 4,

$$\frac{\varphi^i}{\varphi^n} = f^i, \quad i = 1, \ldots, n - 1,$$

where the f^i are inverse demand functions. Hence from (6.4-4) and (6.4-5), the definition of the Antonelli functions (3.2-1), and the chain rule,

$$\psi_j^i(0) = a_{ij}(x^0), \quad i, j = 1, \ldots, n - 1.$$

Since the integrability condition may be stated as $a_{ij} = a_{ji}$, the conclusion is now immediate.

Q.E.D.

It is also clear that if φ is differentiable in a neighborhood of x^0, then the integrability condition can hold at x^0 if and only if $\varphi_j^i(x^0) = \varphi_i^j(x^0)$ for all i and j.

Theorem 6.4-12   *Let x^0 be in E and suppose φ has a differential there. If x^0 is a saturation point, then $J_\varphi(x^0)$ is negative semidefinite. If $\varphi^n > 0$ on Φ_{x^0} and if ψ has a differential at $z = 0$, then $J_\psi(0)$ is also negative semidefinite.*

The definition of negative semidefiniteness used above is that for all vectors $(y_1, \ldots, y_n)$,

$$\sum_{i,\, j=1}^{n} \varphi_j^i(x^0) y_i y_j \leq 0.$$

It is not required that J_φ be symmetric, for this could only occur in the integrable case. Analogous comments apply for negative semidefiniteness of J_ψ. The proof of the first part of the theorem, based on 6.4-6, is identical to that of Theorem 6.2-13 except that P is replaced by φ, h^* by x, and ξ maps $[0, 1]$ into E rather than Γ^* (η is not needed). The second half is proved similarly, except that 6.4-6 must now be expressed in terms of ψ. This is accomplished by virtue of (6.4-10), since φ^n is assumed positive on Φ_{x^0}. The details are left to the reader. Note that 6.4-6 is not strong enough to imply negative definiteness.

Now that saturation points have been defined and their properties studied, attention is focused on a process which enables the consumer to attain them. Let $P \neq 0$ and M be given and suppose x' in E is also in the interior of $B^{\leq}(P, M)$. Consider the system of differential equations

$$(6.4\text{-}13) \qquad\qquad\qquad \frac{dx}{dt} = \varphi(x)$$

defined on $B^{\leq}(P, M)$. If φ satisfies the Lipschitz condition, then there exists a unique, continuous solution $q(t)$ of (6.4-13) in $B^{\leq}(P, M)$ such that $q(0) = x'$, and this is true regardless of whether the integrability condition is satisfied or not.[5] The curve defined by q leaves x' in the orthogonal preference direction, and its tangent at each point, x, contains the ray in the orthogonal preference direction from x. In the integrable case, movement along it continually increases utility at the fastest possible rate.

There are many paths that q can trace out as t increases.[6] If $\bar{E}$ contains a saturation point, $x^0 \neq x'$, and if x^0 is in $B^{\leq}(P, M)$, then it may happen (although it is by no means necessary) that $\lim_{t\to\infty} q(t) = x^0$. Another possibility is that there is an x'' in a bounding hyperplane of $B^{\leq}(P, M)$ and

---

[5] In this case φ satisfies the Lipschitz condition if there exists a number α such that $|\varphi(x) - \varphi(x^0)| \leq \alpha|x - x^0|$ for all x and x^0 in $B^{\leq}(P, M)$. See Hurewicz [12, pp. 26, 28].
[6] See Hurewicz [12, pp. 70–75].

a point t'' such that $q(t'') = x''$ and q is not defined for $t > t''$. Thus q ends at the boundary of $B^{\leq}(P, M)$. In either of these cases write $q[x', x^1]$, where $q(0) = x'$ and $x^1 = x^0$ in the former and $x^1 = x''$ in the latter. The curve $q[x', x^1]$ will be referred to as the *orthogonal segment* from x' to x^1.

If x^1 is not a relative saturation point of $B^{\leq}(P, M)$, first suppose that x^1 is in $B^{=}(P, M) = \Phi_{x^0}$ for some x^0, where $\varphi^n \neq 0$ on the latter. Consider the differential equations

$$\frac{dz}{dt} = \psi_{x^0}(z).$$

If ψ_{x^0} satisfies the Lipschitz condition on Φ_{x^0}, the previous analysis may be repeated here. Hence there may exist a relative orthogonal segment (whose tangents are in relative orthogonal preference directions) from x^1 to some x^2, where x^2 is either the relative saturation point x^0 or on a bounding hyperplane of $B^{=}(P, M)$. If x^1 were not in $B^{=}(P, M)$ but on some other hyperplane bounding $B^{\leq}(P, M)$, a similar analysis would apply in terms of an appropriate differential equation. Continuing in this manner, it may be possible to construct a sequence of segments $q[x', x^1], q[x^1, x^2], \ldots, q[x^{k-1}, x^k]$, where x^k is a relative saturation point in some hyperplane on the boundary of $B^{\leq}(P, M)$. In this case denote the set of all these segments by $Q[x', x'']$, henceforth called the *orthogonal path* from x'. Two examples in which x^2 is a relative saturation point of $B^{\leq}(P, M)$ are illustrated in Figure 6.5. [In diagram (b) the orthogonal path from x' does not exist.] Note that if x' were originally on the boundary of E, orthogonal paths might still be constructed provided there exists an orthogonal preference direction relative to some subset of $\bar{E}$. If not, there is no possibility for such a construction.

The next two theorems provide sufficient conditions for the convergence of orthogonal segments to saturation points. Their proofs are trivial consequences of the stability theory of ordinary differential equations and are not given below.[7]

Theorem 6.4-14 *Let $n > 2$ and suppose that $\bar{E}$ has a saturation point, x^0, contained in E. If $J_{\varphi}(x^0)$ is defined and negative definite, then there exists an open subset, N, of E containing x^0 such that for any other x in N, the orthogonal segment of $q[x, x^0]$ is well defined.*

Theorem 6.4-15 *Let $n > 3$ and suppose that x^0 in $B^{=}(P, M) \cap E$ is a relative saturation point of $B^{\leq}(P, M)$. Assume that $\varphi^n > 0$ on $B^{=}(P, M)$. If $J_{\psi}(0)$ is defined and negative definite, then there exists an open subset, N, of $B^{=}(P, M)$ containing x^0 such that for any other x in N, the relative orthogonal segment $q[x, x^0]$ is well defined.*

[7] See Coddington and Levison [5, pp. 314–315] or Hurewicz [12, pp. 75–84].

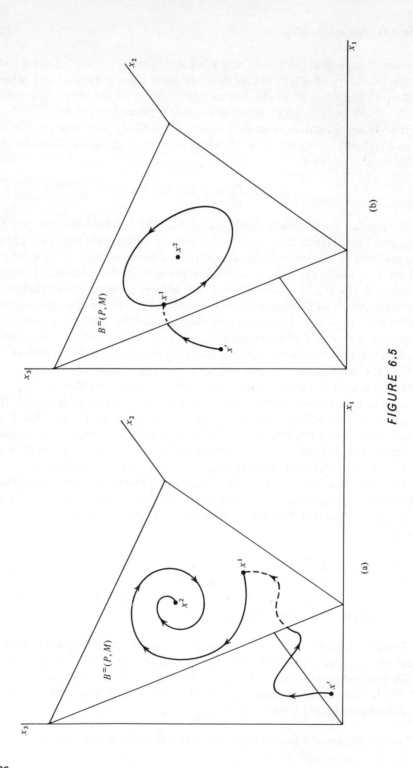

FIGURE 6.5

At this point it is worth digressing for a moment to consider a slightly different line of reasoning studied by Georgescu-Roegen [9] and Samuelson [19]. Although the differential equations discussed thus far can always be integrated uniquely whenever the Lipschitz condition is satisfied, the equations

(6.4-16) $$\varphi(x) \cdot dx = 0,$$

(6.4-17) $$\psi(z) \cdot dz = 0,$$

where dx and dz are vectors, can only be integrated when the integrability condition holds. Then integration yields the indifference surfaces in, respectively, E and Φ_{x^0}, which served as the basis of Chapter 4. But as was indicated there, the integrability condition is always satisfied in two dimensions. Hence (6.4-16) and (6.4-17) can be integrated over any smooth two-dimensional surface. The properties of the resulting integral curves are of interest because they provide information about consumer preferences, but it should be remembered that these curves cannot fit together to form a (indifference) surface unless the integrability condition is met. To illustrate, consider the case in which $B^=(P, M)$ is a two-dimensional plane and for some x^0, ψ_{x^0} is defined, differentiable, and hence (6.4-17) is integrable on it.

Theorem 6.4-18 *Let $n = 3$ and suppose x^0 in $B^=(P, M) \cap E$ is a saturation point relative to $B^<(P, M)$. Assume that $\varphi'' \neq 0$ on Φ_{x^0} and $J_\psi(z)$ is defined on Φ_{x^0} and negative definite at $z = 0$. Then there exists an open subset N of $B^=(P, M)$ containing x^0 such that for any other x in N:*

(a) *If the integrability condition holds on N, then the integral curve of (6.4-17) through x is an ellipsoid around x^0.*

(b) *If the integrability condition is not satisfied on N, then the integral curve through x is a spiral running into x^0 but revolving infinitely many times around it.*

PROOF:
Under the hypotheses of this theorem and the assumptions made earlier, $z = (z_1, z_2)$, $\psi = (\psi^1, \psi^2)$, $B^=(P, M) = \Phi_{x^0}$, $\psi(0) = 0$, and $\psi(z) \neq 0$ for all $z \neq 0$. Equation (6.4-17), in its equivalent parametric form, may be written

$$\frac{dz_1}{dt} = \psi^2(z),$$

$$\frac{dz_2}{dt} = -\psi^1(z),$$

which, since ψ is differentiable, is approximated by

$$\frac{dz_1}{dt} = \psi_1^2(0)z_1 + \psi_2^2(0)z_2,$$

$$\frac{dz_2}{dt} = -\psi_1^1(0)z_1 - \psi_2^1(0)z_2,$$

in some neighborhood of $z = 0$. The characteristic equation of the latter in terms of the dummy variable ϵ is, therefore,

(6.4-19) $\epsilon^2 - (\psi_2^1 - \psi_1^2)\epsilon + (\psi_1^1\psi_2^2 - \psi_2^1\psi_1^2) = 0,$

where ψ_j^i is short for $\psi_j^i(0)$.

If the integrability condition holds on N, then by Theorem 6.4-11, $\psi_2^1 = \psi_1^2$. Hence the roots of (6.4-19) are

$$\epsilon = \pm \sqrt{-(\psi_1^1\psi_2^2 - \psi_2^1\psi_1^2)}.$$

But since $J_z(0)$ is negative definite, the term under the radical is negative. It follows that there exists an open subset of $B^=(P, M)$ in which the integral curves of (6.4-17) are ellipses around $z = 0$ [5, pp. 374–375, 382–383; or 12, pp. 82–83].

If the integrability condition is not satisfied on N, then $\psi_2^1 \neq \psi_1^2$. But any quadratic form derived from $J_\psi(0)$ is identical to one obtained from

$$\begin{bmatrix} \psi_1^1 & \dfrac{\psi_2^1 + \psi_1^2}{2} \\[2ex] \dfrac{\psi_2^1 + \psi_1^2}{2} & \psi_2^2 \end{bmatrix}.$$

Since $J_\psi(0)$ is negative definite, this matrix must have a positive determinant. Hence $4\psi_1^1\psi_2^2 - (\psi_2^1 + \psi_1^2)^2 > 0$ or

$$(\psi_2^1 - \psi_1^2)^2 - 4(\psi_1^1\psi_2^2 - \psi_2^1\psi_1^2) < 0,$$

implying that the discriminant of (6.4-19) is negative. As with part (a), the conclusion of part (b) now follows from the stability theory of ordinary differential equations.

                                                                    Q.E.D.

The ellipse and spiral of Theorem 6.4-18 should not be confused with the curves drawn in Figure 6.5. The latter restricted to $B^=(P, M)$ are the orthogonal trajectories relative to the former.

Picking up the thread of the main argument again, it is now possible to define demand functions under very general circumstances. To do so, the following postulate is introduced:

6.4-20. For $P \neq 0$ and M the rational consumer purchases that bundle of commodities x^0 (if it exists) such that x^0 is a relative saturation point of $B^\leq(P, M)$ and there is an $x' \neq x^0$ in $B^\leq(P, M)$ for which $Q[x, x^0]$ is well defined.

If there exists an x^0 satisfying 6.4-20, write

$$x^0 = h^*(P, M).$$

Thus the consumer may be thought of as starting out in $B^{\leq}(P, M)$ and travel-ing in the "best" (in terms of his local preferences) possible direction looking for a saturation point. If one exists and if there is a way for him to find it, his demand functions are defined at (P, M).[8] Sufficient conditions for h^* to be defined have been given in Theorems 6.4-15 and 6.4-16. Note that only when x^0 is in $B^{=}(P, M)$ will the equality

(6.4-21) $P \cdot h^*(P, M) = M$

hold.

   Properties of h^* are easy to obtain. Clearly, if h^* is defined for (P, M), then it is single valued; for regardless of whether its image is in $B^{=}(P, M)$ or not, saturation points are unique over $B^{\leq}(P, M)$. If $x^0 = h^*(P, M)$ and x^0 is in $B^{=}(P, M)$, then $B^{=}(P, M) = \Phi_{x^0}$. Hence

$$x^0 = h^*(\varphi(x^0), \varphi(x^0) \cdot x^0),$$

so h^* is an "inverse" of φ. Furthermore, h^* is homogeneous of degree zero. If a revealed preference relation, $\tilde{R}$, is defined as in Section 6.2 for (P, M) satisfying (6.4-21), then, by 6.4-6, $\tilde{R}$ is asymmetric. Under the latter con-ditions, if h^* has a differential at (P, M), then S^* is defined and negative semidefinite there. The proof is the same as in Theorem 6.2-13. Of course, s_{ij}^* cannot be given interpretations in terms of either price utility demand functions (Theorem 3.4-3) or derivatives of a support function (6.2-18) unless a utility function, u, exists. But in that case h^* as defined here is identical to its definition there as long as the appropriate assumptions are made on u.

   Thus, where defined, h^* has properties in many ways similar to those given in Section 6.2, the most notable exception being that the integrability condition or strong axiom of revealed preference will not generally hold. With respect to the domain of h^*, it should be pointed out that if $\varphi > 0$ on E, then h^* will map some subset of Γ into E. This would be the case in which a larger bundle of commodities is always locally preferred to a smaller one. It also implies that $\tilde{R}$ is increasing. In general, sufficient conditions for h^* to be defined so that its range contains E are $\varphi^n(x^0) > 0$ and $J_\psi(0)$ exists and is negative definite for all x^0 in E.

   An example similar to one constructed by Gale [8] is now presented to illustrate the theory of this section. Let $n = 3$ and

$$\varphi^1(x) = -4x_1 + x_2 + 4,$$
$$\varphi^2(x) = 3x_1 - 4x_2 + 2,$$
$$\varphi^3(x) = 1,$$

on $\bar{E}$. If $x^0 = (1, 1, 1)$, then Φ_{x^0} is defined by the equation

$$x_1 + x_2 + x_3 = 3.$$

---

[8] This idea was suggested by Professor Hurwicz.

Hence

$$\psi^1(z) = -4z_1 + z_2,$$

$$\psi^2(z) = 3z_1 - 4z_2,$$

for

$$-1 \le z_1 \le 2,$$

$$-1 \le z_2 \le 2,$$

$$-2 \le z_1 + z_2 \le 1.$$

All postulates are easily verified and the integrability condition does not hold. If $(P^0, M^0) = (1, 1, 1, 3)$, then x^0 is a relative saturation point of $B^{\le}(P^0, M^0)$. Let $x = (\frac{3}{2}, \frac{3}{2}, 0)$ in $B^{=}(P^0, M^0) = \Phi_{x^0}$. In the z-coordinate system x^0 is represented by $z = 0$ and x by $z = (\frac{1}{2}, \frac{1}{2})$. The orthogonal segment from x is given by

$$z_1(t) = \frac{3 + \sqrt{3}}{12} \exp\left[(-4 + \sqrt{3})t\right] + \frac{3 - \sqrt{3}}{12} \exp\left[(-4 - \sqrt{3})t\right],$$

$$z_2(t) = \frac{3 + 3\sqrt{3}}{12} \exp\left[(-4 + \sqrt{3})t\right] + \frac{3 - 3\sqrt{3}}{12} \exp\left[(-4 - \sqrt{3})t\right],$$

for $0 \le t < \infty$. Thus $z(0) = (\frac{1}{2}, \frac{1}{2})$ and

$$\lim_{t \to \infty} z(t) = 0,$$

so h^* is defined at (P^0, M^0); i.e.,

$$x^0 = h^*(P^0, M^0).$$

Note also that the integral curves of (6.4-17) in $B^{=}(P, M)$ spiral into x^0.

In addition, let N be a neighborhood of x^0 contained in E. Write $\Theta = \{(P, M): P = \varphi(x), M = P \cdot x, \text{ where } x \text{ is in } E\}$. Then h^* is clearly defined on Θ. Indeed, h^* is computed by inverting φ:

$$h^{*1}(P, M) = -\frac{4}{13} \frac{P_1}{P_3} - \frac{1}{13} \frac{P_2}{P_3} + \frac{18}{13},$$

$$h^{*2}(P, M) = -\frac{3}{13} \frac{P_1}{P_3} - \frac{4}{13} \frac{P_2}{P_3} + \frac{20}{13},$$

$$h^{*3}(P, M) = \frac{M}{P_3} - \frac{18}{13} \frac{P_1}{P_3} - \frac{20}{13} \frac{P_2}{P_3} + \frac{4}{13(P_3)^2} [(P_1)^2 + P_1 P_2 + (P_2)^2].$$

It is easy to verify that $s_{ii}^* < 0$ and, if N is sufficiently small, that $s_{ij}^* \ne s_{ji}^*$ for $i, j = 1, 2, 3$ on Θ.

Finally, suppose h^* is given with the properties derived above. Let $x = h^*(P, M)$, where x is in $\bar{E}$. If (6.4-21) holds, set $\varphi(x) = P$; otherwise define

$\varphi(x) = 0$. Evidently φ satisfies 6.4-3 and 6.4-6, and x is the unique saturation point of $B^{\leq}(P, M)$. By defining directions of preference, antipreference, and indifference according to the sign of $\varphi(x') \cdot (x - x')$ when $\varphi(x') \neq 0$, a local quasi-preference ordering, $\bigcirc_x$, satisfying 6.4-1 and 6.4-2 may be constructed. [Of course, when $\varphi(x') = 0$, all directions emanating from x' are of anti-preference.] Now φ is an "inverse" of h^*. Recall that when studying integrability in Chapter 4, assumptions were made on inverse demand functions which permitted the derivation of h^* and its properties. Following the same practice here, $\bigcirc_x$ obviously generates h^*. Literally, the problem of integrability does not exist in this context.

EXERCISES

6.1 Under the assumptions of Section 6.2 prove the following version of Theorem 6.2-4 without relying on utility functions: if $(P, M) > 0$, then there exists an $\bar{x}$ in $B^=(P, M)$ such that $\bar{x} \bigcirc x$ for all $x \neq \bar{x}$ in $B^{\leq}(P, M)$. [HINT: Show that the family of sets $K_x = B^{\leq}(P, M) \cap C_x^{\geq}$ for x in $B^{\leq}(P, M)$ has the finite intersection property.]

6.2 Show that $H(P, \mu)$ is increasing and linearly homogeneous in P for each μ and that it is increasing in μ for each P.

6.3 Derive the homogeneity of h^* and the negative semidefiniteness of S^* from the properties of H.

6.4 Compute the indirect utility and expenditure functions when $u(x) = -1/x_1 - 1/x_2$. Derive demand functions from both. What is the difference between these two formulations of demand and how is it resolved?

6.5 Let R be the indirect revealed preference relation defined in Section 6.2. Show that R is transitive and increasing.

6.6 Let $\tilde{R}$ be the direct revealed preference relation. Show that the weak axiom of revealed preference implies for all x' and x'', if $x' \tilde{R} x''$, then $x' \tilde{R} [\theta x' + (1 - \theta)x'']$ and $[\theta x' + (1 - \theta)x''] \tilde{R} x''$ for any $0 < \theta < 1$.

6.7 Let R be any relation defined on $\bar{E}$. Prove the following assertions:
a. If R is asymmetric, then R is also irreflexive and $\bar{R}$ is reflexive.
b. R is asymmetric if and only if $\bar{R}$ is total.
c. If R is irreflexive and transitive, then R is also asymmetric.

6.8 In the integrable case of Section 6.4 verify the following:
a. For x sufficiently close to x^0, $\overrightarrow{x^0 x}$ is a direction of antipreference or preference according as $u(x^0) - u(x)$ is positive or negative.
b. Assume 6.4-6. For all x, if $\overrightarrow{x^0 x}$ is a direction of nonpreference, then $u(x^0) > u(x)$. Why is the converse false?

6.9 Let $u(x_1, x_2) = x_1 x_2$. What is the relative saturation point of $B^{\leq}(1, 1, 4)$? Describe the orthogonal paths from $(0, 0)$ and $(2, 0)$.

REFERENCES

[1] Allen, R. G. D., "The Foundations of a Mathematical Theory of Exchange," *Economica* (1932), pp. 197–226.

[2] Allen, R. G. D., "A Reconsideration of the Theory of Value," Part II, *Economica* (1934), pp. 196–219.

[3] Allen, R. G. D., *Mathematical Analysis for Economists* (London: Macmillan, 1938).

[4] Apostol, T. M., *Mathematical Analysis* (Reading, Mass.: Addison-Wesley, 1957).

[5] Coddington, E. A., and N. Levison, *Theory of Ordinary Differential Equations* (New York: McGraw-Hill, 1955).

[6] Evans, G. C., *Mathematical Introduction to Economics* (New York: McGraw-Hill, 1930).

[7] Fisher, I., *Mathematical Investigations in the Theory of Value and Prices* (New Haven: Yale University Press, 1925).

[8] Gale, D., "A Note on Revealed Preference," *Economica* (1960), pp. 348–354.

[9] Georgescu-Roegen, N., "The Pure Theory of Consumer's Behavior," *The Quarterly Journal of Economics* (1936), pp. 545–593.

[10] Georgescu-Roegen, N., "Choice and Revealed Preference," *The Southern Economic Journal* (1954), pp. 119–130.

[11] Houthakker, H. S., "Revealed Preference and the Utility Function," *Economica* (1950), pp. 159–174.

[12] Hurewicz, W., *Lectures on Ordinary Differential Equations* (New York: Wiley, 1958).

[13] Hurwicz, L., and M. K. Richter, "Revealed Preference without Demand Continuity Assumptions," in J. S. Chipman et al. (eds.), *Studies in the Mathematical Foundations of Utility and Demand Theory* (New York: Harcourt, Brace & World, forthcoming).

[14] Hurwicz, L., and H. Uzawa, "On the Integrability of Demand Functions," in J. S. Chipman et al. (eds.), *Studies in the Mathematical Foundations of Utility and Demand Theory* (New York: Harcourt, Brace & World, forthcoming).

[15] Katzner, D. W., "Demand and Exchange Analysis in the Absence of Integrability Conditions," in J. S. Chipman et al. (eds.), *Studies in the Mathematical Foundations of Utility and Demand Theory* (New York: Harcourt, Brace & World, forthcoming).

[16] McKenzie, L., "Demand Theory without a Utility Index," *Review of Economic Studies* v. 24 (1957), pp. 185–189.

[17] Richter, M. K., "Revealed Preference Theory," *Econometrica* (1966), pp. 635–645.

[18] Samuelson, P. A., *Foundations of Economic Analysis* (Cambridge, Mass.: Harvard University Press, 1947).

[19] Samuelson, P. A., "The Problem of Integrability in Utility Theory," *Economica* (1950), pp. 335–385.

[20] Sonnenschein, H. F., "Competitive Equilibrium without Transitive Preferences," in J. S. Chipman et al. (eds.), *Studies in the Mathematical Foundations of Utility and Demand Theory* (New York: Harcourt, Brace & World, forthcoming).

[21] Uzawa, H., "Preference and Rational Choice in the Theory of Consumption," in K. J. Arrow, S. Karlin, and P. Suppes (eds.), *Mathematical Methods in the Social Sciences* (Stanford, Calif.: Stanford University Press, 1960).

7

Odds and Ends

A wide variety of economic problems may be analyzed as modifications, extensions, or applications of the theory of utility maximization. This chapter discusses some of the more important ones. Throughout, the framework is that developed in Chapters 3 and 4.

7.1 LEISURE AND EMPLOYMENT

It is not difficult to extend utility maximization to permit the consumer simultaneously to choose his best commodity bundle and the quantity of labor he will supply. For each unit of work he performs, his income, and hence money available to spend on commodities, increases.

Let the period of time under consideration (recall Section 1.1) be divided into Λ units and suppose t varies over numbers of those units devoted to leisure. The amount of time in employment is then $\Lambda - t$. Use ω to denote the wage per unit of time commanded by the consumer and let it be determined in the same manner as ordinary prices. The budget constraint under these conditions becomes

$$(7.1\text{-}1) \qquad\qquad P \cdot x + \omega t \leq M + \omega \Lambda.$$

Write $\tilde{E}$ for $\{(x, t): x > 0, 0 < t \leq \Lambda\}$. Assume that there is a utility function $u(x, t)$, defined on the closure of $\tilde{E}$ satisfying 3.1-1–3.1-4.

Now let $\tilde{p} = (P_1/\omega, \ldots, P_n/\omega)$, $\tilde{m} = (M/\omega) + \Lambda$, and $\tilde{\Gamma} = \{(\tilde{p}, \tilde{m}): (P, \omega, M) > 0\}$. Then, as in Chapter 3, for each element in $\tilde{\Gamma}$ there is a unique (x, t) in $\tilde{E}$ maximizing u subject to (7.1-1). Denote the mapping so obtained by h and write

$$(x, t) = h(\tilde{p}, \tilde{m}).$$

Note that h is actually $1:1$ on a subset, Θ, of $\tilde{\Gamma}$ and the image of Θ under h is $\tilde{E}$. Clearly on the interior of Θ, h satisfies all the properties implied by utility maximization (Table 3.1) for functions of normalized prices and income. Its properties off of Θ are similar to those off of Γ' derived in the first model of Section 6.1.

In terms of nonnormalized variables, however, there are some subtle changes. As before, define

$$h^*(P, \omega, M + \omega\Lambda) = h\left(\frac{P_1}{\omega}, \ldots, \frac{P_n}{\omega}, \frac{M}{\omega} + \Lambda\right),$$

for $(P, \omega, M) > 0$. Let the derivatives of $h^* = (h^{*1}, \ldots, h^{*n+1})$ be written h_j^{*i}, where $i = 1, \ldots, n + 1$, and $j = 1, \ldots, n + 2$, and

$$(7.1\text{-}2) \qquad s_{ij}^* = h_j^{*i} + h^{*j}h_{n+2}^{*i}, \quad i, j = 1, \ldots, n + 1.$$

Suppose that S^* is the n by n matrix of elements s_{ij}^*, where $i, j = 1, \ldots, n$, and $\mathbb{S}^*$ is the similar matrix for $i, j = 1, \ldots, n + 1$. Since $h_{n+2}^{*i} = h_M^{*i}$ for all i, these are the Slutsky matrices analyzed in Chapter 3. Hence where they exist they have the familiar symmetry and negative definiteness properties. But for $j = n + 1$, the s_{ij}^* of (7.1-2) are not computed, as their counterparts in Chapter 3, by differentiation of h^* with respect to ω. Such a function, $s_{i\omega}^*$, would be defined as

$$s_{i\omega}^* = h_{n+1}^{*i} + \Lambda h_{n+2}^{*i} + h^{*n+1}h_{n+2}^{*i},$$

$$= s_{in+1}^* + \Lambda h_{n+2}^{*i},$$

for $i = 1, \ldots, n + 1$. On the other hand, if $i = n + 1$ and $j \neq n + 1$, then s_{ij}^* is obtained upon differentiation with respect to ω; thus the corresponding $s_{\omega j}^* = s_{n+1j}^*$. It follows that replacing the last row and column of $\mathbb{S}^*$ by, respectively, the $s_{\omega j}^*$ and the $s_{i\omega}^*$, will in general destroy its symmetry and negative semidefiniteness. Furthermore, the interpretation in terms of price–utility demand functions (Theorem 3.4-3) holds for all s_{ij}^* but not the $s_{i\omega}^*$.

Finally, the consumer's labor supply function is given by

$$t = \Lambda - h^{*n+1}(P, \omega, M + \omega\Lambda).$$

Its properties are easily derived from those of h^*. The problem of integrability in the context of this analysis is left to the reader.

7.2 CHANGES IN TASTES AND QUALITY

Variation in both individual preferences and quality of commodities may be studied by introducing parameters, say $\zeta = (\zeta_1, \ldots, \zeta_n) > 0$, into the utility function. Thus consider $\bar{G}(\zeta_1 x_1, \ldots, \zeta_n x_n)$ defined for all $(x, \zeta) \geq 0$

such that $\bar{G}$ satisfies 3.1-1–3.1-4 on $\bar{E}$. Since only one parameter will be permitted to vary at a time, no generality is lost by restricting attention to, say,

$$G(\zeta_1 x_1, x_2, \ldots, x_n) \equiv \bar{G}(\zeta_1 x_1, \zeta_2^0 x_1, \ldots, \zeta_n^0 x_n),$$

where the ζ_j^0 for $j = 2, \ldots, n$ are fixed. Writing

$$u(x, \zeta_1) \equiv G(\zeta_1 x_1, x_2, \ldots, x_n),$$

u is twice continuously differentiable for all $(x, \zeta_1) > 0$, and as a function of x satisfies 3.1-1–3.1-4 on $\bar{E}$. Now for each value of $\zeta_1 > 0$, demand functions $h^*(P, M, \zeta_1)$ are defined on Γ^*, which as functions of (P, M) have all properties listed in Table 3.1. The Slutsky functions (3.2-7) are written $s_{ij}^*(P, M, \zeta_1)$, where $i, j = 1, \ldots, n$. In what follows behavioral implications of changes in ζ_1 are deduced.

Let $\partial^2 G / \partial x_i \partial \zeta_1$ denote the cross-partial derivative of G with respect to first x_i and then ζ_1; it is distinct from G_{i1}, which represents the cross-partial derivative with respect to arguments i and 1. The symbol u_{ij} is defined as usual for $i, j = 1, \ldots, n$. Differentiating u_i partially with respect to ζ_1 when x_j alone is thought of as functionally dependent on ζ_1 gives

$$u_{i1} \frac{\partial x_1}{\partial \zeta_1} + \frac{\partial^2 G}{\partial x_i \partial \zeta_1}, \quad i = 1, \ldots, n, i = 1,$$

$$u_{ij} \frac{\partial x_j}{\partial \zeta_1}, \qquad i = 1, \ldots, n, j \neq 1.$$

It follows as in the proof of Lemma 3.2-9 that differentiating equilibrium conditions (3.2-10) with respect to ζ_1 and solving for the derivative, $h_{\zeta_1}^{*i}$, of h^{*i} with respect to ζ_1,

$$(7.2\text{-}1) \quad h_{\zeta_1}^{*i}(P, M, \zeta_1) = -\sum_{j=1}^{n} \delta_j(P, M, \zeta_1) s_{ji}^*(P, M, \zeta_1), \quad i = 1, \ldots, n,$$

for (P, M) in Ω^*, where

$$\delta_j = \frac{1}{\lambda^*} \frac{\partial^2 G}{\partial x_j \partial \zeta_1}, \quad j = 1, \ldots, n.$$

Thus $h_{\zeta_1}^{*i}$ is a linear combination of the ith column of the Slutsky matrix S^*.

It is clear that in order for (7.2-1) to be a meaningful restriction on behavior, it must be invariant under increasing transformations of u. Let T be such a transformation whose derivative $T' > 0$ everywhere. Let its second derivative T'' exist and write

$$\tilde{G}(\zeta_1 x_1, x_2, \ldots, x_n) \equiv T(G(\zeta_1 x_1, x_2, \ldots, x_n)).$$

Then

$$\frac{\partial^2 \tilde{G}}{\partial x_i \partial \zeta_1} = x_1 G_1 T'' u_i + T' \frac{\partial^2 G}{\partial x_i \partial \zeta_1}, \quad i = 1, \ldots, n.$$

Note that the marginal utility of income associated with $\tilde{G}$ is $\tilde{\lambda}^* = T'\lambda^*$, and none of the s_{ji}^* are changed by T. Hence, using $\tilde{G}$ in the preceding argument instead of G,

$$h_{\zeta_1}^{*i} = -\sum_{j=1}^{n} \frac{1}{\lambda^*} \frac{\partial^2 G}{\partial x_j \, \partial \zeta_1} s_{ji}^* - \frac{x_1 G_1 T''}{\tilde{\lambda}^*} \sum_{j=1}^{n} u_j s_{ji}^*,$$

where $i = 1, \ldots, n$. But again from the equilibrium conditions the sum in the right-hand term reduces to $\lambda^* \sum_{j=1}^{n} P_j s_{ji}^*$, which vanishes by the homogeneity of h^* (recall the proof of Exercise 3.3). Therefore, (7.2-1) is invariant under T. A similar argument shows that

(7.2-2) $$\sum_{i=1}^{n} P_i h_{\zeta_1}^{*i} = 0.$$

The parameter ζ_1 can be interpreted either as an indicator of tastes or quality. In terms of tastes, a rise of commodity 1 in the individual's preference ranking while relative positions of all other goods remain unchanged would appear as an increase in ζ_1. The latter, of course, implies greater utility, since

$$\frac{\partial u}{\partial \zeta_1} = x_1 G_1 > 0,$$

for all ζ_1. Its impact on demand is given by (7.2-1) and (7.2-2), but the sign of $h_{\zeta_1}^{*i}$ cannot be determined without further information about u. The reason for ambiguity is that the consumer might now actually be satisfied with less of the first good since he likes it more. Whether or not this is, in fact, the case depends on the precise nature of his preferences. Regarding ζ_1 as a quality index of commodity 1, where better quality is reflected in a higher value of ζ_1 and hence greater utility, similar conclusions may be drawn. Note that the units in which good 1 is measured are not altered; quality changes affect only shapes of utility functions.

For the special case in which u is strongly separable and

$$u(x, \zeta_1) = V(v^1(\zeta_1 x_1) + v^2(x_{(1)})),$$

where $x_{(1)} = (x_2, \ldots, x_n)$, (7.2-1) reduces to

$$h_{\zeta_1}^{*i}(P, M, \zeta_1) = -\delta_1(P, M, \zeta_1) s_{1i}^*(P, M, \zeta_1), \quad i = 1, \ldots, n,$$

for (P, M) in Ω^*. Thus, since $s_{11}^* \le 0$, if increases in ζ_1 increase marginal utility u_1, then

$$h_{\zeta_1}^{*1}(P, M, \zeta_1) > 0.$$

This case was originally studied by Ichimura [9]; the more general relation (7.2-1) is due to Tintner [17].

7.3 AGGREGATION

Although aggregates may be constructed in many ways to serve many purposes, only two highly specific types are considered here. The first is concerned with aggregation over individuals, the second over commodities and prices. Both will be used in the remaining sections of this chapter.

Let there be K individuals, each with utility function u^k defined on $\bar{E}$ and satisfying 3.1-1–3.1-4. Of course $k = 1, \ldots, K$. Demand functions derived from u^k are written h^k and defined on $\Gamma^k = \{(p, m^k): p > 0, m^k > 0\}$, where m^k is the income of individual k. In this context the symbol h^k is a vector and should not be confused with the single function h^i studied in earlier chapters. Similarly, s_{ij}^k is his appropriate Slutsky function. Now let

$$Y = \sum_{k=1}^{K} m^k,$$

and d_k be each persons share in the total; i.e.,

$$d_k = \frac{m^k}{Y}, \quad k = 1, \ldots, K.$$

The vector $d = (d_1, \ldots, d_K)$ represents the distribution of income over these consumers. Market demand functions are thus defined as

$$H(p, Y, d) = \sum_{k=1}^{K} h^k(p, d_k Y),$$

on $\Gamma^H = \{(p, Y): p > 0, Y > 0\}$ for each $d > 0$ such that $|d| = 1$. Denote their corresponding Slutsky functions by s_{ij}^H. The first question to be considered, then, is: under what conditions does there exist a utility function u^H defined on $\bar{E}$ which generates H? In other words, when can market demand functions be obtained from an aggregate community preference ordering in the same manner that individual functions are derived? One answer is provided by Theorem 7.3-1.

Theorem 7.3-1 *Let h^k (i.e., its inverse) satisfy 4.3-1–4.3-3 on Γ^k for $k = 1, \ldots, K$. If there are functions φ such that*

$$h^k(p, m^k) = m^k \varphi(p),$$

for every k, then there exists a utility generator u^H of H. Furthermore, u^H is defined on $\bar{E}$, satisfies 3.1-1–3.1-4, is a monotone transformation of a linearly homogeneous function, and does not depend on the distribution of income, d.

PROOF:

If each h^k has the required form,

$$H(p, Y, d) = Y\varphi(p),$$

(7.3-2)
$$s_{ij}^H(p, Y, d) = \sum_{k=1}^{K} s_{ij}^k(p, d_k Y), \quad i, j = 1, \ldots, n.$$

Let $d^0 > 0$ be given where $|d^0| = 1$. Then $H(p, Y, d^0)$ clearly maps Γ^H onto E. The hypothesis implies that each $n - 1$ by $n - 1$ matrix of functions s_{ij}^k is negative definite (Theorem 3.2-13). Hence the $n - 1$ by $n - 1$ matrix of s_{ij}^H is also. As in Theorem 3.2-13, it follows that the Jacobian of H is nonzero on Γ^H. Therefore, $H(p, Y, d^0)$ is a 1:1 correspondence from Γ^H to E. Furthermore, its inverse satisfies 4.3-1–4.3-3. By Theorem 4.3-6, there exists a utility generator, u^H, of H defined on $\bar{E}$ and satisfying 3.1-1–3.1-4. From (7.3-2) and Theorem 5.1-3, u^H is a monotone transformation of a linearly homogeneous function. Evidently u^H is independent of d^0.

Q.E.D.

Combining commodities and prices into composites is the second form of aggregation to be considered here. Let u defined on $\bar{E}$ satisfy 3.1-1–3.1-4 and generate h^*. Suppose goods $r + 1, \ldots, n$, where $1 < r < n$ are lumped into one along with their corresponding prices. Denote these composites by $\bar{x}$ and $\bar{P}$, respectively. Write $x_{\bar{r}} = (x_1, \ldots, x_r)$, $x_{(\bar{r})} = (x_{r+1}, \ldots, x_n)$, $P_{\bar{r}} = (P_1, \ldots, P_r)$, and $P_{(\bar{r})} = (P_{r+1}, \ldots, P_n)$. The problem is to obtain conditions under which there exist functions ξ, ψ, and a utility function $\bar{u}$ defined for all $x_{(\bar{r})} > 0$, $P_{(\bar{r})} > 0$, and $(x_{\bar{r}}, \bar{x}) > 0$, respectively, such that $\bar{u}$ satisfies 3.1-1–3.1-4 on its domain,

$$\bar{x} = \xi(x_{(\bar{r})}),$$
$$\bar{P} = \psi(P_{(\bar{r})}),$$

and if x maximizes u over $B^\leq(P, M)$, then at the maximum,

(7.3-3) $$\bar{P}\bar{x} = P_{(\bar{r})} \cdot x_{(\bar{r})},$$

(7.3-4) $$\frac{\bar{u}_i(x_{\bar{r}}, \bar{x})}{\bar{u}_{r+1}(x_{\bar{r}}, \bar{x})} = \frac{P_i}{\bar{P}}, \quad i = 1, \ldots, r,$$

where $\bar{u}_{r+1}$ is the derivative of $\bar{u}$ with respect to $\bar{x}$. When such functions exist $\bar{x}$ is called a *composite commodity* and $\bar{P}$ its *composite price*. Note that (7.3-3) says expenditure on the composite commodity is the sum of expenditure on its components and that (7.3-4) is analogous to the first-order constrained maximization conditions for ordinary commodities. Thus composites may be treated in the same manner as any commodity and price, and the concept of demand for a group of commodities (i.e., composite commodity) as a function of an aggregate price (i.e., composite price) has a well-defined meaning.

There are many approaches to the question raised above. Hicks [6] has observed that for any fixed $P_{(\bar{r})}^0 > 0$, over the domain

$$\Gamma_{P_{(\bar{r})}^0} = \{(P, M): P_{\bar{r}} > 0, M > 0 \text{ and } P_{(\bar{r})} = \theta P_{(\bar{r})}^0 \text{ for some } \theta > 0\},$$

the functions

(7.3-5) $$\xi(x_{(\bar{r})}) = P_{(\bar{r})}^0 \cdot x_{(\bar{r})},$$

where $x_v = h^{*v}(P, M)$ for $v = r + 1, \ldots, n$ and

(7.3-6) $$\psi(P_{(\bar{r})}) = \theta,$$

satisfy the conditions enabling them to be used as composites:

Theorem 7.3-7   *Assume that 4.3-1–4.3-3 are satisfied on E. Then there exists a $\bar{u}$ such that (7.3-5) and (7.3-6) define a composite commodity and price on $\Gamma_{P_{(\bar{r})}^0}$.*

PROOF:
Write $\bar{P} = \theta$ and define

$$\bar{h}^i(P_r, \bar{P}, M) = \begin{cases} h^{*i}(P_{\bar{r}}, \theta P_{(\bar{r})}^0, M), & \text{if } i = 1, \ldots, r, \\ \sum_{v=r+1}^{n} P_v^0 h^{*v}(P_{\bar{r}}, \theta P_{(\bar{r})}^0, M), & \text{if } i = r + 1, \end{cases}$$

for all $(P_{\bar{r}}, \bar{P}, M) > 0$. Define the Slutsky functions $\bar{s}_{ij}$ for $i, j = 1, \ldots, r + 1$, with respect to $\bar{h} = (\bar{h}^1, \ldots, \bar{h}^{r+1})$ in the usual manner [as in (3.2-7)]. Then

$$\bar{s}_{ij} = \begin{cases} s_{ij}^*, & \text{if } i, j \neq r + 1, \\ \sum_{v=r+1}^{n} P_v^0 s_{iv}^*, & \text{if } i \neq r + 1, j = r + 1, \\ \sum_{v=r+1}^{n} P_v^0 s_{vj}^*, & \text{if } i = r + 1, j \neq r + 1, \\ \sum_{v=r+1}^{n} \sum_{\epsilon=r+1}^{n} P_v^0 P_\epsilon^0 s_{v\epsilon}^*, & \text{if } i, j = r + 1, \end{cases}$$

where s_{ij}^* are the Slutsky functions obtained from h^*. Letting

$$\bar{x} = \bar{h}^{r+1}(P_{\bar{r}}, \bar{P}, M) = \xi(x_{(\bar{r})}),$$

it follows as in the proof of Theorem 7.3-1 that in terms of $\bar{h} = (\bar{h}^1, \ldots, \bar{h}^{r+1})$, 4.3-1–4.3-3 hold for all $(x_{\bar{r}}, \bar{x}) > 0$. By Theorem 4.3-6 there exists a function $\bar{u}$ satisfying 3.1-1–3.1-4, (7.3-4), and generating $\bar{h}$. Since (7.3-3) is obviously valid, the proof is complete.

Q.E.D.

Thus composites may be constructed among commodities whose prices change in the same proportion. Note that $\bar{h}^{r+1}$ is the demand for the composite commodity. On the other hand, Gorman [5] has shown that by assuming a special form of separability, price proportionality is not required.

Theorem 7.3-8 *If there are twice continuously differentiable functions $\bar{u}$ and ξ, where $\bar{u}$ satisfies 3.1-1–3.1-4 on its domain, ξ is homogeneous of degree one, and*

$$u(x) = \bar{u}(x_{\bar{r}}, \xi(x_{(\bar{r})})),$$

on E, then there exists a function ψ such that (7.3-3) and (7.3-4) are satisfied. Furthermore, ψ is also homogeneous of degree one.

PROOF:

From the theory of weak separability (Section 5.2) and the fact that ξ is homogeneous of degree one (recall Theorem 5.1-1), demand functions for commodities $r + 1, \ldots, n$, may be written in terms of nonnormalized variables as

(7.3-9) $x_{(\bar{r})} = M_{(\bar{r})}\varphi(P_{(\bar{r})}),$

for an appropriate φ. Here $M_{(\bar{r})}$ represents expenditure on commodities $r + 1, \ldots, n$. Substituting (7.3-9) for $x_{(\bar{r})}$ in $\xi(x_{(\bar{r})})$, define ψ by

$$\psi(P_{(\bar{r})}) = \frac{P_j}{\xi_j(\varphi(P_{(\bar{r})}))},$$

for any $j = r + 1, \ldots, n$, where subscripts on ξ denote derivatives. Write $\bar{x} = \xi(x_{(\bar{r})})$ and $\bar{P} = \psi(P_{(\bar{r})})$. Since ξ is linearly homogeneous, ξ_j is homogeneous of degree zero. This justifies omitting $M_{(\bar{r})}$ from the denominator above and implies that ψ is linearly homogeneous. Also

$$\psi(P_{(\bar{r})}) = \frac{\bar{u}_{r+1}P_j}{\bar{u}_{r+1}\xi_j} = \frac{\bar{u}_{r+1}}{\lambda^*},$$

by the equilibrium conditions (3.1-17), and hence ψ is independent of j. It follows, again from (3.1-17), that (7.3-4) is satisfied. Also

$$P_{(\bar{r})} \cdot x_{(\bar{r})} = \left[\sum_{j=r+1}^{n} \xi_j x_j \right] \psi = \bar{P}\bar{x},$$

by Euler's theorem, thereby proving (7.3-3).

                                                                                          Q.E.D.

Maximizing $\bar{u}(x_{\bar{r}}, \bar{x})$ subject to $P_{\bar{r}} \cdot x_{\bar{r}} + \bar{P}\bar{x} = M$ now gives, in particular, demand for the composite commodity as a function of $P_{\bar{r}}$, M, and the composite price. It has all the empirical properties of the Slutsky theory.

A generalization of Theorem 7.3-8 suggests an interesting interpretation of the consumers decision-making process when his utility function is weakly separable. In the notation of Section 5.2, if

$$u(x) = V(v^1(x_{\bar{1}}), \ldots, v^{\pi}(x_{\bar{\pi}})),$$

where $V(z_1, \ldots, z_{\pi})$ satisfies 3.1-1–3.1-4 for all $z = (z_1, \ldots, z_{\pi}) > 0$ and each v^i is linearly homogeneous, then it follows as in Theorem 7.3-8 that all of the z_i's may be regarded as composite commodities whose corresponding composite prices are $\bar{P} = (\bar{P}_1, \ldots, \bar{P}_{\pi})$. Then, to determine utility maximizing commodity bundles given (P, M), the consumer may first maximize $V(z)$ subject to

$$\bar{P} \cdot z \le M,$$

thus obtaining quantities of the composites, z^0, to be purchased. But by (7.3-3) income spent on a composite commodity is the same as income spent on the group of goods making up that composite. Hence the optimal purchases within each group may now be found by maximizing each v^i subject to

$$P_{\bar{i}} \cdot x_{\bar{i}} \le \bar{P} z_i^0.$$

This two-stage procedure yields the same results as single-stage maximization and at the same time allows the consumer to make decisions by first determining his expenditure on broad groups of commodities and then allocating funds within each group.

Still a third approach to composites which involves neither price proportionality nor separability is to define $\bar{x}$ implicitly by the system of equations

$$x_j = \eta^j(\bar{x}), \quad j = r + 1, \ldots, n,$$

where $\eta = (\eta^{r+1}, \ldots, \eta^n)$ is a vector of functions with positive, continuous derivatives for all $\bar{x} > 0$. Once η is fixed, ξ may be specified in any number of ways as long as

$$\bar{x} = \xi(\eta(\bar{x})),$$

and $\bar{u}$ may be obtained by

(7.3-10) $$\bar{u}(x_{\bar{r}}, \bar{x}) = u(x_{\bar{r}}, \eta(\bar{x})).$$

This procedure has its origins with Leontief [11]. The next result provides sufficient conditions for (7.3-3) and (7.3-4) to be satisfied.

Theorem 7.3-11 *For any positive constants* α_j, *let* $\eta^j(\bar{x}) = \alpha_j \bar{x}$, *where* $j = r + 1, \ldots, n$, *and set*

$$\bar{P} = \psi(P_{(\bar{r})}) = \sum_{j=r+1}^{n} \alpha_j P_j.$$

Then $\bar{x}$ *and* $\bar{P}$ *are, respectively, composite commodity and price.*

PROOF:

Clearly $\bar{u}$ as defined in (7.3-10) satisfies 3.1-1–3.1-4 on its domain. Equation (7.3-3) is equally obvious. Furthermore,

$$\frac{\bar{u}_i}{\bar{u}_{r+1}} = \frac{u_i}{\sum\limits_{j=r+1}^{n} \alpha_j u_j} = \frac{P_i}{\bar{P}}, \quad i = 1, \ldots, r,$$

by the equilibrium conditions (3.1-17).

Q.E.D.

It is clear from the proof of Theorem 7.3-11 that for each $\alpha = (\alpha_{r+1}, \ldots, \alpha_n)$, relation (7.3-4) can be satisfied only for utility maximizing vectors lying in the set

$$Q_\alpha = \{x : x_{\bar{r}} > 0, x_{(\bar{r})} = \bar{x}\alpha \text{ for } \bar{x} > 0\}.$$

The notion of price proportionality used by Hicks is therefore replaced by quantity proportionality here.

Geometrically this approach has an interesting and simple interpretation. Letting $n = 3$ and $r = 1$, the equations

$$x_j = \alpha_j \bar{x}, \quad j = 2, 3,$$

define a plane Q_α in the commodity space as in Figure 7.1. If

$$\xi(x_{(\bar{1})}) = \sqrt{(x_2)^2 + (x_3)^2}$$

(implying $\alpha_2^2 + \alpha_3^2 = 1$), then the unit length on the line labeled $\bar{x}$ represents one unit of the composite commodity. Thus use of composites in this case shrinks the commodity space into a plane. Now the intersection of indifference surfaces and budget planes with Q_α yield indifference curves and budget lines in that space. The original consumer choice problem is therefore reduced to a completely analogous two-dimensional situation. Equation (7.3-4) is, after all, nothing more than the statement that an indifference curve is tangent to a budget line in Q_α. A similar interpretation may be given in the general case.

As with the first two analyses of composites, demand functions, $\bar{h}$, for $(x_{\bar{r}}, \bar{x})$ may be obtained, this time by maximizing $\bar{u}$ subject to

$$P_{\bar{r}} \cdot x_{\bar{r}} + \bar{P}\bar{x} = M.$$

It is clear that

$$\bar{h}^i(P_{\bar{r}}, \bar{P}, M) = \begin{cases} h^{*i}(P, M), & \text{if } i = 1, \ldots, r, \\ \dfrac{1}{\bar{P}} \sum\limits_{j=r+1}^{n} P_j h^{*j}(P, M), & \text{if } i = r+1, \end{cases}$$

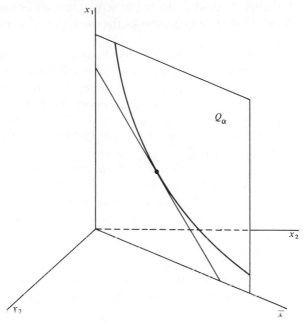

FIGURE 7.1

on Γ^* where $\bar{P} = \sum_{j=r+1}^{n} \alpha_j P_j$ and h^* is generated by u. Note that $\bar{h}$ must exhibit all the properties implied by utility maximization and that $\bar{h}^{r+1}$ is once again a demand function for the group $r + 1, \ldots, n$.

Apart from giving the concept "demand for a group of goods" legitimate meaning, composites are important because they permit considerable geometric and analytic simplification. This is true regardless of the way in which they are defined. Thus Hicks [6] has been able to obtain many of the familiar implications of utility maximization by analyzing a two-dimensional situation in which one commodity is a composite of all except that under specific scrutiny. Another example of their use will be presented in Section 7.5. Note also that it is possible to combine the results obtained here to study the demand for a group of commodities by a group of consumers.

7.4 COMPLEMENTARITY

The idea that some commodities are in certain ways related to others is both intriguing and elusive. Elusiveness arises in that to be truly meaningful, such notions must be consistent with intuition, have properties rendering them useful, and, at the same time, be reflected in observable economic phenomena. Although somewhat limited in scope, one set of such concepts is developed here. It in no way precludes the existence of a more general approach.

Intuitively, two commodities are usually thought of as complements if they "go with" or "belong to" one another. Thus left shoes go with right shoes and, for many people, cream goes with coffee. Goods which are "very complementary" tend to be desired in fixed proportions. But not all individuals may feel the same way about it. Sam may put three drops of cream in each cup of coffee but Sylvia prefers hers black. Coffee and cream are therefore complements for him but they do not stand in that relationship for her. Similarly, two goods are substitutes if one can be used as an "equal replacement" for the other. Five nickels, for example, are commonly regarded as a substitute for one quarter. Once again the idea of fixed proportions is present and individuals may disagree over what they consider to be substitutes.

In cases which are not so extreme, the proportions involved need not be fixed. An individual may like to drink both tea and coffee, being indifferent between various proportions along a strictly convex indifference curve. Nevertheless, he may feel that tea and coffee are more like substitutes to him than complements. Many pairs of commodities, then, may exhibit in the mind of the consumer some degree of complementarity or substitutability. Goods which do not are often called independent.

To enhance their usefulness and give depth to their meaning, there are at least five properties that definitions of relationships between commodities might possess[1]:

7.4-1. *Intuition.* Concepts should be related to individual preferences according to the intuitive notions presented above.

7.4-2. *Symmetry.* If commodities i and j stand in a specific relationship with each other, then commodities j and i should also stand in that relationship.

7.4-3. *Dimensionality.* Relationships between commodities should not depend on the dimension of the commodity space. If, for example, two goods are regarded as complements in an n-commodity world, they should still be capable of being regarded as such in isolation.

7.4-4. *Universality.* Any pair of commodities should be capable of being declared complements, substitutes, or independent under the proposed definition. It should also be possible for all pairs of goods to stand in the same relationship.

7.4-5. *Observability.* It should be possible to determine the relationship in which any individual holds any pair of goods by observing his market activity.

[1] This kind of approach was suggested by Professor Pollak.

Of course, if 7.4-5 does not hold, then the definitions are empirically meaningless, for it is impossible to discern if such relationships in fact exist.

Although the appeal of 7.4-1–7.4-5 is immediately obvious, few definitions satisfy all simultaneously. The well-known notion of Auspitz and Lieben that goods i and j are complements, independent, or substitutes according as the derivative

$$u_{ij}(x) \gtreqless 0,$$

is not invariant over increasing transformations of u. In general, then, it is impossible to express this concept either in terms of preference orderings or demand functions so intuition and observability are violated. Alternatively calling i and j complements, independent, or substitutes according as

(7.4-6) $$h_j^{*i}(P, M) \gtreqless 0,$$

also runs into trouble since it is possible to have both $h_j^{*i} > 0$ and $h_i^{*j} \leq 0$ simultaneously (this is true of the demand functions in Exercise 3.6). To correct the lack of symmetry Hicks and Allen [7] have suggested replacing (7.4-6) by

$$s_{ij}^*(P, M) \lesseqgtr 0$$

But since $s_{ii}^* \leq 0$ for every i (Theorem 3.2-12) and $\sum_{j=1}^n P_j s_{ij}^* = 0$ by Euler's theorem (recall the proof of Exercise 3.3), it follows according to this criterion that there can be no complements in any two-commodity world, nor can all goods be complements in general.[2] Dimensionality and universality are not satisfied.

One approach whose concepts do have all properties 7.4-1–7.4-5 has its origins with Fisher [4]. It is developed now starting with a two-commodity world. The idea is to determine a scale over which a measure of the degree of complementarity, σ, may range. As σ varies both indifference map and demand functions change. At the lower extreme, $\sigma = 0$, the two goods are *perfect complements* and at the upper end, $\sigma = \infty$, they are *perfect substitutes*. As σ increases from zero they are designated *complements* up to a point and *substitutes* thereafter. At the dividing line the commodities are called *independent*. Sufficient conditions for such a scale to exist are given below.

Theorem 7.4-7 *Let $n = 2$ and α, γ, and σ be constants, where $\alpha > 0$, $0 < \gamma < 1$, and $0 \leq \sigma \leq \infty$. If preferences can be represented on $\bar{E}$ by*

(7.4-8) $$u(x, \sigma) = \alpha[\gamma x_1^{(\sigma-1)/\sigma} + (1 - \gamma)x_2^{(\sigma-1)/\sigma}]^{\sigma/(\sigma-1)},$$

then, as a measure of the degree of complementarity, σ satisfies 7.4-1–7.4-5.

---

[2] Examples in which $s_{ij}^* > 0$ for all $i \neq j$ were discussed in Sections 5.2 and 5.4.

PROOF:

First observe that

(7.4-9) $$\lim_{\sigma \to 0} u(x, \sigma) = \min [\alpha x_1, \alpha x_2],$$

(7.4-10) $$\lim_{\sigma \to \infty} u(x, \sigma) = \alpha[\gamma x_1 + (1 - \gamma)x_2],$$

are, respectively, the cases of perfect complements and perfect substitutes.[3] These utility functions have been analyzed in Section 6.1. For $0 < \sigma < \infty$ demand functions generated by u are

$$h^{*1}(P, M, \sigma) = \frac{M}{P_1 + [(1 - \gamma)/\gamma]^\sigma P_1^\sigma P_2^{1-\sigma}},$$

$$h^{*2}(P, M, \sigma) = \frac{M}{P_2} - \frac{M}{P_2 + [(1 - \gamma)/\gamma]^\sigma P_1^{\sigma-1} P_2^{2-\sigma}}$$

on Γ^*. Clearly as σ goes to zero and infinity $h^*(P, M, \sigma)$ approaches that generated by the utility functions of (7.4-9) and (7.4-10). Therefore, observability holds. The remaining properties are trivially satisfied.

Q.E.D.

Under the hypotheses of Theorem 7.4-7, σ may be defined as *the degree of complementarity* between goods 1 and 2. Although the dividing line between substitutes and complements is somewhat arbitrary, there is good reason for setting it at $\sigma = 1$. In that case

$$u(x, 1) = \alpha x_1^\gamma x_2^{1-\gamma},$$

and hence $\log u(x, 1)$ is Bergson with $b = 0$ (see Sections 2.4 and 5.2). Not only are the indifference curves geometrically appealing as the "midpoint" between (7.4-9) and (7.4-10), but the demand function h^{*i} does not depend on P_j where $i \neq j$ and $i, j = 1, 2$. This suggests that $\sigma = 1$ is "properly" designated as the case of independence.

To illustrate what might happen if preferences cannot be represented by a utility function of the form of (7.4-8), consider

$$u(x, \sigma) = x_1^\sigma + x_2,$$

where $0 \leq \sigma \leq 1$. Here

(7.4-11) $$u(x, 0) = 1 + x_2,$$

(7.4-12) $$u(x, 1) = x_1 + x_2,$$

which have the same indifference maps as, respectively, (7.4-9) with αx_1 replaced by ∞, and (7.4-10) with $\gamma = \frac{1}{2}$. Hence the notions of perfect comple-

---

[3] For proofs of (7.4-9) and (7.4-10) the reader is referred to Arrow et al. [2].

ment and substitute are consistent with intuition. Now demand functions for $0 < \sigma < 1$ are

$$h^{*1}(P, M, \sigma) = \left(\frac{P_1}{\sigma P_2}\right)^{1/\sigma - 1},$$

$$h^{*2}(P, M, \sigma) = \frac{M}{P_2} - \frac{P_1}{P_2}\left(\frac{P_1}{\sigma P_2}\right)^{1/\sigma - 1},$$

whence

$$\lim_{\sigma \to 0} h^*(P, M, \sigma) = \left(0, \frac{M}{P_2}\right),$$

$$\lim_{\sigma \to 1} h^*(P, M, \sigma) = (\infty, -\infty),$$

on Γ^*. The former is generated by (7.4-11) but the latter could not possibly come from (7.4-12). Therefore, σ cannot be used to measure the degree of complementarity: observability does not hold.

Generalizing these notions to more than two commodities is not at all difficult. Write $x_{(i,j)}$ for x without its ith and jth component.

Theorem 7.4-13 *Let α, γ, and σ_{ij} be constants where $\alpha > 0$, $0 < \gamma < 1$, $\sigma_{ij} = \sigma_{ji}$, $0 \le \sigma_{ij} \le \infty$, and $i, j - 1, \ldots, n$. If preferences can be represented on E by*

$$u(x, \sigma_{ij}) = V(x_{(i,j)}, \alpha[\gamma x_i^{(\sigma_{ij} - 1)/\sigma_{ij}} + (1 - \gamma)x_j^{(\sigma_{ij} - 1)/\sigma_{ij}}]^{\sigma_{ij}/\sigma_{ij} - 1}),$$

then, as a measure of the degree of complementarity between i and j, σ_{ij} satisfies 7.4-1–7.4-5.

The proof is an easy application of the theory of weak separability (Section 5.2) in light of Theorem 7.4-7. It is also possible to define complementarity in terms of triplets of commodities or any n-tuple, for that matter. In such cases (7.4-8) may be replaced by its appropriate generalization due to McFadden [12] or Uzawa [18].

When there is more than one individual, complementarity can be defined at the aggregate level provided there is a "general consensus" among consumers about the relationships among commodities. If no such agreement exists, it is unreasonable to expect group notions of complementarity to have any meaning. By means of an example, consider first the problems involved in applying ideas developed thus far to aggregates of individuals. Let there be two commodities and two consumers,

$$u(x) = \alpha x_1 + \gamma x_2,$$

$$u(x) = \gamma x_1 + \alpha x_2,$$

who have identical incomes. Suppose $\alpha > \gamma$. Both individuals regard goods 1 and 2 as perfect substitutes and so it is tempting to assert that the "group" of both persons (a separate entity) feels similarly. But according to the definition of complementarity given earlier, group behavior is incompatible with this reasoning. For the market demand functions are

$$\left. \begin{array}{l} H^{*1}(P, M) = \dfrac{M}{P_1} \\[2ex] H^{*2}(P, M) = 0 \end{array} \right\} \quad \text{if } \dfrac{P_1}{P_2} > \dfrac{\alpha}{\gamma},$$

$$\left. \begin{array}{l} H^{*1}(P, M) = \dfrac{M}{2P_1} \\[2ex] H^{*2}(P, M) = \dfrac{M}{2P_2} \end{array} \right\} \quad \text{if } \dfrac{\alpha}{\gamma} > \dfrac{P_1}{P_2} > \dfrac{\gamma}{\alpha},$$

$$\left. \begin{array}{l} H^{*1}(P, M) = 0 \\[2ex] H^{*2}(P, M) = \dfrac{M}{P_2} \end{array} \right\} \quad \text{if } \dfrac{\gamma}{\alpha} > \dfrac{P_1}{P_2}.$$

Now on the subset Γ' of Γ^* for which $\alpha/\gamma > P_1/P_2 > \gamma/\alpha$, market demand is generated by $u^H(x) = \sqrt{x_1 x_2}$. But if α is very large and γ very small, Γ' will be most of Γ^*, and thus it is unlikely that empirical observation will reveal zero values of either H^{*i}. For all practical purposes, then, the group behaves as if it considers these commodities independent.

At least in the above case there is a single parameter, $\sigma = 1$, which can be used, if not misleadingly, to indicate the presence of complementarity. But generally there will be no unique parameter indicating group feelings unless some additional assumption such as identical utility functions for all individuals is made. If $\sigma < \infty$ for all persons, one way out is to measure the degree of complementarity felt by the group by averaging all complementarity parameters of its individual members. Using the same scale for the average as for ordinary parameters, the concepts of group complements, substitutes, and independent goods can then be given rigorous meaning consistent with the notion of general consensus. Although the degree of complementarity now depends critically on the weights used in averaging, the smaller the variance in individual parameters, the better the measure. This would, furthermore, eliminate the dilemma raised by the previous example. Averages could easily be computed when there are more than two commodities provided all individual preference orderings are representable as in Theorem 7.4-13.

7.5 WELFARE

Welfare analysis is concerned with determining in which of two situations, say, (P', M') and (P'', M''), a consumer or group is better off. For a single individual the answer may be deduced from his indirect utility function. Thus if $l(P', M') > l(P'', M'')$, welfare is greater when (P', M') prevails. A similar conclusion may be phrased in terms of derivatives, provided they exist: if, for example, $l_i(P', M') < 0$ for some i, small reductions in P_i' also improve welfare.

The assumptions underlying the theory of utility maximization themselves have specific welfare implications for the consumer. To begin with, he is better off when prices fall or income rises.

Theorem 7.5-1 *For all (P', M') and (P'', M'') in Γ^*, if either*

(a) $p'' \geq p', p'' \neq p'$ and $M' \geq M''$, or
(b) $p'' \geq p'$ and $M' > M''$,

then $l(P', M') > l(P'', M'')$. Furthermore, $l_i(P, M) < 0$ for $i = 1, \ldots, n$, and $l_M(P, M) > 0$ on Ω^*.

PROOF:

If $P'' \geq P', P'' \neq P'$ and $M' = M''$, then the argument of Theorem 3.5-4 shows that $l(P', M') > l(P'', M'')$. If $P' = P''$ and $M' > M''$, let $x' = h^*(P', M')$ and $x'' = h^*(P'', M'')$. Then x'' is in $B^s(P', M')$, so $u(x') > u(x'')$. Thus again $l(P', M') > l(P'', M'')$. Applying these facts under hypothesis (a),

$$l(P', M') > l(P'', M') \geq l(P'', M''),$$

and under (b),

$$l(P', M') > l(P', M'') \geq l(P'', M'').$$

To prove the second half of the theorem recall that on Ω^*,

$$l_M(P, M) = \lambda^*(P, M) > 0,$$

by Theorems 3.5-2 and 3.1-16. Hence by Theorem 3.5-3, $l_i(P, M) < 0$ for $i = 1, \ldots, n$ on Ω^*.

Q.E.D.

When $P'' \not\geq P'$ welfare comparisons are still easily made if any of the three hypotheses which permit construction of composite commodities and prices as discussed in Section 7.3 are satisfied. For under those conditions, Theorem 7.5-1 may be applied to the indirect utility function defined in terms of the $\bar{u}$ of that section. Hence if a composite price at P' is lower than at P'' with remaining prices unchanged, and if $M' = M''$, then welfare must be higher at (P', M'); and this is true regardless of how the components which make up the composite stand in relation to each other.

In still more general cases when composites cannot be obtained, if h^* is known and properties 4.3-1–4.3-3 hold, Theorem 4.3-6 guarantees the existence of a utility generator, u, of h^*. Computing l from u will permit direct comparison of (P', M') and (P'', M''). But proving existence of u is one thing and, unfortunately, finding a specific utility function which does the job is quite another. In practice it may be very difficult, if not impossible, to do so. It is therefore natural to look for other ways in which to make welfare comparisons. One technique is based on the notion of consumer's surplus.

Although there are many different definitions of consumer's surplus, only that dating to Dupuit and later popularized by Marshall is considered here.[4] Others may be found in Samuelson [15]. Consider first the Marshallian demand curve illustrated in Figure 7.2 and suppose the consumer were to purchase x_i' at P_i'. Then for the increment Δx_i he must only pay $P_i' \Delta x_i$, when in fact he is willing to pay, approximately, $P_i'' \Delta x_i$. Hence the difference, area *abcd*, may be considered a surplus obtained by purchasing Δx_i at the lower price. *Consumer's surplus* at x_i' is therefore the sum of all incremental surpluses or the area (shaded region) under the demand curve over $P_i > P_i'$, whenever it is finite. The gain in consumer's surplus by moving from P_i'' to P_i' is the area under the demand curve over $P_i' \le P_i \le P_i''$.

The usefulness of consumer's surplus lies in that it is related to differences in utility evaluated at (P', M') and (P'', M'').

Theorem 7.5-2   *Let l be differentiable on Γ^*. Then for any (P', M') and (P'', M'') in Γ^*,*

$$l(P', M') - l(P'', M'')$$
$$= \int_{M''}^{M'} l_M(P'', M)dM - \sum_{i=1}^{n} \int_{P_i''}^{P_i'} l_M(P^i, M')h^{*i}(P^i, M')dP_i,$$

where $P^i = (P_1'', \ldots, P_{i-1}'', P_i, P_{i+1}', \ldots, P_n')$, for each i.

PROOF:
  Since

$$l(P', M') - l(P'', M'')$$
$$= l(P'', M') - l(P'', M'') + \sum_{i=1}^{n} [l(P'^i, M') - l(P''^i, M')],$$

where $P'^i = (P_1'', \ldots, P_{i-1}'', P_i', P_{i+1}', \ldots, P_n')$ and $P''^i = (P_1'', \ldots, P_{i-1}'', P_i'', P_{i+1}', \ldots, P_n')$, it follows from the fundamental theorem of the integral calculus [1, p. 215] that

$$l(P', M') - l(P'', M'') = \int_{M''}^{M'} l_M(P'', M)dM + \sum_{i=1}^{n} \int_{P_i''}^{P_i'} l_i(P^i, M')dP_i.$$

Applying Theorem 3.5-3 now yields the desired result.

Q.E.D.

---

[4] See, for example, Hotelling [8, pp. 243–245].

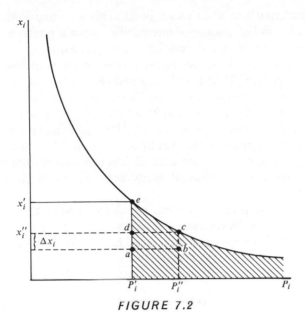

FIGURE 7.2

Thus, for example, if there exists a utility representation whose marginal utility of income is constant with respect to all prices (recall Section 5.4), and if l is interpreted to be the associated indirect utility function so that $l_M = \beta/M$, where $\beta > 0$, then Theorem 7.5-2 implies

$$(7.5\text{-}3) \quad l(P', M') - l(P'', M'')$$

$$= \beta \left[\log M' - \log M'' - \frac{1}{M'} \sum_{i=1}^{n} \int_{P_i''}^{P_i'} h^{*i}(P^i, M') dP_i \right].$$

The bracketed term on the right can be computed and its sign deduced. Since $\beta > 0$, it is possible to determine whether the consumer considers himself better off with (P', M') or (P'', M''). Note that the integrals in (7.5-3) yield areas similar to that under the demand curve between P_i' and P_i'' in Figure 7.2; as such their relationship to consumer's surplus is clear.

Although the assumptions of Chapters 3 and 4 have served as the basis of analysis to this point, the first part of Theorem 7.5-1 clearly holds for the revealed preference model of Sections 6.2 and 6.3. An analogous result can be stated even when the integrability condition is not satisfied as in Section 6.4. Thus if $x' = h^*(P', M')$ and $x'' = h^*(P'', M'')$ where $M' \geq P' \cdot x''$, then x'' is in $B^{\leq}(P', M')$, so $\overrightarrow{x'x''}$ is a direction of nonpreference. By 6.4-6 and the discussion following Theorem 6.4-7, $\overrightarrow{x''x'}$ is a direction of preference. Therefore, if x' is close enough to x'', $x' \ominus_{x'} x''$ and $x' \ominus_{x''} x''$ from 6.4-1, so x'

is locally "preferred" to x'' at either point. This assertion is the best that can be hoped for in the absence of integrability, since a preference ordering, the basis of comparison in Theorem 7.5-1, does not exist.

Several of the above conclusions carry over to cases in which there is more than one person. Thus if (P', M') and (P'', M'') or if corresponding composite and noncomposite prices and incomes satisfy the hypotheses of Theorem 7.5-1 for each person, then $l(P', M') > l(P'', M'')$ for all individuals. Hence community welfare is greater at (P', M'). But in most situations some consumers' utility increases while that of others diminishes, and so to make any kind of group welfare assertions at all, it is necessary to assume cardinal utility scales and use interpersonal utility comparisons. Such a procedure will now be demonstrated.

Let there be K persons and denote by x^k commodity bundles in $\bar{E}$ for each $k = 1, \ldots, K$. A distribution of goods among these people is given by $y = (x^1, \ldots, x^k)$. Suppose each individual has a cardinal utility function $u^k(x^k)$ on $\bar{E}$. Write $\bar{E}_y = \{y: y \geq 0\}$ and $u^y(y) = (u^1(x^1), \ldots, u^K(x^K))$. A *welfare function*, W, is defined on $\bar{E}_y$ by specifying a function F such that

$$W(y) = F(u^y(y)).$$

If the vector of demand functions of each consumer is now written h^{*k} as in Section 7.3, if Y is a vector representing the income distribution $(M^1, \ldots, M^K)$, and if $h^{*y} = (h^{*1}, \ldots, h^{*K})$, then the *indirect welfare function* is

$$W(h^{*y}(P, Y)),$$

defined for all $(P, Y) > 0$. Hence by comparing $W(h^{*y}(P', Y'))$ and $W(h^{*y}(P'', Y''))$ appropriate welfare assertions can be made.

Actually, the assumption of cardinality is not really needed to define W. But as pointed out in Section 2.5, cardinality does ensure that regardless of the specific utility representation u^k, unit lengths of utility expressed in terms of any scale are constant as utility levels vary. By choosing F, a way of weighting and combining each persons preferences into one is specified. If representations change, with underlying orderings and F fixed, then the weights assigned to each person shift. Thus cardinality guarantees that any weighting scheme obtained from some base by changing utility representations (preference orderings and F held fixed) does not weigh individuals differently across the domain of F. This would not be so, for example, if $u^1 + u^2$ were changed to $u^1 + (u^2)^2$. For in the latter case, individual 2 is given more weight as u^2 rises. Weighting schemes together with the method of combination implied by F are frequently labeled *interpersonal utility comparisons*. It is clear that the theory of demand is of no help in determining which method of interpersonal utility comparisons is "best." In the last analysis, this will depend on the analyst's personal values.

As with individual utility representations, computation of community welfare functions from observed market data may be impractical. Therefore, it again becomes worthwhile to indicate when group welfare comparisons can be made in terms of consumer's surplus. This is easily done if, for example, F takes the form

$$F(\mu_1, \ldots, \mu_K) = \sum_{k=1}^{K} d_k \mu_k,$$

where μ_k varies over the range of u^k for each k. For then

(7.5-4) $W(h^{*y}(P', Y')) - W(h^{*y}(P'', Y''))$

$$= \sum_{k=1}^{K} d_k [l^k(P', M'^k) - l^k(P'', M''^k)],$$

where l^k is the indirect utility function associated with u^k. Under conditions discussed earlier, the right-hand side can be reduced to areas beneath demand curves by using (7.5-3). Thus if β in (7.5-3) is assumed to be the same for all persons, the sign of (7.5-4) can be determined.

7.6 CHARACTERISTICS

In concluding this chapter it is worth considering briefly a novel approach to demand theory recently developed by Lancaster [10]. Only a simplified version is outlined below.

The originality of Lancaster's analysis lies in that he does not assume consumers order the commodity space according to their preferences. Rather, each commodity possesses certain characteristics which are the focal point of the consumer's interest. The sole object of buying commodities is to obtain these characteristics. For example, food has, primarily, nutritional characteristics, but it has aesthetic ones as well. The difference between two chairs, identical except for color, is in their color characteristics. Other characteristics such as style and material are held in common.

Formally, let the total number of characteristics attainable from all goods in the economy be fixed at π. Write c_j for quantities of the jth characteristic and $c = (c_1, \ldots, c_\pi)$. Assume that associated with each commodity bundle, x, is a specific vector of characteristics and let τ be the function describing this relationship. Thus

(7.6-1) $c = \tau(x),$

on $\bar{E}$. Finally, suppose the consumer has a preference ordering defined on the space of characteristics which is representable by, say, $v(c)$. The idea is to analyze the consumer's market behavior as if he decided on purchases by maximizing v subject to (7.6-1) and the usual budget constraint $P \cdot x \leq M$. Now defining u by

$$u(x) = v(\tau(x)),$$

something similar to a utility function is obtained. And if the maximization procedure is to have any meaning, hypotheses such as 3.1-1–3.1-4 or 6.2-1–6.2-3 must be assumed. Hence demand functions may be defined having properties akin to those discussed in earlier chapters.

Although inserting characteristics as an intermediary between commodities and utility seems to yield the same empirical results as when they are absent, there is, nevertheless, considerable potential in this method. For, as Lancaster has suggested, several economic problems, until now insoluble by traditional means, can be handled at the nonobservable level in terms of characteristics (for example, the distinction between durable and nondurable goods). But until the solutions are translated into specific properties of demand functions which cannot be obtained by additionally restricting preference orderings as in Chapter 5, they will remain sterile figments of the theorist's imagination. This new approach, however, has barely been explored. It is much too early to tell if it will live up to expectations.

EXERCISES

7.1 Discuss the impact of changes in ζ_1 on the demand for commodity 1 when $\zeta_2^0 = 1$ and
a. $u(x, \zeta_1) = \log \zeta_1 x_1 + \log x_2$,
b. $u(x, \zeta_1) = \sqrt{x_1 \zeta_1} + \sqrt{x_2}$,
c. $u(x, \zeta_1) = \zeta_1 x_1 + \sqrt{x_2}$.

7.2 Verify the assertion in the proof of Theorem 7.3-1 that the $n - 1$ by $n - 1$ matrix of terms s_{ij}^H is negative definite.

7.3 Consider two individuals with utility functions

$$u^1(x) = T^1(x_1 x_2),$$

$$u^2(x) = T^2(x_1 x_2),$$

where T^1 and T^2 are arbitrary, increasing transformations. Find a utility generator, u^H, of the implied market demand functions. Why in this particular case does u^H not depend on the relative position of each individual in the income distribution?

7.4 Consider the Gorman definition of composites based on separability (Theorem 7.3-8). What is the relationship between the demand functions for all commodities generated by $u(x)$ and those for the first r goods and the composite generated by $\bar{u}(x_{\bar{r}}, \bar{x})$?

7.5 Assume utility to be cardinal and suppose u is quasi-linear with respect to x_n, where the coefficient of x_n is unity. Show the Auspitz–Leiben definition of complementarity reduces to the observable, inverse demand conditions

$$f_j^i(x) = f_i^j(x) \gtreqless 0, \quad i, j \neq n,$$

according as i and j are complements, independent, or substitutes. (See Schultz [16, pp. 575–578].) Note that $f_n^i = 0$ for each i, and hence this criterion implies that the first $n - 1$ goods are independent of the last. Furthermore, these results are true regardless of the (cardinal) choice of u.

REFERENCES

[1] Apostol, T. M., *Mathematical Analysis* (Reading, Mass.: Addison-Wesley, 1957).

[2] Arrow, K. J., et al., "Capital–Labor Substitution and Economic Efficiency," *The Review of Economics and Statistics* (1961), pp. 225–249.

[3] Basemann, R. L., "A Theory of Demand with Variable Consumer Preferences," *Econometrica* (1956), pp. 47–58.

[4] Fisher, I., *Mathematical Investigations in the Theory of Value and Prices* (New Haven: Yale University Press, 1925).

[5] Gorman, W. M., "Separable Utility and Aggregation," *Econometrica* (1959), pp. 469–481.

[6] Hicks, J. R., *Value and Capital* (London: Oxford University Press, 1939).

[7] Hicks, J. R., and R. G. D. Allen, "A Reconsideration of the Theory of Value," *Economica* (1934), pp. 52–76, 196–219.

[8] Hotelling, H., "General Welfare in Relation to Problems of Taxation and of Railway and Utility Rates," *Econometrica* (1938), pp. 242–269.

[9] Ichimura, S., "A Critical Note on the Definition of Related Goods," *Review of Economic Studies*, v. 18 (1951), pp. 179–183.

[10] Lancaster, K. J., "A New Approach to Consumer Theory," *The Journal of Political Economy* (1966), pp. 132–157.

[11] Leontief, W., "Composite Commodities and the Problem of Index Numbers," *Econometrica* (1936), pp. 39–59.

[12] McFadden, D., "Constant Elasticity of Substitution Production Functions," *Review of Economic Studies* (1963), pp. 73–83.

[13] Morishima, M., "The Problem of Intrinsic Complementarity and Separability of Goods," *Metroeconomica* (1959), pp. 188–202.

[14] Pearce, I. F., *A Contribution to Demand Analysis* (London: Oxford University Press, 1964).

[15] Samuelson, P. A., *Foundations of Economic Analysis* (Cambridge, Mass.: Harvard University Press, 1947).

[16] Schultz, H., *The Theory and Measurement of Demand* (Chicago: University of Chicago Press, 1938).

[17] Tintner, G., "Complementarity and Shifts in Demand," *Metroeconomica* (1952), pp. 1–4.

[18] Uzawa, H., "Production Functions with Constant Elasticities of Substitution," *Review of Economic Studies* (1962), pp. 291–299.

Stochastic Demand Theory

By the phrase "stochastic demand theory" is meant a theory of demand in which random elements of one form or another influence market behavior. Its purpose is to incorporate the many facets of uncertainty which enter ordinary, everyday life. For example, there are many consumers who bet on the outcome of future random events such as horse races. An individual might be unsure of his preferences and so "errors" could appear in his decision making, or his preferences may be sensitive to outside random "shocks" like weather changes. In addition, consumers purchase stocks, bonds, and other assets, not for current consumption, whose yield and value in the future are governed by unforeseen events. There are, of course, many other ways in which uncertainties affect market behavior, but this chapter is only concerned with these. Once again the underlying theoretical foundation is that of Chapter 3 and Section 6.1, although weaker frameworks as discussed in Chapter 6 could easily be substituted.

8.1 RISK-NEUTRAL GAMBLES

The kinds of gambling situations considered here are those which may be described as if, to participate in them, the consumer buys a lottery ticket entitling him to one of several prizes, depending on the outcome of some future random event. Betting at the roulette wheel or racetrack and purchasing, say, fire or theft insurance are a few of many activities which may be so classified. The probabilities of winning each prize may be known or the consumer may have to make a subjective estimate of them, but in either case they are bound to influence his behavior.

In all gambles the consumer is assumed to be neutral in his attitude toward risk; he neither avoids nor courts it. The fact that he has come to the race-track already indicates he is willing to accept the risks involved in placing bets. Thus his general philosophies concerned with avoiding or favoring risk in everyday life should not influence his preferences among lotteries. The point will be further clarified below.

At the outset it is assumed that all prizes available in any lottery are vectors in the commodity space, $\bar{E}$. This requirement is by no means necessary, but it does simplify matters by permitting use of notation and results derived in earlier chapters. Thus a *lottery* L consists of, say, prizes $x^1, \ldots, x^\pi$, and nonnegative probabilities $q_1, \ldots, q_\pi$, where π is an integer, x^k is in $\bar{E}$ for every $k = 1, \ldots, \pi$, and

(8.1-1) $$\sum_{k=1}^{\pi} q_k = 1.$$

Writing

$$L = \sum_{k=1}^{\pi} q_k x^k,$$

it is clear that L is in $\bar{E}$. Thus every point of $\bar{E}$ may be thought of as either a prize or any one of an infinite number of lotteries.

Let there be a utility function so that every vector x in $\bar{E}$, as a prize, has a utility value associated with it. But what about lotteries? Since the consumer is neutral toward risk, the fact that the purchase of a lottery involves an assumption of risk is of no consequence. From the point of view of preferences, lotteries and prizes should be ordered in a single consistent pattern which does not depend on which is which. Thus it is natural to assign to lotteries (points) in $\bar{E}$ the same utility values they would have if they were regarded as prizes. On the other hand, intuition strongly suggests that the utility of a lottery ought to be the expected utility of the prizes it contains; that is, in the above notation,

(8.1-2) $$\sum_{k=1}^{\pi} q_k u(x^k).$$

Von Neumann and Morgenstern [5] were the first to give conditions on preference orderings under which these two notions are equivalent.

Equivalence, of course, means that for any π

(8.1-3) $$u\left(\sum_{k=1}^{\pi} q_k x^k \right) = \sum_{k=1}^{\pi} q_k u(x^k),$$

for all nonnegative probabilities $q_1, \ldots, q_\pi$ satisfying (8.1-1). But this, in turn, is identical to u being linear (recall Section 2.3). It follows under the hypotheses of Theorem 2.3-4 that a necessary and sufficient condition for there to exist a utility representation satisfying (8.1-3) is that the underlying preference ordering of prizes be linear.[1] Furthermore, the only increasing transformations of u which preserve linearity are themselves linear. By Theorem 2.5-2, u must also be cardinal.

With these ideas in mind, rigorous content may now be given to the concept of risk neutrality. In doing so it is also convenient to formalize notions of "risk aversion" and "risk favor" as well. Since all are defined in terms of shapes of utility functions which vary with nonlinear increasing transformations, it is necessary to assume cardinality. Whenever u is concave, the consumer is referred to as a *risk averter*, since the expected utility of any lottery, say, $L = \theta x' + (1 - \theta)x''$, where $0 < \theta < 1$, is less than the utility of the point L regarded as a prize; that is,

$$u(L) > \theta u(x') + (1 - \theta)u(x'').$$

Thus if the consumer had a choice between a chance of obtaining x' as opposed to x'' and the sure prospect L, even though one (but not both) of $u(x')$ and $u(x'')$ may be larger than $u(L)$, he would still prefer the latter. Similarly, he is a *risk favorer* if u is convex and *risk neutral* if u is linear. It is easily possible for the same utility function to exhibit all three properties, each over different regions of the commodity space. Note also that the results of the preceding paragraph give nothing more than necessary and sufficient conditions under which a risk-neutral utility representation exists.

The translation of risk neutrality into market behavior leaves something to be desired. For, as indicated in Section 6.1, demand functions generated by a linear utility function either lead the consumer to bundles which contain only one commodity (or an appropriate, corresponding lottery), or they are not single valued. It is unreasonable to expect such activity to be observed except in extraordinary cases. The way out, of course, is to abandon risk neutrality. If specific points of $\bar{E}$ are designated as lotteries and the remainder as prizes, then assuming the existence of a utility function satisfying, say, 6.1-1–6.1-3, appropriate demand functions may be derived. Finally, as pointed out in Section 6.1, a risk favorer will have almost the same demand functions as a consumer who is risk neutral. It is unlikely that empirical observation will reveal the difference between them.

8.2 ERRORS AND SHOCKS

It has been remarked earlier that efforts to test the validity of demand theory have not provided it with much support. A possible explanation is that observable conclusions of the theory have not been interpreted correctly

---

[1] Interestingly enough, this result is intimately related to the existence of a strongly separable utility function. See Debreu [1].

in light of existing data. By recognizing that the consumer may misjudge his preferences or permit random shocks to alter them, new interpretations of the implications of utility maximization may be given which could provide a more appropriate foundation to serve as the basis of empirical tests. But in any case, adding these factors to the theory can only increase its generality and applicability; they therefore have importance in their own right as well. To introduce them use will be made of the so-called "constant" and "random utility" models recently developed by psychologists.[2]

Considering the former first, imagine a case in which the consumer, when faced with an ordinary market situation, finds his preferences somewhat vague. The preferences exist, to be sure, but he is not completely aware of what they are. Nevertheless, he must still make a decision even in the face of such uncertainty. On these occasions the consumer will not always pick the utility-maximizing bundle from his budget set.

Formally, let there be a utility function, satisfying 3.1-1–3.1-4 and generating $h^*(P, M)$ defined on Γ^*. Let ϵ denote elements of a sample space $\mathscr{E}$ and ρ a probability measure on it. Now actual consumer purchases depend on prices, income, and the random error ϵ turning up in the sample space. Thus assume that for each point of $\Gamma^* \times \mathscr{E}$ there is a unique x in E reflecting his choice. Denote this correspondence by $g = (g^1, \ldots, g^n)$, so that

$$(8.2\text{-}1) \qquad\qquad x = g(P, M, \epsilon),$$

for all (P, M, ϵ) in $\Gamma^* \times \mathscr{E}$. It is clear that the constraint

$$P \cdot g(P, M, \epsilon) \leq M$$

must be satisfied everywhere. Suppose that for all (P, M), as a function of ϵ alone, g is measurable. Then since g is positive, it is also integrable [3, p. 118]. Assume

$$(8.2\text{-}2) \qquad\qquad h^*(P, M) = \int_{\mathscr{E}} g(P, M, \epsilon)d\rho,$$

on Γ^*, where integration is understood to be in the sense of Lebesque. Thus, for each (P, M), $g(P, M, \epsilon)$ is a vector of random variables with means $h^*(P, M)$. Suppose their variances are also finite.

The meaning of requirement (8.2-2) is that even when the consumer is not sure of his preferences, if he were to choose from the same budget set many times, "on the average" he would choose the utility maximizing bundle.

Under these circumstances observations of market activity take on a new meaning. For if, say, ϵ_t is realized in the sample space, then $g(P, M, \epsilon_t)$, where ϵ_t is now a fixed parameter, is observed. But as functions of (P, M), it is not necessary that $g(P, M, \epsilon_t)$ have any of the properties of Table 3.1

---

[2] See, for example, Luce and Suppes [4, sec. 5].

earlier attributed to demand functions because they are not derived from utility maximization. On the other hand, any collection of observations $\{g^i(P, M, \epsilon_t)\}$, where $t = 1, \ldots, T$, is a sequence of identically distributed random variables. Assuming all observations are independent and setting

$$(8.2\text{-}3) \qquad \bar{g}(P, M, T) = \frac{1}{T} \sum_{t=1}^{T} g(P, M, \epsilon_t),$$

the following result is a trivial consequence of the strong law of large numbers [8, p. 108].

Theorem 8.2-4 *For all (P, M) in Γ^*,*

$$\lim_{T \to \infty} \bar{g}(P, M, T) = h^*(P, M),$$

with probability 1.

Thus, although the consumer may appear to be irrational upon observation of one $g(P, M, \epsilon_t)$, repeated observations may reveal that his "average" demand functions, $\bar{g}$, approximate those derived from utility maximization as T becomes large. Observing only one $g(P, M, \epsilon_t)$ which violates the Slutsky restrictions does not, therefore, refute demand theory.

Although the conditions under which demand theory might be rejected are matters for statistical analysis, it is worth examining briefly a simple example. Thus consider any i and $\delta > 0$. From the hypotheses of Theorem 8.2-4 and Chebyshev's inequality, at each (P, M) the probability that[3]

$$|g^i(P, M, T) - h^{*i}(P, M)| < \delta,$$

is at least as great as $1 - \sigma^2/T\delta^2$, where σ^2 is the variance of every $g^i(P, M, \epsilon_t)$. For simplicity assume that σ^2 does not depend on (P, M). Then knowing σ^2 it is possible to determine the number of observations, T^0, required to ensure the probability will be no less than, say, 0.95 that $\bar{g}^i$ and h^{*i} differ by no more than some predetermined δ on Γ^*. Checking the properties of $\bar{g}^i(P, M, T^0)$ could then lead to rejection if they did not approximate those of rational behavior.[4] When σ^2 is not known, application of the central limit theorem or an assumption about the kind of probability distributions involved, such as normality, would lead to alternative tests.[5]

Rather than assume the individual has fixed preferences but makes errors in determining his optimal commodity bundle as in the constant utility model, suppose now that his preferences themselves are subject to random

---

[3] See Wilks [8, p. 100].
[4] Actually, properties of $\bar{g}$ stated in terms of the revealed preference relation may be more appropriate here since they do not require $\bar{g}$ to be differentiable.
[5] See Wilks [8, p. 257–258].

shocks. This is the random utility case mentioned earlier. Thus a sudden thunderstorm may increase his desire relative to other commodities for a raincoat and umbrella or a headache may induce him to buy aspirin. Randomness is once again introduced into his behavior but for a different reason. Note the similarity to the analysis of changes in tastes in Section 7.2.

Owing to difficulties which arise from integration, several of the following assumptions do not remain valid under arbitrary, increasing transformations of utility functions. Thus, as in Chapter 5, these hypotheses should be interpreted only as requiring the existence of a representation with the desired properties.

Let the utility function be

$$u(x, \epsilon),$$

where, as a function of x, u satisfies, say, 6.1-1–6.1-3 for each ϵ in the sample space $\mathscr{E}$. Assume $\mathscr{E}$ is connected. Let ρ again denote a probability measure on $\mathscr{E}$. Note that if u has the form

$$u(x, \epsilon) = V(v^1(x), v^2(\epsilon))$$

for some scalar-valued functions V, v^1, and v^2, then the underlying preference ordering does not depend on ϵ, and random shocks, no matter how violent, have no effect on market activity. Supposing, in general, that u is integrable for each x, the *expected utility function, $\bar{u}$,* is given by

$$\bar{u}(x) = \int_{\mathscr{E}} u(x, \epsilon) d\rho,$$

on E. Frequently $\bar{u}$ may be extended continuously to $\bar{E}$.

Without further restrictions $\bar{u}$ need not have properties which permit its use as a utility function. For example, if

$$u(x, \epsilon) = x_1^{\epsilon} \log x_1 + x_2^{\epsilon} \log x_2,$$

and ϵ is distributed uniformly on the closed interval $\mathscr{E} = [\frac{1}{4}, \frac{1}{2}]$, then it is not hard to show that 6.1-1–6.1-3 are satisfied on $\bar{E}$ for each ϵ in $\mathscr{E}$. But in this case

$$\bar{u}(x) = 4[(x_1)^{1/2} - (x_1)^{1/4} + (x_2)^{1/2} - (x_2)^{1/4}],$$

whose first derivatives $\bar{u}_1$ and $\bar{u}_2$ are not positive everywhere on E. The additional assumption to be required here is as follows:

8.2-5. For some $r > 0$ there exists continuous functions $\varphi^1, \ldots, \varphi^r$ defined on $\mathscr{E}$ and an appropriate function V such that
(a) For all x in $\bar{E}$,

$$u(x, \epsilon) = V(x, \varphi^1(\epsilon_1), \ldots, \varphi^r(\epsilon_r)),$$

whenever $\epsilon_i = \epsilon$ for all $i = 1, \ldots, r$.

(b) For all x in $\bar{E}$,

$$\int_{\mathscr{E}} V(x, \varphi(\epsilon))d\rho = V\left(x, \int_{\mathscr{E}} \varphi(\epsilon)d\rho\right),$$

where $\varphi(\epsilon) = (\varphi^1(\epsilon_1), \ldots, \varphi^r(\epsilon_r))$.

(c) For each $(\epsilon_1, \ldots, \epsilon_r)$, as a function of x, V satisfies 6.1-1–6.1-3.

This is more of an assumption about how random shocks affect preferences rather than about preferences themselves. It implies that $\bar{u}$ is defined on $\bar{E}$.

Theorem 8.2-6 $\bar{u}$ *satisfies 6.1-1–6.1-3 on $\bar{E}$.*

PROOF:

Since φ^i is continuous, by Theorem C.3 there exists an ϵ_i^0 in $\mathscr{E}$ such that

$$\varphi^i(\epsilon_i^0) = \int_{\mathscr{E}} \varphi^i(\epsilon_i)d\rho, \quad i = 1, \ldots, r.$$

Hence, from 8.2-5 it follows that

$$\bar{u}(x) = V(x, \varphi^1(\epsilon_1^0), \ldots, \varphi^r(\epsilon_r^0)),$$

for all x in $\bar{E}$. The conclusion is now evident from the assumed properties of V [8.2-5(c)].

Q.E.D.

For each ϵ in $\mathscr{E}$, $u(x, \epsilon)$ generates demand functions

(8.2-7) $$x = g(P, M, \epsilon),$$

defined on $\Gamma^* \times \mathscr{E}$. Now (8.2-7) differs from (8.2-1) in that for each ϵ the former must exhibit the general properties of demand functions on Γ^* derived in Section 6.1 because they are obtained from utility maximization. The latter need not. Assume as before that for all (P, M) in Γ^* the random variables g have finite means,

$$\int_{\mathscr{E}} g(P, M, \epsilon)d\rho,$$

and variances. Since $\bar{u}$ is also a utility function, it, too, generates demand functions, h^*, having similar properties. Suppose

(8.2-8) $$h^*(P, M) = \int_{\mathscr{E}} g(P, M, \epsilon)d\rho,$$

on an appropriate subset Γ' of Γ^*. The nature of Γ' will become apparent from the example at the end of this section. The interpretation of (8.2-8) is analogous to that of (8.2-2): the consumer's "average choice" is the same as that chosen from his "average preference ordering."

Turning once again to empirical implications, if it is possible to observe one relationship between (P, M) and x, say $g(P, M, \epsilon_t)$, then properties may be checked for concurrence with the traditional theory. But if the observations are taken over an interval of time, it is quite likely that random disturbances may have altered the consumer's preferences. Combining observations to estimate his demand functions may then lead to the conclusion that he is irrational when, in reality, each one of his choices comes from a different utility-maximizing relationship. Yet, defining the average demand functions $\bar{g}$ as in (8.2-3), Theorem 8.2-4 restricted to Γ' remains valid in this case. As before, rational behavior therefore implies that $\bar{g}$ must approximate the functions h^* derived from the maximization of some $\bar{u}$ as T becomes large.

To illustrate the random utility model let

$$u(x, \epsilon) = x_1 x_2 + \epsilon(x_1 + x_2),$$

where ϵ is distributed uniformly on $[0, 1]$. Then u satisfies all hypotheses and

$$g^1(P, M, \epsilon) = \begin{cases} \dfrac{M + (P_2 - P_1)\epsilon}{2P_1}, & \text{if } \epsilon < \min\left(\dfrac{M}{P_1 - P_2}, \dfrac{M}{P_2 - P_1}\right), \\[3mm] 0, & \text{if } \dfrac{M}{P_2 - P_1} > \epsilon \geq \dfrac{M}{P_1 - P_2}, \\[3mm] \dfrac{M}{P_1}, & \text{if } \dfrac{M}{P_1 - P_2} > \epsilon \geq \dfrac{M}{P_2 - P_1}, \end{cases}$$

$$g^2(P, M, \epsilon) = \begin{cases} \dfrac{M + (P_1 - P_2)\epsilon}{2P_2}, & \text{if } \epsilon < \min\left(\dfrac{M}{P_1 - P_2}, \dfrac{M}{P_2 - P_1}\right), \\[3mm] \dfrac{M}{P_2}, & \text{if } \dfrac{M}{P_2 - P_1} > \epsilon \geq \dfrac{M}{P_1 - P_2}, \\[3mm] 0, & \text{if } \dfrac{M}{P_1 - P_2} > \epsilon \geq \dfrac{M}{P_2 - P_1}. \end{cases}$$

Now

$$\bar{u}(x) = x_1 x_2 + \tfrac{1}{2}(x_1 + x_2),$$

and hence h^* is the same as g given above with ϵ replaced by $\tfrac{1}{2}$. It follows that (8.2-8) and Theorem 8.2-4 are valid on the subset

$$\Gamma' = \{(P, M): P_1 - P_2 \leq M \text{ and } P_2 - P_1 \leq M\},$$

but nowhere else in Γ^*.

Note in the above example the relationship for inverse demand functions analogous to (8.2-8) is not valid. Furthermore, if

$$u(x, \epsilon) = \epsilon \log x_1 + \log x_2,$$

just the reverse is true: it holds for inverse demand functions but not direct ones. Hence (8.2-8) is neither necessary nor sufficient for the corresponding relationship between inverses.

8.3 PORTFOLIO SELECTION

The problem of portfolio selection is frequently viewed as one of purchasing assets with uncertain yields in such a manner that the expected utility of the return to the portfolio is maximized for a given risk. More precisely, let x_i vary over the number of units of asset i to be held during the period under consideration and denote its yield per unit (a random variable) by ϵ_i. Writing $x = (x_1, \ldots, x_n)$ and $\epsilon = (\epsilon_1, \ldots, \epsilon_n)$, the total return, R, to the portfolio becomes

$$R = \epsilon \cdot x.$$

Assuming that the consumer cannot borrow and that yields are never nega tive, $x \geq 0$, $\epsilon \geq 0$, and hence $R \geq 0$.

Let there be a utility function $u(R)$ defined for all $R \geq 0$. As in Section 8.1, the terms "risk averter," "risk favorer," and "risk neutral" may be applied depending on the shape of u. Let $\mathscr{E}$ be an n-dimensional sample space over which ϵ varies and suppose ρ is a probability measure on it. The probabilities may either be "known" or subjective estimates made by the consumer. Then $u(R) = u(\epsilon \cdot x)$ is quite similar to that of the random utility model of the previous section. Assume that for each x in $\bar{E}$, as a function of ϵ, u is integrable. Then the expected utility function

$$\bar{u}(x) = \int_{\mathscr{E}} u(\epsilon \cdot x) d\rho,$$

is defined on $\bar{E}$. The postulate of rationality in this context is that purchases are made so as to maximize $\bar{u}$ subject to the standard constraint $P \cdot x \leq M$, where P_i is the price per unit of the ith asset and M is the quantity of money the consumer has decided, by some independent means, to spend.

Now the properties of $\bar{u}$ could be derived from those of u as in Theorem 8.2-6. But there are $u(x, \epsilon)$ not satisfying 6.1-1–6.1-3 as functions of x whose expected utility function does. Since the latter is all that is important here, it is reasonable to begin the analysis by requiring $\bar{u}$ to have these properties and let the matter go at that. The demand functions so obtained have been discussed in Section 6.1.

Although the reactions of the consumer to changes in market prices of assets and changes in the money he is willing to spend on them are therefore analyzed in the usual fashion, nothing has yet been said about the effects of variations in the underlying probability distribution on market behavior. If, for example, the consumer reassesses his estimates of the probabilities of obtaining various yields, his purchases will almost certainly be altered. To study this problem it will be assumed for concreteness that u is quadratic; thus

$$u(R) = R - \tfrac{1}{2}\alpha R^2,$$

where α is a positive constant. The argument is only outlined below and details are left to the reader.

Let μ_i denote the mean of ϵ_i and σ_{ii} its variance. Write σ_{ij} for the covariance between ϵ_i and ϵ_j and let the variance, covariance matrix of ϵ be $\|\sigma_{ij}\|$. Changes in probability distributions will be thought of as changes in $\mu = (\mu_1, \ldots, \mu_n)$ and $\|\sigma_{ij}\|$ only. The μ_i and σ_{ij} are assumed finite and allowed to range over appropriately chosen open, connected sets. This, together with the earlier requirement that $\epsilon \geq 0$, implies that $\mu_i > 0$ and $\sigma_{ii} > 0$ for all i. The last condition states that there are no riskless assets. Finally, the standard hypothesis that $\|\sigma_{ij}\|$ is symmetric and positive definite is imposed here.

Under the above specifications, for given values of μ and $\|\sigma_{ij}\|$,

$$\bar{u}(x) = \sum_{i=1}^{n} \mu_i x_i - \tfrac{1}{2}\alpha \sum_{i,j=1}^{n} (\sigma_{ij} + \mu_i \mu_j) x_i x_j,$$

on $\bar{E}$. Since the second-order derivatives are $\bar{u}_{ij} = -\alpha(\sigma_{ij} + \mu_i \mu_j)$, for all i and j, and since $\|\sigma_{ij}\|$ is positive definite, it follows that the Hessian matrix of $\bar{u}$ is negative definite. As in Theorem B.5-2, $\bar{u}$ is strictly concave on $\bar{E}$. It is also clear that $\bar{u}$ has a unique global maximum at some x^0 and that indifference surfaces are portions of ellipsoids around that point. Thus 6.1-1–6.1-3 are satisfied on the subset D of $\bar{E}$ on which the first-order derivatives $\bar{u}_i > 0$. From now on attention will be confined to D.

Let $\tilde{\Gamma}$ be the subset of Γ^* such that if it contains (P, M), then the utility-maximizing bundle of commodities over $B^{\leq}(P, M)$ is in both E and $B^{=}(P, M)$. Thus demand functions h^* are defined on $\tilde{\Gamma}$, which, in terms of (P, M), have the usual properties. (Note that h^* can be extended to Γ^* in the obvious manner.) But in this case, h^* (and $\tilde{\Gamma}$, too) also depends on μ and $\|\sigma_{ij}\|$; i.e.,

$$x = h^*(P, M, \mu, \|\sigma_{ij}\|).$$

A similar example was the subject matter of Exercise 5.9. To analyze the effects of changes in the underlying probability distribution on market behavior, then, the derivatives $h^{*k}_{\mu_j}$ and $h^{*k}_{\sigma_{ij}}$ will be studied. Because of the special form of $\bar{u}$, the latter always exist.

By differentiating equilibrium conditions (3.2-10) with respect to σ_{ij} as in the proof of Lemma 3.2-9, it is not hard to show that

$$h^{*k}_{\sigma_{ij}} = \frac{\alpha(|U^{ik}|h^{*j} + |U^{jk}|h^{*i})}{|U|}, \quad i, j, k = 1, \ldots, n,$$

where U and U^{ik} are the matrices of Chapter 3 defined with respect to $\bar{u}$. Hence, from Lemma 3.2-9 itself,

$$h^{*k}_{\sigma_{ij}} = \frac{\alpha}{\lambda^*}(s^*_{ik}h^{*j} + s^*_{jk}h^{*i})$$

for all i, j, k. The properties of S^* therefore imply that all matrices obtained by letting i and j vary for each k in $h^{*k}_{\sigma_{ij}}$ are symmetric. Furthermore,

$$h^{*k}_{\sigma_{kk}} < 0,$$

for any k, whence the conclusion that as an asset becomes more risky, its demand falls.

The effects of changes in μ are not so clear-cut. For by again differentiating (3.2-10), this time with respect to μ_j, and solving for $h^{*k}_{\mu_j}$,

$$h^{*k}_{\mu_j} = \alpha \frac{h^{*j}}{\lambda^*} \sum_{i=1}^{n} \mu_i s^*_{ik} + \alpha \frac{s^*_{jk}}{\lambda^*} \left[\sum_{i=1}^{n} \mu_i h^{*i} - 1 \right],$$

for all k and j. Even when $k = j$, the sign of this expression could, in general, go either way.

Matters are not complicated very much by letting one asset, say the nth, be cash. In the quadratic utility case, this means that $\epsilon_n = \mu_n = 1$ and $\sigma_{in} = \sigma_{ni} = 0$ for all i. Only the matrix consisting of the first $n - 1$ rows and columns of $\|\sigma_{ij}\|$ can now be assumed positive definite. The resulting changes in the above analysis are left to the reader.

8.4 LIQUIDITY PREFERENCE

An alternative approach to portfolio selection which emphasizes the possibility of capital gain is due to Tobin [7]. Instead of the consumer being faced with expected returns and variances he cannot influence, he is now required to choose among them. In so doing his demand for speculative cash balances, i.e., liquidity preference, is determined along with that for the assets themselves. Thus portfolios are selected on the basis of their ability to provide the most desirable probability distribution or risk rather than because they maximize the expected utility of their return. What is desirable among probability distributions, of course, depends on the consumer's preferences for holding different compositions of risk.

The liquidity preference problem is studied now in isolation, without reference to ordinary commodities or the usual budget constraint. It will be integrated into the more general setting in Chapter 9.

Let there be n assets, with the nth designated as cash. Write β_i for that fraction of the total value of the portfolio consisting of asset i and suppose $r_i \geq 0$ is the rate of interest paid on i during the period. If γ_i represents the per-dollar capital gain or loss, then the return to each dollar of the portfolio is

$$\sum_{i=1}^{n-1} \epsilon_i,$$

where

(8.4-1) $\epsilon_i = \beta_i(r_i + \gamma_i), \quad i = 1, \ldots, n-1,$

$\gamma_i \geq 0$ for every $i \neq n$, and

$$\sum_{i=1}^{n} \beta_i = 1.$$

There is, of course, no return to or capital gain from holding cash.

Assume that $(\gamma_1, \ldots, \gamma_{n-1})$ is a vector of random variables with zero means and variance, covariance matrix $\|(\sigma_{ij}^\gamma)^2\|$. Thus σ_{ii}^γ is the standard deviation of γ_i and σ_{ij}^γ is the square root of the covariance of γ_i with γ_j. The matrix of the latter is written $\|\sigma_{ij}^\gamma\|$. Now $(\epsilon_1, \ldots, \epsilon_{n-1})$ is also a random variable. Denote its means and variance, covariance matrix by, respectively, $\mu = (\mu_1, \ldots, \mu_{n-1})$ and $\|(\sigma_{ij})^2\|$. Then, from (8.4-1),

$$\mu_i = \beta_i r_i,$$

$$\sigma_{ij} = \sqrt{\beta_i \beta_j}\, \sigma_{ij}^\gamma,$$

where $i, j = 1, \ldots, n-1$. It follows that

$$0 \leq \mu_i,$$

(8.4-2) $0 \leq \sigma_{ij} \leq \sigma_{ij}^\gamma,$

(8.4-3) $\sqrt{r_i r_j}\, \sigma_{ij} = \sqrt{\mu_i \mu_j}\, \sigma_{ij}^\gamma,$

for all i and j distinct from n.

As in the previous section, suppose each specification of μ and $\|\sigma_{ij}\|$ corresponds to a unique probability distribution. Let there be a utility function, $u(\mu, \|\sigma_{ij}\|)$, defined over the nonnegative orthant of Euclidian $(n^2 + n)$-space: u is nothing more than a representation of the consumer's preferences for holding different kinds of risk. If u is assumed to satisfy appropriate smoothness, monotonicity, and convexity requirements, then maximization of u subject to (8.4-2) and (8.4-3) yields "demand" functions for probability distributions. That is, μ and $\|\sigma_{ij}\|$ may be expressed as functions of $r = (r_1, \ldots, r_{n-1})$ and $\|\sigma_{ij}^\gamma\|$, which have properties corresponding to the assumptions made on u. The analysis runs along lines suggested in earlier chapters.

As an illustration of this technique the case $n = 2$ is instructive. To simplify notation write r for r_1, γ for γ_1, σ^γ for σ_{11}^γ, ϵ for ϵ_1, μ for μ_1, σ for σ_{11}, and let $z = (\mu, \sigma)$. Thus ϵ is a scalar, random variable with mean μ and standard deviation σ, where

(8.4-4) $$\mu = \beta_1 r,$$

(8.4-5) $$0 \leq \sigma \leq \sigma^\gamma,$$

(8.4-6) $$r\sigma = \mu\sigma^\gamma.$$

Recalling the notation of Chapter 3, $E = \{z : z > 0\}$ and $\bar{E}$ is its closure. Assume that u is defined on $\bar{E}$ such that

8.4-7. u is twice continuously differentiable on E and continuous where finite on $\bar{E}$.

8.4-8. u is strictly quasi-concave.

8.4-9. $u_1(z) > 0$ and $u_2(z) < 0$ on E, and u_1 is defined and positive for all $(z_1, 0)$, where $z_1 > 0$.

Note that 8.4-7 and 8.4-8 are identical to, respectively, 3.1-1 and 3.1-3. But the indifference map generated by u must look something like that pictured in Figure 8.1 (the arrow points in a direction of increasing utility). Such a consumer may be designated a *risk averter* in the sense that remaining on the same indifference curve, he will accept greater risk (variance) only upon compensation by an increased expected capital gain. This is a different notion of risk aversion from that discussed in Section 8.1.

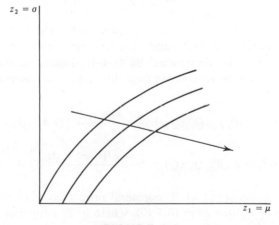

FIGURE 8.1

Now in the special case considered here, indifference curves as functions of z_1 are increasing and strictly concave, while as functions of z_2 are increasing and strictly convex. It follows from Corollary B.2-8 that the matrix, U, as defined in Section 3.1, has the properties asserted in Theorem 3.1-10.

Consider the constraint

$$(-\sigma^\gamma)\mu + r\sigma = \tau,$$

where $-\sigma^\gamma$, r, and τ are parameters. This is identical to the ordinary budget constraint with prices replaced by $(-\sigma^\gamma, r)$, income by τ, and quantities by (μ, σ). Let $\Gamma^* = \{(-\sigma^\gamma, r, \tau): \sigma^\gamma > 0 \text{ and } r > 0\}$. Then the postulate of rationality, (3.1-12), applied here, defines a $1:1$ correspondence between a subset Γ' of Γ^* and some subset of $\bar{E}$; it is denoted by $g = (g^1, g^2)$:

$$z = g(-\sigma^\gamma, r, \tau).$$

Using the properties of U indicated above and the argument of Chapter 3, g on Γ' is subject to all the implications of utility maximization listed in Table 3.1. Note that the Slutsky functions in this case are of the form

$$s_{ij}^g(-\sigma^\gamma, r, \tau) = g_j^i(-\sigma^\gamma, r, \tau) + g^j(-\sigma^\gamma, r, \tau)g_3^i(-\sigma^\gamma, r, \tau),$$

where g_3^i is the derivative of g^i with respect to its third argument.

Let Γ'' be the subset of Γ' on which $\tau = 0$ and $g^2(-\sigma^\gamma, r, 0) \le \sigma^\gamma$. Then 8.4-7–8.4-9 imply that Γ'' is not empty. In addition, each of its points satisfies both constraints (8.4-5) and (8.4-6). Therefore, g on Γ'' is the demand for probability distributions sought after. The properties of g on Γ'' are exactly those stated above.

Continuing with this simplified model, suppose the value of the consumer's portfolio at the beginning of the period is Q and he has decided, by some independent means, to change it during the period by ΔQ. Assume further that β_1^0 and β_2^0, where $0 \le \beta_1^0 \le 1$ and $\beta_1^0 + \beta_2^0 = 1$, are, respectively, the fraction of bonds (asset 1) and cash previously held by him. Then given values for σ^γ and r, the optimal μ and σ are obtained through g, and hence new fractions β_1 and β_2 are determined by (8.4-4). Therefore, the demand for bonds, h^{*1}, and that for speculative cash, h^{*2} (liquidity preference), are given by

$$h^{*1}(\sigma^\gamma, r; \beta_1^0, \beta_2^0, Q, \Delta Q) = \frac{g^1(-\sigma^\gamma, r, 0)}{r}(Q + \Delta Q) - \beta_1^0 Q,$$

(8.4-10)

$$h^{*2}(\sigma^\gamma, r; \beta_1^0, \beta_2^0, Q, \Delta Q) = \frac{r - g^1(-\sigma^\gamma, r, 0)}{r}(Q + \Delta Q) - \beta_2^0 Q,$$

defined on an appropriate set. The general properties of $h^* = (h^{*1}, h^{*2})$ are thus: h^* may be written as in (8.4-10), where g^1 is a function satisfying the restrictions previously indicated.

Since $h^{*1} + h^{*2} \equiv \Delta Q$, the derivatives of h^{*1} must have opposite signs from those of h^{*2}. But it generally will be impossible to deduce the signs of either. This ambiguity disappears, however, if, for example,

(8.4-11) $$u(\mu, \sigma) = \mu - \tfrac{1}{2}\alpha(\sigma^2 + \mu^2),$$

where α is a positive constant. For, restricting u to the subset of $\bar{E}$ on which 8.4-7–8.4-9 are satisfied,

(8.4-12)
$$g^1(-\sigma^\gamma, r, 0) = \frac{r^2}{2\alpha[(-\sigma^\gamma)^2 - r^2]},$$
$$g^2(-\sigma^\gamma, r, 0) = -\frac{r(-\sigma^\gamma)}{2\alpha[(-\sigma^\gamma)^2 - r^2]},$$

on the appropriate Γ'. Since the ranges of (8.4-12) are nonnegative,

(8.4-13) $$\sigma^\gamma \geq r.$$

Combining (8.4-10), (8.4-12), and (8.4-13) it is not hard to show that

$$h_r^{*1} > 0, \qquad h_{\sigma^\gamma}^{*1} < 0,$$
$$h_r^{*2} < 0, \qquad h_{\sigma^\gamma}^{*2} > 0,$$

on Γ'. Thus, in particular, the demand for speculative cash balances is a downward-sloping function of the interest rate when remaining variables are fixed. Note also that (8.4-11) may be interpreted as an expected utility function obtained by integrating

(8.4-14) $$\tilde{u}(\epsilon) = \epsilon - \alpha\epsilon^2.$$

In this case, then, selecting a portfolio by choosing the best risk-bearing position is equivalent to optimizing its expected return. The approach of the last section has become identical to that employed here.

Similar demand functions, $h^{*1}, \ldots, h^{*n}$, may be defined when there are more than two assets and their general properties stated in terms of the g^i.

REFERENCES

[1] Debreu, G., "Topological Methods in Cardinal Utility," in K. J. Arrow, S. Karlin, and P. Suppes (eds.), *Mathematical Methods in the Social Sciences* (Stanford, Calif.: Stanford University Press, 1960), pp. 16–26.

[2] Friedman, M., and L. J. Savage, "The Utility Analysis of Choices Involving Risk," *Journal of Political Economy* (1948), pp. 297–304.

[3] Loève, M., *Probability Theory*, 3rd ed. (Princeton, N.J.: Van Nostrand, 1963).

[4] Luce, R. D., and P. Suppes, "Preference, Utility and Subjective Probability," in R. D. Luce, R. R. Bush and E. Galanter (eds.), *Handbook of Mathematical Psychology*, v. 3 (New York: Wiley, 1965), pp. 249–410.

[5] Neumann, J. von, and O. Morgenstern, *Theory of Games and Economic Behavior* (Princeton, N.J.: Princeton University Press, 1944).

[6] Royama, S., and K. Hamada, "Substitution and Complementarity in the Choice of Risky Assets," in D. D. Hester and J. Tobin, (eds.), *Risk Aversion and Portfolio Choice* (New York: Wiley, 1967), pp. 27–40.

[7] Tobin, J., "Liquidity Preference as Behavior Towards Risk," *Review of Economic Studies* (1958), pp. 65–86.

[8] Wilks, S. S., *Mathematical Statistics* (New York: Wiley, 1962).

9

Economic Man

It is commonplace that during any given period of time a consumer's decisions concerning what to buy, how much to work and save, and what to do with his savings are interrelated. In this concluding chapter, these problems are all treated as part of a unified whole whose solution is obtained upon the maximization of a single utility function. In so doing, many of the elements of demand theory discussed earlier are brought together. The argument is only briefly sketched below.

It is well to begin by reviewing and clarifying the concepts to be used and the notation symbolizing them. As usual, x denotes a vector of n quantities of commodities available for consumption during the period, and P is a vector of current commodity prices. Quantities of a composite commodity, written y, are interpreted to be units of future consumption which the consumer can purchase now as savings.[1] The precise construction of y is of no importance in this context. Since future prices are never known in advance, it is reasonable to regard next period's price of the composite commodity as a random variable, whose expected value, F, is somehow estimated. Thus the current price of future consumption becomes $F/(1 + r)$, where r is the rate of interest. For simplicity assume there is no causal relationship between F and P. The period of time under consideration is divided into Λ units, t varies over quantities of leisure, and ω is the wage per unit of time spent at labor. As in Section 8.4, μ and σ correspond uniquely to probability distributions reflecting the yield and risk of holding assets, σ^γ is the variance of capital gain, Q the value of the consumer's portfolio at the beginning of the period, and β_1 and β_2, respectively, the fraction of bonds and cash contained in it. Finally, let M be nonwage income received during the period and write z for (x, y, t, μ, σ).

---

[1] See Leser, C. E. V., "The Consumer's Demand for Money," *Econometrica* (1943), pp. 123–140.

Let there be a utility function, u, defined on the nonnegative orthant of Euclidean $(n + 4)$-space, $\bar{E}$, such that

9.1. u has continuous, second-order, partial derivatives on E and is continuous where finite on $\bar{E}$.

9.2. $u_i(z) > 0$ for $i = 1, \ldots, n + 3$ and $u_{n+4}(z) < 0$ on E.

9.3. $u_i(z)$ is defined and positive for all $(x, y, t, \mu) > 0$ and $\sigma = 0$, $i = 1, \ldots, n + 3$.

9.4. u is strictly quasi-concave.

The consumer is constrained by

$$(9.5) \qquad P \cdot x + \frac{1 + F}{r} y = M + (\Lambda - t)\omega, \quad 0 \le t \le \Lambda,$$

and, as in Section 8.4,

$$(9.6) \qquad \mu = \beta r, \quad 0 \le \sigma \le \sigma^\gamma, \quad r\sigma = \mu\sigma^\gamma.$$

Thus maximizing u subject to (9.5) and (9.6) yields simultaneously his demand for commodities, future consumption, bonds, and speculative cash balances, together with his supply of labor. The properties of these functions are obtained by applying the techniques developed in earlier chapters. Note, and this can be modified without great difficulty, that the requirement that y be positive precludes borrowing by the consumer.

It is not necessary to pursue matters in such generality here. The point can be made simply and efficiently by adding a separability assumption so that

$$u(z) = V(v^1(x, y, t), v^2(\mu, \sigma)).$$

For, in this case, maximizing u subject to (9.5) and (9.6) is equivalent to maximizing v^1 subject to the former and v^2 subject to the latter. Thus the demand for commodities and future consumption, and the supply of labor, are written

$$(x, y, \Lambda - t) = h^{*\bar{1}}\left(P, \frac{1 + F}{r}, M + \omega\Lambda\right),$$

where $h^{*\bar{1}} = (h^{*1}, \ldots, h^{*n+2})$ is a vector of functions whose properties are explicitly given in Section 7.1. The demand for bonds, b, and cash, c, are similarly

$$(b, c) = h^{*\bar{2}}\left(r, \sigma^\gamma, \beta_1^0, \beta_2^0, Q, \frac{1 + F}{r} y\right),$$

where $h^{*\bar{2}} = (h^{*n+3}, h^{*n+4})$ is the vector of (8.4-10) with ΔQ (the amount of funds added to the portfolio during the period) replaced by $[(1 + F)/r]y$, and where β_1^0 and β_2^0 are the fractions of bonds and cash inherited from the last period. The properties of $h^{*\bar{2}}$ are elucidated in Section 8.4.

A key feature of this model is that the variable representing savings, y, and those reflecting probability distributions of risk, (μ, σ), are independent of each other. Thus the decision of how much to save is treated separately from that concerning the form in which savings are to be held. Such an individual is not a "target" saver: he is not trying to secure a certain quantity of money with which to begin the next period. If he were aiming at a target, there would be no reason for him to speculate by holding cash. He need only loan out that sum of money sufficient to provide him with the desired amount at the going rate of interest. Instead, the consumer here is saving just to have some unspecified fund available in the future. Perhaps the quantity set aside is not as important as participation in the act itself, for he considers it worthwhile to save whatever he thinks he can. Meanwhile the composition of his total portfolio (i.e., past assets plus current savings) depends on his present preferences for holding different probability distributions of risk. Requiring this dichotomy between the decisions to save and select a portfolio is one way of making the demand for speculative cash meaningful. Furthermore, if a consumer is not sure of the timing of his expenditures and income receipts during the period, at some point he may unexpectedly run out of money. To insure himself against the resulting embarrassment and inconvenience he may want to hold cash as a precaution. Thus designating one commodity, say the nth, as money records the fact that holding precautionary balances provide him with utility. The demand for that commodity, h^{*n}, is his demand for precautionary cash balances. Therefore, the consumer's consumption, k^1, and total savings, k^2, functions are given by

$$k^1(\xi) = \sum_{i=1}^{n-1} P_i h^{*i}(\xi),$$

$$k^2(\xi) = P_n h^{*n}(\xi) + \frac{1+F}{r} h^{*n+1}(\xi),$$

where $\xi = (P, (1 + F)/r, M + \omega\Lambda)$. Properties of k^1 and k^2 may be obtained from those of h^{*1}.

These ideas are easily illustrated. Thus if

$$u(z) = x_1 x_2 yt + (\mu - \sigma^2)\sqrt{x_1 x_2 yt},$$

simple calculations reveal that

$$h^{*i}(\xi) = \frac{1}{3P_i}(M + \omega\Lambda), \quad i = 1, 2,$$

$$h^{*3}(\xi) = \frac{1}{3F}(M + \omega\Lambda)(1 + r),$$

$$h^{*4}(\eta) = \frac{r}{2(\sigma^r)^2}\left[Q + \frac{M + \omega\Lambda}{3}\right] - \beta_1^0 Q,$$

$$h^{*5}(\eta) = \left[1 - \frac{r}{2(\sigma^r)^2}\right]\left[Q + \frac{M + \omega\Lambda}{3}\right] - \beta_2^0 Q,$$

where $\eta = (r, \sigma^\gamma, \beta_1^0, \beta_2^0, Q, \xi)$, and h^{*3} has been substituted into h^{*4} and h^{*5} so that the latter depend on ξ rather than $[(1 + F)/r]y$. Furthermore,

$$k^1(\xi) = \tfrac{1}{3}(M + \omega\Lambda),$$

$$k^2(\xi) = \tfrac{2}{3}(M + \omega\Lambda).$$

In many respects this model gives a good deal of information about the behavior of static economic man. A considerable number of his everyday decision-making problems are included and the implications of their rational solutions in terms of the rules he must follow in reacting to parameter changes (expressed as properties of demand functions) are worked out in rather explicit detail. There is, further, a wide range of assumptions over which the analysis may be carried out, from requirements as weak as those in non-integrable situations to the relatively rigid restrictions of separability.

Nevertheless, serious difficulties remain. For example, although all commodities are bought in whole units or simple fractions thereof, most of the commodity space consists of vectors whose coordinates are irrational numbers or rational ones which never appear on the market. Thus the commodity space really should be a collection of isolated points. But what rational behavior might be like under these conditions is an open question. Alternatively, a place must be found for many omitted but still ordinary phenomena such as bequests, a wide variety of transactions costs, and consumer credit. Furthermore, the theory treats all goods alike in spite of the fact that each commodity has its own peculiar properties. Magazines are different from food, durables from nondurables. These differences do influence consumer behavior, but there is no way as yet to incorporate such effects into demand functions themselves. Other omissions include failure to account for the appearance or disappearance of commodities on the market, failure to analyze the consumer's choice of occupation, and so on. As pointed out in Section 7.5, the notion of characteristics may prove to be useful in one or more of these contexts provided the analysis can be translated into observable phenomena. In any case, considerable time and energy will undoubtedly be spent on questions such as these in the future.

Appendix

The purpose of this appendix is to catalogue in a more or less self-contained manner various mathematical results which are not conveniently available in the economics literature. Although the subject matter is restricted to that which is required by the text, considerable additional effort is devoted to a detailed development of convex functions and their properties. There is little similarity between notation used here and that employed in the text.

A. Relations[1]

In this section basic results concerning (1) extensions of orderings and (2) isomorphisms between partially ordered sets and the real line are derived. The latter (due to Cantor) is considered first.

Let D be a set. A *binary relation* R on D is a set of ordered pairs:

$$R = \{\langle x, y\rangle : x \text{ and } y \text{ are in } D\}.$$

The notation $x \, R \, y$ means $\langle x, y\rangle$ is in R. The *complement* of R is denoted by $\bar{R}$ and defined by

$$\bar{R} = \{\langle x, y\rangle : x \text{ and } y \text{ are in } D \text{ and } \langle x, y\rangle \text{ is not in } R\}.$$

Thus for all x and y in D, either $x \, R \, y$ or $x \, \bar{R} \, y$, but both cannot occur simultaneously. A relation may exhibit one or more of a multitude of properties. As examples, R may be

(1) *Reflexive*: For all x in D, $x \, R \, x$.
(2) *Irreflexive*: For all x in D, $x \, \bar{R} \, x$.

---

[1] This section has been based on Birkoff [5, chs. 1, 3]. See also Halmos [13].

(3) *Symmetric*: For all x and y in D, if $x\,R\,y$, then $y\,R\,x$.

(4) *Antisymmetric*: For all x and y in D, if $x\,R\,y$ and $y\,R\,x$, then $x = y$.

(5) *Asymmetric*: For all x and y in D, if $x\,R\,y$, then $y\,\bar{R}\,x$.

(6) *Acyclic*: For any sequence of points $x^1, \ldots, x^n$, in D, if $x^1\,R\,x^2, \ldots$, $x^{n-1}\,R\,x^n$, then $x^n\,\bar{R}\,x^1$.

(7) *Transitive*: For any x, y, and z in D, if $x\,R\,y$ and $y\,R\,z$, then $x\,R\,z$.

(8) *Total*: For all x and y in D, either $x\,R\,y$ or $y\,R\,x$.

An *equivalence relation* is a binary relation which is reflexive, symmetric, and transitive. An equivalence relation on D partitions D into mutually exclusive and exhaustive *equivalence classes*.

A *partial ordering* of D, written $\geqslant$, is a relation on D which is reflexive, antisymmetric, and transitive. If a partial order on D is total, then D is called a *chain*. The rational and real numbers are chains ordered by $\geq$.

Let D be a chain and $S \subseteq D$ (i.e., S is a subset of D). If for every x and y in $D - S$ such that $x \geqslant y$ there exists a distinct z in S for which $x \geqslant z \geqslant y$, then S is *order-dense*[2] in D. Note that the set of rational numbers is order-dense in the reals.

Let D and D' be sets. Let θ be a function mapping D into D'. If each element of D corresponds under θ to a unique element of D', and if each element of D' corresponds under θ^{-1} to a unique element of D, then θ is called a *1:1 correspondence*. Let D and D' be partially ordered by R and R', respectively. Then D and D' are *isomorphic* if and only if there exists a 1:1 correspondence φ between them such that

(1) For all x and y in D, if $x\,R\,y$, then $\varphi(x)\,R'\,\varphi(y)$.

(2) For all $\varphi(x)$ and $\varphi(y)$ in D', if $\varphi(x)\,R'\,\varphi(y)$, then $x\,R\,y$.

In this case φ is called an *isomorphism* between D and D'. Every finite chain of, say, n elements is isomorphic with the chain of integers $\{1, \ldots, n\}$ ordered by $\geq$.

Lemma A-1 *Any countable*[3] *chain D is isomorphic with a subchain of the chain of rational numbers.*

PROOF:

Enumerate the rationals and elements of D as, respectively, $\{r_1, r_2, \ldots\}$ and $\{x_1, x_2, \ldots\}$. An induction argument shows that for any n, either

(1) $x_n \geqslant x_i$ for all $i = 1, \ldots, n - 1$,

(2) $x_n \leqslant x_i$ for all $i = 1, \ldots, n - 1$, or

(3) $x_i \leqslant x_n \leqslant x_j$ for some greatest x_i and least x_j, where $i, j < n$.

---

[2] The notation x is in $D - S$ means that x is in D but not in S.

[3] A set is countable if and only if there exists a 1:1 correspondence between it and a subset of the positive integers.

Define $\varphi(x_1) = 0$ and set

$$\varphi(x_n) = \begin{cases} n & \text{in case (1),} \\ -n & \text{in case (2),} \\ r_k & \text{in case (3),} \end{cases}$$

where r_k is the first rational in $\{r_1, r_2, \ldots\}$ which has the same order relation to $\varphi(x_1), \ldots, \varphi(x_{n-1})$ as x_n has to $x_1, \ldots, x_{n-1}$. Such an r_k will always exist, because between any two rationals there exists a third. The function φ is the desired isomorphism.

Q.E.D.

Theorem A-2 (Cantor)   *A chain D is isomorphic with a subchain of the chain of real numbers if and only if D contains a countable, order-dense subset.*

PROOF:

Suppose D contains a countable, order-dense subset S. Without loss of generality assume that whenever they exist, S contains its least upper and greatest lower bounds.[4] By Lemma A-1 there is an isomorphism φ mapping S into a subchain $\varphi(S)$ of the rationals. The next step is to extend φ to D. Thus let x be in $D - S$. Since S is order-dense in D, there are sets

$$A_x = \{s: s \text{ is in } S \text{ and } s \leq x\},$$

$$B_x = \{s: s \text{ is in } S \text{ and } x \leq s\}.$$

Then $A_x \cup B_x = S$, $A_x \cap B_x = \varnothing$, and x is uniquely determined by this partition.[5] Now let

$$a = \underset{A_x}{\text{l.u.b.}} \; \varphi(s),$$

$$b = \underset{B_x}{\text{g.l.b.}} \; \varphi(s),$$

where l.u.b.$_{A_x}$ and g.l.b.$_{B_x}$ are, respectively, the least upper and greatest lower bounds taken over all s in A_x and B_x. Defining

$$\varphi(x) = \tfrac{1}{2}(a + b),$$

D is seen to be isomorphic with a subchain of the real numbers.

To prove the second part of the theorem assume that D is isomorphic with a subchain of the real numbers. Denote the isomorphism by φ. Let $I = \{I_1, I_2, \ldots\}$ be the set of all closed intervals on the real line whose end points are rational and which contain at least one image point of D under φ. Choose one image point $\varphi(x_i)$ from each I_i and set $A = \cup_i \{x_i\}$. Thus A is countable. Now let $B = \{y: y$ is in D and there exists an x in D where $x \neq y$ such that

---

[4] An upper bound of S under $\geqslant$ is an element x in D such that $x \geqslant s$ for all s in S. The least upper bound is an element x^0 in D such that $x \geqslant x^0$ for all upper bounds x.

[5] The symbols $\cup$, $\cap$, and $\varnothing$ mean union, intersection, and empty set, respectively.

no I_i in I is contained in the open interval $(\varphi(x), \varphi(y))\}$. Then B contains all points of D which are mapped into the end points of finite open intervals of the real line. Hence B is countable; so is $A \cup B$. It remains to show that $A \cup B$ is order-dense in D.

To this end let x and y be in $D - (A \cup B)$ and suppose $x \gneqq y$. Then $\varphi(x) \geq \varphi(y)$. Since x and y are not in B, there is an I_i contained in $(\varphi(x), \varphi(y))$. But there is also a distinct z in A such that $\varphi(z)$ is in I_i; i.e., $\varphi(x) \geq \varphi(z) \geq \varphi(y)$. Hence $x \gneqq z \gneqq y$.

Q.E.D.

Consider now an irreflexive and transitive relation R on D. Suppose a and b are in D, where $a \neq b$ and neither $\langle a, b \rangle$ nor $\langle b, a \rangle$ are in R. Let R^1 be the single element set $R^1 = \{\langle a, b \rangle\}$. Let R^2 consist of those pairs $\langle u, v \rangle$ not in $R \cup R^1$ which, for some x in D, both $\langle u, x \rangle$ and $\langle x, v \rangle$ are in $R \cup R^1$. Similarly, let R^3 be all pairs $\langle y, z \rangle$ not in $R \cup R^1 \cup R^2$ such that for some w in D, $R \cup R^1 \cup R^2$ contains both $\langle y, w \rangle$ and $\langle w, z \rangle$. Define

$$R' = R \cup R^1 \cup R^2 \cup R^3.$$

The proof of the following lemma is straightforward but very tedious and therefore omitted.

Lemma A-3   *R' is irreflexive and transitive on D.*

Theorem A-4   *If R is an irreflexive and transitive relation on D, then R can be extended to an irreflexive, transitive, and total relation on D.*

PROOF:

Let $Q = \{T: T$ is an irreflexive and transitive relation on D which contains $R\}$. Then $Q \neq \varnothing$ and Q is partially ordered by set inclusion $(\subseteq)$ such that every chain in Q has an upper bound. By Zorn's lemma [13, p. 62] there is a maximal element M in Q. If M were not total, then by Lemma A-3 there would exist a relation T in Q such that T is irreflexive and transitive, $M \subseteq T$ and $M \neq T$. This contradicts the maximality of M.

Q.E.D.

Corollary A-5   *Any reflexive and transitive relation on D can be extended to a reflexive, transitive, and total relation on D.*

PROOF:

Let R be reflexive and transitive on D and set $X = \{\langle x, x \rangle : x$ is in $D\}$. Consider the relation $\rho = R - X$. This is irreflexive and transitive and hence by Theorem A-4 may be extended to an irreflexive, transitive, and total relation, ρ' on D. But then $\rho' \cup X$ is the desired extension of R.

Q.E.D.

B.   Convex Functions

B.1   DEFINITIONS

Let $f(x)$ be a real-valued function defined on a subset D of Euclidean n-space, where x is used to denote n-dimensional vectors $(x_1, \ldots, x_n)$. Unless otherwise stated, D is assumed *convex*; that is, for all x' and x'' in D and any real number θ between (or equal to) 0 and 1, the point $\theta x' + (1 - \theta)x''$ lies in D. If for all distinct x' and x'' in D and all θ, where $0 < \theta < 1$,

(B.1-1) $$\theta f(x') + (1 - \theta)f(x'') > f(\theta x' + (1 - \theta)x''),$$

then f is called *strictly convex*. When $>$ is replaced by $\geq$ in (B.1-1), f is referred to as just *convex*. Reversing these inequalities f becomes, respectively, *strictly concave* and *concave*. Note that the sum of two convex (or concave) functions is always convex (or concave), but this need not be true of their difference. Also, f is convex if and only if $-f$ is concave; thus the general properties of concave functions are readily obtained from those of convex ones. Throughout this section D will be assumed open and f differentiable[6] on it. The partial derivative of f with respect to its ith argument is written f_i. Equivalent definitions of strict convexity are now considered; analogous assertions for convex functions are left to the reader.

Lemma B.1-2   *f is strictly convex if and only if*

(B.1-3) $$f(x') - f(x'') > \sum_{i=1}^{n} f_i(x'')(x_i' - x_i''),$$

for all distinct x' and x'' in D.

PROOF:

Suppose f is strictly convex. Choose distinct x' and x'' in D and θ^0, where $0 < \theta^0 < 1$. Then from (B.1-1) there is an $\epsilon > 0$ such that

$$f(x') - f(x'') = \frac{f(x'' + \theta^0[x' - x'']) - f(x'')}{\theta^0} + \epsilon.$$

Applying (B.1-1) to the numerator for all θ and letting θ approach zero,

$$f(x') - f(x'') \geq \frac{1}{\theta^0} \lim_{\theta \to 0} \left[\frac{f(x'' + \theta\theta^0[x' - x'']) - f(x'')}{\theta} \right] + \epsilon,$$

which, since f is differentiable,

$$= \sum_{i=1}^{n} f_i(x'')(x_i' - x_i'') + \epsilon.$$

This proves (B.1-3).

[6] A function is differentiable on D if it has a differential at every point of D. See Section B.4.

To go the other way, note that for any distinct x' and x'' in D and θ, where $0 < \theta < 1$,

$$\theta f(x') + (1 - \theta)f(x'') - f(\theta x' + (1 - \theta)x'')$$

$$= \theta \left[f(x') - f(x'') - \frac{f(x'' + \theta[x' - x'']) - f(x'')}{\theta} \right].$$

Applying (B.1-3) to the numerator of the fraction in this expression,

$$\theta f(x') + (1 - \theta)f(x'') - f(\theta x' + (1 - \theta)x'')$$

$$> \theta \left[f(x') - f(x'') - \sum_{i=1}^{n} f_i(x'')(x_i' - x_i'') \right],$$

which is positive, by (B.1-3).

Q.E.D.

Lemma B. 1-4 *f is strictly convex if and only if*

$$\sum_{i=1}^{n} [f_i(x') - f_i(x'')](x_i' - x_i'') > 0,$$

for any distinct x' and x'' in D.

Proof:

If f is strictly convex, then by applying Lemma B.1-2 twice to distinct x' and x'' in D gives

$$f(x') - f(x'') > \sum_{i=1}^{n} f_i(x'')(x_i' - x_i''),$$

$$f(x'') - f(x') > \sum_{i=1}^{n} f_i(x')(x_i'' - x_i').$$

Adding these inequalities completes the first half of the proof.

Conversely, if x' and x'' are distinct in D, let z be the function $z(\theta) = x'' + \theta(x' - x'')$, where $0 \le \theta \le 1$. Since D is convex, $z(\theta)$ is in D for each θ. Hence, by the mean value theorem [2, p. 117], there is a θ^0 such that $0 < \theta^0 < 1$ and

$$f(x') - f(x'') - \sum_{i=1}^{n} f_i(x'')(x_i' - x_i'') = \sum_{i=1}^{n} [f_i(z(\theta^0)) - f_i(x'')](x_i' - x_i'')$$

$$= \frac{1}{\theta^0} \sum_{i=1}^{n} [f_i(z(\theta^0)) - f_i(x'')](z^i(\theta^0) - x_i''),$$

where z^i is the ith component of z. By hypothesis, this last expression is strictly positive, so by Lemma B.1-2, f is strictly convex.

Q.E.D.

Lemma B.1-5 *Let f be strictly convex on D. Then for all x' and x" in D and*
$i = 1, \ldots, n$,

$$f_i(x') = f_i(x'')$$

if and only if x' = x".

PROOF:
If $x' = x''$, then of course $f_i(x') = f_i(x'')$ for each i. If x' and x'' are distinct,
then Lemma B.1-4 implies that $f_i(x') \neq f_i(x'')$ for some i.

Q.E.D.

Lemma B.1-6 *Let $\{f^\alpha: \alpha \text{ is in } A\}$, where A is some indexing set, be a*
family of convex functions defined on D. Let[7]

$$g(x) = \sup_A f^\alpha(x),$$

and

$$\Psi = \{x: |g(x)| < \infty\}.$$

Then Ψ is convex and g is convex on Ψ.

PROOF:
Let x' and x'' be in Ψ. Then $g(x') < \infty$, $g(x'') < \infty$ and for every α in A,

$$f^\alpha(\theta x' + (1 - \theta)x'') \leq \theta f^\alpha(x') + (1 - \theta)f^\alpha(x'')$$
$$\leq \theta g(x') + (1 - \theta)g(x'')$$
$$< \infty.$$

Hence

$$g(\theta x' + (1 - \theta)x'') = \sup_A f^\alpha(\theta x' + (1 - \theta)x'')$$
$$\leq \theta g(x') + (1 - \theta)g(x'')$$
$$< \infty.$$

Therefore, $\theta x' + (1 - \theta)x''$ is in Ψ and g is convex on Ψ.

Q.E.D.

B.2 CONVEX FUNCTIONS OF A SINGLE VARIABLE[8]

From now on, it is no longer assumed that f is differentiable. Indeed, much
of what follows will be an investigation into the differential properties of
convex functions. For functions of one variable, these are simple to state and
prove. Since they have interest in their own right and are used in the proofs
of the general theorems in later sections, the important results are presented
here.

---

[7] $\sup_A f^\alpha(x)$ means the supremum of $f^\alpha(x)$ taken over all α in A.
[8] This section is taken from Bourbaki [7, pp. 19–22, 46–50]. © Hermann, Paris, 1949.
Translated and reprinted by permission of Hermann.

In this section f is a function defined on an interval D. Its left and right derivatives, if they exist, are written f_l and f_r, respectively. Open, closed, and half-open intervals between points a and b are denoted, respectively, by (a, b), $[a, b]$, and $(a, b]$ or $[a, b)$. The first two lemmas are known results from analysis and their proofs are not repeated here.[9]

Lemma B.2-1 *Let f be continuous on a closed, bounded interval $[a, b]$, and have a derivative (finite or not) from the right at all points of $[a, b) - A$, where A is at most countable and $A \subseteq [a, b]$. For f to be monotone nondecreasing, it is necessary and sufficient that $f_r(x) \geq 0$ on $[a, b) - A$. For f to be monotone increasing, it is necessary and sufficient that $f_r(x) \geq 0$ for all x in $[a, b) - A$ and that $f_r(x) > 0$ on a set $B \subseteq [a, b]$, where B is dense in $[a, b]$.*[10]

Lemma B.2-2 *Let f and g be continuous on $[a, b]$ and have finite derivatives from the right at all points of $[a, b) - A$, where A is at most countable and $A \subseteq [a, b]$. Let there exist finite numbers m and M such that*

$$mg_r(x) \leq f_r(x) \leq Mg_r(x),$$

for all x in $[a, b) - A$. Then

$$m[g(b) - g(a)] \leq f(b) - f(a) \leq M[g(b) - g(a)].$$

Lemma B.2-3 *f is convex (or strictly convex) on an interval D if and only if for any point a in D,*

$$\frac{f(x) - f(a)}{x - a}, \quad x \neq a,$$

is a monotone-nondecreasing (or monotone-increasing) function of x on D.

PROOF:

Let x, y, and a be in D and suppose $y > x > a$. Then

$$\frac{x - a}{y - a} y + \left(1 - \frac{x - a}{y - a}\right) a = x.$$

Thus f is convex if and only if

$$\frac{x - a}{y - a} f(y) + \left(1 - \frac{x - a}{y - a}\right) f(a) \geq f(x)$$

or

$$\frac{f(y) - f(a)}{y - a} \geq \frac{f(x) - f(a)}{x - a}.$$

A similar argument holds for strict convexity and when $y < a < x$ or $a < x < y$.

Q.E.D.

---

[9] Proofs are given by Bourbaki [7, pp. 19–22].
[10] A set $B \subseteq D$ is dense in D if every x in $D - B$ is a limit point of B.

Lemma B.2-4 *Let f be convex on a closed interval D. At all points of the interior of D, f is continuous, has finite derivatives from the left and from the right and $f_l(x) \le f_r(x)$. At the left endpoint of D (if there is one), f_r is bounded from above and at the right end point, f_l is bounded from below.*

PROOF:

Let x, x', y, y', and a be in D such that $y' < y < a < x < x'$. Then from Lemma B.2-3,

$$\frac{f(y') - f(a)}{y' - a} \le \frac{f(y) - f(a)}{y - a} \le \frac{f(x) - f(a)}{x - a} \le \frac{f(x') - f(a)}{x' - a}.$$

Letting x and y approach a from above and below, respectively, f_l and f_r exist and

$$\frac{f(y') - f(a)}{y' - a} \le f_l(a) \le f_r(a) \le \frac{f(x') - f(a)}{x' - a}.$$

Thus if a is a left endpoint, f_r is bounded from above, and if a is a right endpoint, f_l is bounded from below. The existence of right and left derivatives at a in the interior of D imply the right and left continuity of f at a. Hence f is continuous at a.

Q.E.D.

Lemma B.2-5 *Let f be convex (or strictly convex) on D. If a and b are in the interior of D and $a < b$, then*

$$f_r(a) \le \frac{f(b) - f(a)}{b - a} \le f_l(b) \qquad \left[or \qquad f_r(a) < \frac{f(b) - f(a)}{b - a} < f_l(b) \right].$$

PROOF:

Let x and y be in D where $x > a$ and $y < b$. Then, as in the proof of Lemma B.2-4,

$$f_r(a) \le \frac{f(x) - f(a)}{x - a},$$

$$f_l(b) \ge \frac{f(y) - f(b)}{y - b}.$$

Setting $x = b$ and $y = a$ yields the desired inequality for convex f. Letting $x = y = c$, where $a < c < b$ in these two inequalities and noting

$$\frac{f(c) - f(a)}{c - a} < \frac{f(b) - f(a)}{b - a} = \frac{f(a) - f(b)}{a - b} < \frac{f(c) - f(b)}{c - b} = \frac{f(b) - f(c)}{b - c},$$

from Lemma B.2-3, gives the result for strict convexity.

Q.E.D.

Lemma B.2-6 *If f is convex (or strictly convex) on D, then*

(a) f_r *and* f_l *are monotone nondecreasing (or monotone increasing) in the interior of D,*

(b) *The set of points of D, where f is not differentiable [i.e., where* $f_r(x) \neq f_l(x)$], *is at most countable.*

PROOF:

(a) Let x and y be in D and $x < y$. Then by Lemmas B.2-4 and B.2-5,

$$f_l(x) \le f_r(x) \le f_l(y) \le f_r(y),$$

from which the conclusion follows. A similar argument holds for strict convexity.

(b) By Lemma B.2-4, $f_l(x) \le f_r(x)$ for all x in the interior of D. Let $A = \{x : f_l(x) < f_r(x)\}$ and for x in A, let I_x be the open interval $(f_l(x), f_r(x))$. Thus if a and b are in A and $a < b$, then $u < v$ for all u in I_a and v in I_b. Hence I_a and I_b are nonempty, disjoint, open intervals. Since there are only a countable number of such intervals on the real line, A must be countable.

Q.E.D.

Theorem B.2-7 *f is convex (or strictly convex) on an open interval D if and only if*

(a) *f is continuous on D.*

(b) *The derivative f' exists for all x in D − A, where A is at most countable.*

(c) *f' is monotone nondecreasing (or monotone increasing) on D − A.*

PROOF:

Necessity follows from Lemmas B.2-4 and B.2-6. To prove sufficiency suppose that (a)–(c) hold but f is not convex. By Lemma B.2-3, there are points a, b, and c in D such that $a < c < b$ and

$$\frac{f(c) - f(a)}{c - a} = \frac{f(a) - f(c)}{a - c} > \frac{f(b) - f(c)}{b - c}.$$

Let $m = \inf_{[c,b]-A} f'(x)$ and $M = \sup_{[a,c]-A} f'(x)$. Consider the function $g(x) = x$ on D. Then on $[c, b] - A$,

$$m = mg_r(x) \le f'(x) = f_r(x),$$

and on $[a, c] - A$,

$$f_r(x) = f'(x) \le Mg_r(x) = M.$$

Now, by Lemma B.2-2,

$$\frac{f(c) - f(a)}{c - a} \le M,$$

$$\frac{f(b) - f(c)}{b - c} \ge m,$$

which, from the above, implies $M > m$, contradicting the supposition that f' is monotone nondecreasing.

If f' is monotone increasing, then indeed f' is monotone nondecreasing, so by the above argument, f is convex. Thus if f were not strictly convex, it would have to have a linear segment on some interval $I \subseteq D$. But then f' would be constant on I, contrary to assumption.

Q.E.D.

Corollary B.2-8 *Let f be continuous and have a second derivative f'' on an open interval D.*

(a) *For f to be convex on D, it is necessary and sufficient that $f''(x) \geq 0$ for all x in D.*

(b) *For f to be strictly convex on D, it is necessary and sufficient that $f''(x) \geq 0$ for all x in D and $f''(x) > 0$ for all x in B, where B is a dense subset of D.*

This result follows immediately from Theorem B.2-7 and Lemma B.2-1. Note that strict convexity can never imply that $f''(x) > 0$ on all of D, as the example $f(x) = x^4$ shows. For in this case $f''(0) = 0$ even though f is strictly convex on the entire real line.

Of course, if f is a function of n variables, it is also a function of the single variable, say x_i, whenever the remaining variables are held fixed. Hence Theorem B.2-7 and Corollary B.2-8 apply with D appropriately redefined and f' and f'' replaced by the first- and second-order partial derivatives f_i and f_{ii}.

B.3 A DIGRESSION [11]

To prove many of the theorems in following sections, properties of directional derivatives and homogeneous-subadditive functions are needed. These preliminary results are given here.

The *right directional derivative* of f at a point x (an n-dimensional vector) in D in the direction y is defined as

$$f'(x; y) = \lim_{t \downarrow 0} \frac{f(x + ty) - f(x)}{t},$$

whenever this limit exists. The *left directional derivative* at x in the direction y is $-f'(x; -y)$. The *directional derivative* at x in the direction y is defined as $f'(x; y)$ whenever

$$f'(x; y) = -f'(x; -y).$$

[11] Most of the propositions in this section may be found in Bonnesen and Fenchel [6, pp. 15–28]. © Springer-Verlag, Berlin, 1934. Translated and reprinted by permission of Springer-Verlag.

If the directional derivative of f exists at x in all directions, then all partial derivatives of f exist at x.

Lemma B.3-1 *If at x in D, $f'(x; y)$ is a linear function of y for all directions y, then the partial derivatives f_i exist and*

$$f'(x; y) = \sum_{i=1}^{n} f_i(x) y_i,$$

for all y.

PROOF:

Since $f'(x; y)$ is linear in y,

$$f'(x; y) = \sum_{i=1}^{n} g^i(x) y_i,$$

for some functions g_i. Therefore, $f'(x; y) = -f'(x; -y)$ so the partial derivatives f_i exist at x. Let u^i be the vector with one in the ith position and zeros elsewhere. Then for each i,

$$f_i(x) = \lim_{t \to 0} \frac{f(x + tu^i) - f(x)}{t} = f'(x; u^i) = g^i(x).$$

Q.E.D.

This lemma does not imply that if $f'(x; y)$ is linear in y for all y, then f has a differential at x. (See Section B.4.)

A function g defined on Euclidean n-space (denoted by E^n) is said to be *homogeneous-subadditive* if and only if

(B.3-2) $g(\lambda x) = \lambda g(x)$,   for all real $\lambda \geq 0$ and x in E^n,

(B.3-3) $g(x + y) \leq g(x) + g(y)$,   for all x and y in E^n.

It is clear that homogeneous-subadditive functions are convex.

Let g be homogeneous-subadditive. A vector x in E^n is a *direction of linearity* of g provided (B.3-2) holds for all real λ, i.e., if

(B.3-4) $g(x) = -g(-x)$.

Lemma B.3-5 *Let g be homogeneous-subadditive on E^n. If x and y are directions of linearity of g, then so is $\lambda x + \mu y$ for any real λ and μ, and, furthermore,*

$$g(\lambda x + \mu y) = \lambda g(x) + \mu g(y).$$

PROOF:

Using (B.3-2) and (B.3-3),

$$0 = g(0) = g(\tfrac{1}{2} z + \tfrac{1}{2}(-z)) \leq \tfrac{1}{2} g(z) + \tfrac{1}{2} g(-z),$$

for any z. Setting $z = \lambda x + \mu y$ implies

$$-g(-\lambda x - \mu y) \leq g(\lambda x + \mu y).$$

But also using (B.3-2)–(B.3-4),

$$g(\lambda x + \mu y) \leq \lambda g(x) + \mu g(y)$$
$$= -g(-\lambda x) - g(-\mu y)$$
$$\leq -g(-\lambda x - \mu y),$$

which completes the proof.

Q.E.D.

Corollary B.3-6 *If $y^1, \ldots, y^m$ are directions of linearity of g, then so is $\sum_{i=1}^m \alpha_i y^i$ for all real numbers α_i and*

$$g\left(\sum_{i=1}^m \alpha_i y^i\right) = \sum_{i=1}^m \alpha_i g(y^i).$$

This corollary follows from Lemma B.3-5 and an easy induction argument on m.

Corollary B.3-7 *If g has n linearly independent directions of linearity, then*

$$g(x) = \sum_{i=1}^n k_i x_i,$$

where the k_i are constants.

PROOF:

Any x in E^n is a linear combination of any set of n linearly independent vectors. Hence by Corollary B.3-6 every x in E^n is a direction of linearity of g. In particular, this is true of the unit vectors u^i which have ones as their ith components and zeros elsewhere. Set $k_i = g(u^i)$ and note that for any x in E^n,

$$x = \sum_{i=1}^n x_i u^i.$$

Thus replacing y^i by u^i and α_i by x_i in Corollary B.3-6 gives the desired result.

Q.E.D.

The preceding corollary may be used to demonstrate that a function f which is both concave and convex on E^n must be *linear*; i.e.,

$$f(x) = \sum_{i=1}^n k_i x_i + b,$$

where b and the k_i are constants. For if $g(x) = f(x) - f(0)$, then simultaneous concavity and convexity of f implies g is homogeneous-subadditive and

$$g(\theta x' + (1 - \theta)x'') = \theta g(x') + (1 - \theta)g(x''),$$

for any x' and x'' in E^n and $0 \le \theta \le 1$. Setting $x' = x$, $x'' = -x$, and $\theta = \frac{1}{2}$ gives, since $g(0) = 0$,

$$g(x) = -g(-x),$$

for all x in E^n. Therefore, g has n linearly independent directions of linearity and the conclusion follows immediately upon application of Corollary B.3-7.

Lemma B.3-8 *If g is convex on E^n and $g'(x; y)$ exists for all y, then as a function of y, $g'(x; y)$ is homogeneous-subadditive (and hence convex) on E^n.*

PROOF:
For any $\lambda > 0$ and $t > 0$,

$$\frac{g(x + t\lambda y) - g(x)}{t} = \lambda \frac{g(x + t\lambda y) - g(x)}{\lambda t}.$$

Taking the limit as t approaches zero proves (B.3-2). If $\lambda = 0$ a similar argument holds. Now, replacing x' by $x + 2ty$ and x'' by $x + 2tz$ and setting $\theta = \frac{1}{2}$ in (B.1-1) gives, for $t > 0$,

$$g(x + t[y + z]) \le \tfrac{1}{2}g(x + 2ty) + \tfrac{1}{2}g(x + 2tz).$$

Subtracting $g(x)$ from both sides, dividing by t, and letting t approach zero proves (B.3-3).

Q.E.D.

Lemma B.3-9 *Let g be homogeneous-subadditive on E^n and suppose that $g'(x; y)$ exists for all y. If z is a direction of linearity of g, then z is also a direction of linearity of $g'(x; y)$ thought of as a function of y.*

PROOF:
The hypothesis implies that g is convex. Hence by Lemma B.3-8, $g'(x; y)$ as a function of y is homogeneous-subadditive. Now for any $t > 0$,

$$\begin{aligned}
2g(x) &= g([x + tz] + [x - tz]) \\
&\le g(x + tz) + g(x - tz) \\
&\le 2g(x),
\end{aligned}$$

by (B.3-2)–(B.3-4). Therefore,

$$\frac{g(x + tz) - g(x)}{t} = -\frac{g(x - tz) - g(x)}{t},$$

so, as t approaches zero,

$$g'(x; z) = -g'(x; -z).$$

Q.E.D.

Lemma B.3-10 *Let* g *be homogeneous-subadditive on* E^n *and suppose* $g'(x; y)$ *exists for all* y. *Then*

(a) $g'(x; y) \leq g(y)$ *for all* y.
(b) x *is a direction of linearity of* $g'(x; y)$ *thought of as a function of* y *and*

$$g'(x; x) = -g'(x; -x) = g(x).$$

PROOF:

Using (B.3-2) and (B.3-3), for any $t > 0$,

$$\frac{g(x + ty) - g(x)}{t} \leq \frac{g(x) + g(ty) - g(x)}{t} = g(y).$$

Letting t go to zero proves (a). To prove (b) note that for $0 < t < 1$,

$$g(x + tx) + g(x - tx) = 2g(x),$$

so

$$\frac{g(x + tx) - g(x)}{t} = -\frac{g(x - tx) - g(x)}{t},$$

from which it follows that

$$g'(x; x) = -g'(x; -x).$$

Also

$$g'(x; x) = \lim_{t \downarrow 0} \frac{g([1 + t]x) - g(x)}{t}$$
$$= \lim_{t \downarrow 0} g(x)$$
$$= g(x).$$

Q.E.D.

Note that the last part of Lemma B.3-10 is a statement of Euler's theorem.

B.4 CONTINUITY AND DIFFERENTIABILITY[12]

The aim of this section is to prove continuity and existence of first-order derivatives of convex functions. Once again D is a convex subset of E^n and f is defined on it.

Lemma B.4-1 *Let* $x^1, \ldots, x^m$ *be in* D *and* $\lambda_1, \ldots, \lambda_m$ *be nonnegative real numbers such that* $\sum_{i=1}^{m} \lambda_i = 1$. *If* f *is convex in* D *then*

$$f\left(\sum_{i=1}^{m} \lambda_i x^i \right) \leq \sum_{i=1}^{m} \lambda_i f(x^i).$$

[12] This section follows in part the development in Fenchel [9]. See especially pp. 58, 59, 61, 62, 74, 75, 79–82, 85–87.

PROOF:

The argument proceeds by induction. If $\lambda_1 = 1$ or if $m = 1$, the lemma is trivial. Thus suppose $\lambda_1 < 1$ and assume the lemma true for $m - 1$. Then

$$f\left(\sum_{i=1}^{m} \lambda_i x^i\right) = f\left(\lambda_1 x^1 + (1 - \lambda_1)\sum_{i=2}^{m} \frac{\lambda_i}{1 - \lambda_1} x^i\right),$$

which, since f is convex,

$$\leq \lambda_1 f(x^1) + (1 - \lambda_1) f\left(\sum_{i=2}^{m} \frac{\lambda_i}{1 - \lambda_1} x^i\right).$$

Upon application of the induction hypothesis, this becomes

$$f\left(\sum_{i=1}^{m} \lambda_i x^i\right) \leq \lambda_1 f(x^1) + (1 - \lambda_1)\sum_{i=2}^{m} \frac{\lambda_i}{1 - \lambda_1} f(x^i)$$

$$= \sum_{i=1}^{m} \lambda_i f(x^i).$$

Q.E.D.

Lemma B.4-2 *Let D' be a compact subset of D. If f is convex on D, then f is bounded from above on D'.*

PROOF:

By the Heine–Borel theorem [12, pp. 52, 146], D' can be covered by a finite number of n-simplexes $A_1, \ldots, A_m$, where $A_j \subseteq D$ for each j. If $v^{0j}, \ldots, v^{nj}$ are the vertices of A_j, and if x is in A_j, then

$$x = \sum_{i=0}^{n} \lambda_i v^{ij},$$

for some set of nonnegative numbers $\lambda_0, \ldots, \lambda_n$ such that $\sum_{i=0}^{n} \lambda_i = 1$. By Lemma B.4-1,

$$f(x) \leq \sum_{i=0}^{n} \lambda_i f(v^{ij}).$$

Let $M_j = \max_i f(v^{ij})$. Then $f(x) \leq M_j$ for all x in A_j. Thus setting $M = \max_j M_j$, $f(x) \leq M$ for all x in D'.

Q.E.D.

Lemma B.4-3 *If f is convex on D, it is bounded from below on every bounded subset of D.*

PROOF:

Let $A \subseteq D$ be bounded. Let x^0 be in the relative interior of D. Then there is a number M_1 such that $|y - x^0| < M_1$ for all y in A.

Let $\delta > 0$ be sufficiently small so that the closed ball $B = \{x: |x - x^0| \leq \delta\}$ is contained in the relative interior of D. Let y be in A and let z be on the line segment joining y and x^0 such that $|z - x^0| = \delta$ and z is not between x^0 and y. Then z is in B and

$$x^0 = \frac{\delta}{|y - x^0| + \delta} y + \frac{|y - x^0|}{|y - x^0| + \delta} z.$$

Since B is compact, by Lemma B.4-2 there is a number M_2 such that $f(z) \leq M_2$ on B. Hence by the convexity of f and the fact that $|y - x^0| < M_1$,

$$f(x^0) \leq \frac{\delta}{|y - x^0| + \delta} f(y) + \frac{M_1 M_2}{|y - x^0| + \delta}.$$

Therefore,

$$\delta f(y) \geq (|y - x^0| + \delta)(f(x^0) - M_1 M_2)$$

$$\geq \begin{cases} -M_1 M_2, & \text{if } f(x^0) \geq 0, \\ (M_1 + \delta)(f(x^0) - M_1 M_2), & \text{if } f(x^0) < 0. \end{cases}$$

Q.E.D.

Lemma B.4-4 *Let B be the unit ball having the same dimensionality as D. Let D' be a compact subset in the relative interior of D and let $\delta > 0$ be such that $D'' = D' + \delta B$ is also in the relative interior[13] of D. If f is convex on D, then there exist numbers M and m such that for any x in D' and y for which $|y| \leq \delta$,*

$$|f(x + y) - f(x)| \leq \frac{M - m}{\delta} |y|.$$

PROOF:

If $y = 0$, the lemma is trivial. If $y \neq 0$, then by Lemmas B.4-2 and B.4-3, there exist numbers M and m such that

$$m \leq f(x) \leq M,$$

for all x in D'. Consider x in D' and $|y| \leq \delta$. Then $x + y$ is in D'' and as a function of the scalar variable t, $f(x + ty)$ is convex in the interval

$$-\frac{\delta}{|y|} \leq t \leq \frac{\delta}{|y|}.$$

By Lemma B.2-3, for any t in this interval,

$$\frac{f(x) - f(x - [\delta/|y|]y)}{\delta} |y| \leq \frac{f(x + ty) - f(x)}{t} \leq \frac{f(x + [\delta/|y|]y) - f(x)}{\delta} |y|.$$

---

[13] Here $D'' = \{x + \delta b: x \text{ is in } D' \text{ and } b \text{ is in } B\}$.

In particular, at $t = 1$,

$$-\frac{M - m}{\delta} |y| \le f(x + y) - f(x) \le \frac{M + m}{\delta} |y|,$$

from which the desired inequality follows.

Q.E.D.

Theorem B.4-5 *If f is convex on D, then it is continuous in the relative interior of D.*

PROOF:

Let x^0 be in the relative interior of D. Then there is a $\delta_1 > 0$ such that the ball $B = \{y: |y - x^0| \le \delta_1\}$ is also contained in the relative interior of D. By Lemmas B.4-2 and B.4-3 there exist numbers M and m such that

$$m \le f(x) \le M,$$

for all x in B. If $m = M$, then f is constant on B and continuous at x^0.

If $m < M$, let $\epsilon > 0$ be given. Choose

$$\delta = \min\left(\delta_1, \frac{\epsilon \delta_1}{M - m}\right).$$

Then if $|y| < \delta$, by Lemma B.4-4,

$$|f(x^0 + y) - f(x^0)| \le \frac{M - m}{\delta_1} |y|$$

$$< \frac{M - m}{\delta_1} \frac{\epsilon \delta_1}{M - m}$$

$$= \epsilon.$$

Q.E.D.

Let A be a set and consider points x contained in it. The *ray* from any point z through x in A is given by

$$r_x = \{(1 - \theta)z + \theta x: \theta \ge 0\}.$$

Define the *projecting cone* of A from z as

$$P_z(A) = \bigcup_A r_x.$$

Lemma B.4-6 *If f is convex on D, then the right directional derivative $f'(x; y)$ exists and is either finite or $-\infty$ for any x in D and y such that $x + y$ is in $P_x(D)$. Also $f'(x; y)$ is finite in the relative interior of D.*

PROOF:

If x is in D and y is such that $x + y$ is in $P_x(D)$, then $f'(x; y)$ is the right derivative of $f(x + ty)$ thought of as a function of the scalar variable t evaluated at $t = 0$. Since $f(x + ty)$ is defined and convex in some interval $0 \leq t < t^0$, $f'(x; y)$ exists and is bounded from above by Lemma B.2-4. When x is in the relative interior of D, then $f(x + ty)$ is defined and convex on some interval containing $t = 0$ in its interior. Hence by Lemma B.2-4, $f'(x; y) > -\infty$.

Q.E.D.

Lemma B.4-7 *If f is convex on D, then*[14]

$$f(x) \geq f(x^0) + f'(x^0; x - x^0),$$

for all x^0 and x in D.

PROOF:

By Lemma B.4-6 either $f'(x^0; x - x^0)$ is finite or $-\infty$. In the latter case there is nothing to prove. Otherwise, let x^0 and x be in D. Then as a function of t alone, $f(x^0 + t[x - x^0])$ is convex on $0 \leq t \leq 1$. Hence by Lemma B.2-3,

$$\frac{f(x^0 + t[x - x^0]) - f(x^0)}{t} \geq f'(x^0; x - x^0),$$

and setting $t = 1$ completes the proof.

Q.E.D.

The function f defined on D is said to have a *differential* at x^0 in the relative interior of D provided there exists a function (the differential) $d(x^0; z)$ defined for each z in E^n such that d is linear in z and for any $\epsilon > 0$ there is a $\delta > 0$ such that whenever $|y - x^0| < \delta$,

$$|f(y) - f(x^0) - d(x^0; y - x^0)| < \epsilon |y - x^0|.$$

If f has a differential at x^0, then all partial derivatives f_i exist at x^0 and [2, pp. 107–109]

$$d(x^0; z) = f'(x^0; z) = \sum_{i=1}^{n} f_i(x^0) z_i.$$

Lemma B.4-8 *Let f be convex on D and x^0 a point in its relative interior. If $f'(x^0; y)$ is a linear function of y for all directions y, then f has a differential at x^0.*

---

[14] Apart from the strict convexity, this lemma differs from Lemma B.1-2 in that differentiability of f is not assumed.

PROOF:

Let $A = \{u: |u| = 1\}$ and $B = \{y: y_i = \pm 1$ for $i = 1, \ldots, n\}$. Then B has 2^n elements; i.e., $B = \{y^1, \ldots, y^{2^n}\}$. The convex hull of B is $C = \{x: x = \sum_{i=1}^{2^n} \lambda_i y^i$, where $\sum_{i=1}^{2^n} \lambda_i = 1$ and for each i, $\lambda_i \geq 0$ and y^i is in $B\}$. Note that $A \subseteq C$.

Let $\epsilon > 0$ be given. Since $f'(x^0; y^i)$ exists and is finite for the direction y^i in B (Lemma B.4-6), there is a $\delta_i > 0$ such that for $0 < t < \delta_i$,

$$f(x^0 + ty^i) - f(x^0) - tf'(x^0; y^i) \leq \epsilon t.$$

Now the expression left of the inequality is nonnegative by Lemma B.4-7 and the linearity in y of $f'(x^0; y)$. Hence

(B.4-9) $$|f(x^0 + ty^i) - f(x^0) - tf'(x^0; y^i)| \leq \epsilon t.$$

Repeat this argument for each y^i in B and let $\delta = \min_i \delta_i$. Then (B.4-9) holds for all $0 < t < \delta$ and y^i in B.

Now, since f is convex and since from Lemma B.3-8, $f'(x^0; -ty) = -tf'(x^0; y)$ is a convex function of y, $f(x^0 + ty) - f(x^0) - tf'(x^0; y)$ is also a convex function of y. Thus if y is in C, Lemma B.4-1 together with (B.4-9) imply that for $0 < t < \delta$,

$$|f(x^0 + ty) - f(x^0) - tf'(x^0; y)| \leq \left| \sum_{i=1}^{2^n} \lambda_i [f(x^0 + ty^i) - f(x^0) - tf'(x^0; y^i)] \right|$$

$$\leq \left| \sum_{i=1}^{2^n} \lambda_i \epsilon t \right|$$

$$= \epsilon |t|.$$

Since $A \subseteq C$, this is true for all points of A. But because $|u| = 1$ and $f'(x^0; y)$ is linear in y, it follows that for all u in A and $0 < t < \delta$,

(B.4-10) $$|f(x^0 + tu) - f(x^0) - f'(x^0; tu)| \leq \epsilon |tu|.$$

Replacing t and u by $-t$ and $-u$, and noting that the inequality trivially holds for $t = 0$ leads to the conclusion that (B.4-10) is valid for all u in A and $|t| < \delta$.

Q.E.D.

The function f defined on D is *lower semicontinuous* at x^0 in D if and only if $\lim \inf_{x \to x^0} f(x) = f(x^0)$. It is *upper semicontinuous* there if $\lim \sup_{x \to x^0} f(x) = f(x^0)$. Clearly f is continuous at x^0 if and only if it is both upper and lower semicontinuous at x^0 [12, p. 63].

Theorem B.4-11 *Let f be convex on a relatively open convex set D of dimension $m \leq n$. Let y be a vector in the linear manifold L of smallest dimension containing D. Then $f'(x; y)$ is an upper semicontinuous function of x*

*on D. The differential of f for any direction y in L exists everywhere in D with
the possible exception of a subset of m-dimensional Lebesque measure zero.
Where it exists, the differential is a continuous function of x.*

PROOF:

Let y be in L. Since f is continuous in the relative interior of D (Theorem
B.4-5),

$$G_t(x) = \frac{f(x + [1/t]y) - f(x)}{1/t},$$

as a function of x is also continuous there. But the G_t are nondecreasing as
$t \to \infty$ (Lemma B.2-3) and

$$f'(x; y) = \lim_{t \to \infty} G_t(x)$$

always exists (Lemma B.4-6). Therefore, as a function of x, $f'(x; y)$ is upper
semicontinuous [12, p. 130].

Now, as a function of y, $f'(x; y)$ is homogeneous-subadditive (Lemma
B.3-8). Hence

$$f'(x; y) + f'(x; -y) > f'(x; 0) = 0.$$

Let $A = \{x : f'(x; y) + f'(x; -y) > 0\}$. Then A is measurable. By Lemma
B.4-8 the differential of f exists and equals $f'(x; y)$ provided x is not in A.
It is now shown that A has zero measure.

As a function of t, $f(x + ty)$ has a derivative except possibly on a countable
set (Theorem B.2-7). Hence the intersection of A with any line in D parallel
to the vector y must be at most countable. By Fubini's theorem A has zero
measure [12, p. 218].

Finally, in the same manner that $f'(x; y)$ is upper semicontinuous at x, it
follows that $-f'(x; -y)$ is lower semicontinuous at x. But for x not in A,
$f'(x; y) = -f'(x; -y)$, so $f'(x; y)$ is continuous on $D - A$.

Q.E.D.

Corollary B.4-12 *If f is convex on an open convex set D, then f is continuously
differentiable except possibly for a set of measure zero on D.*

This result follows immediately from Theorem B.4-11.

It is also true that convex functions have second-order differentials except
possibly for a set of zero measure. For functions of one variable this follows
immediately from Theorem B.2-7, part (c). For functions of several variables
the proof is complicated and not presented here.[15]

---

[15] See Alexandroff [1].

B.5 HESSIANS[16]

Let f be defined on an open, convex set D and have continuous partial derivatives of the second order everywhere in D. At each x in D the *Hessian matrix* of f is given by

$$F(x) = \begin{bmatrix} f_{11}(x) & \cdots & f_{1n}(x) \\ \vdots & & \vdots \\ f_{n1}(x) & \cdots & f_{nn}(x) \end{bmatrix},$$

where f_{ij} is the second-order partial derivative of f with respect to its ith and then jth arguments. If for all vectors $y \neq 0$ the matrix product

$$yF(x)y' = \sum_{i,j=1}^{n} f_{ij}(x)y_i y_j > 0,$$

where y' denotes the transpose of y, then $F(x)$ is called *positive definite*. If only the weak inequality "$\geq$" holds, $F(x)$ is *positive semidefinite*. Reversing the inequalities, F becomes, respectively, *negative definite* and *semidefinite*. Attention is now focused on characterizing convexity in terms of the definiteness of F.

Theorem B.5-1   *If f is strictly convex on D, then F is positive semidefinite there.*

PROOF:

Let x be in D and let y be a given direction. Then there is a $\delta_1 > 0$ such that $x + ty$ is in D for all $0 < t < \delta_1$. For these values of t, Lemma B.1-2 implies

$$f(x + ty) - f(x) - t\sum_{i=1}^{n} f_i(x)y_i > 0.$$

By the mean value theorem, for each t there is a t' such that this inequality may be written

$$t\sum_{i=1}^{n} [f_i(x + t'y) - f_i(x)]y_i > 0$$

where $0 < t' < t$. A second application of the mean value theorem yields a t'' where $0 < t'' < t'$ such that

$$tt'\sum_{i,j=1}^{n} f_{ij}(x + t''y)y_i y_j > 0.$$

Thus, since $tt' > 0$,

$$\sum_{i,j=1}^{n} f_{ij}(x + t''y)y_i y_j > 0.$$

[16] The results in this section are due to Bernstein and Toupin [4].

Now as t approaches zero, so does t''. Since the second partial derivatives of f are continuous,

$$\sum_{i,j=1}^{n} f_{ij}(x)y_iy_j = \lim_{t''\to 0}\sum_{i,j=1}^{n} f_{ij}(x + t''y)y_iy_j \geq 0.$$

Since y was arbitrary, the theorem is proved.

Q.E.D.

The conclusion of Theorem B.5-1 holds if f is assumed to be only convex.

Theorem B.5-2 *If F is positive definite on D, then f is strictly convex there.*

PROOF:

Let x' and x'' be distinct points of D. Set $y = (x' - x'')$ so, since D is convex, $x'' + ty$ is in D for all $0 \leq t \leq 1$. As in the proof of Theorem B.5-1, for each such t, there are numbers t' and t'', where $0 < t'' < t' < t$, such that

$$f(x') - f(x'') - \sum_{i=1}^{n} f_i(x'')(x'_i - x''_i) = tt'\sum_{i,j=1}^{n} f_{ij}(x'' + t''y)y_iy_j.$$

Since the right side of this equality is positive by hypothesis, Lemma B.1-2 implies that f is strictly convex.

Q.E.D.

Clearly Theorem B.5-2 is still valid if the words "positive definite" and "strictly convex" are replaced by "positive semidefinite" and "convex," respectively. This and previous remarks show that f is convex if and only if its Hessian is positive semidefinite. In view of the definitions given in Section B.1, analogous assertions can be made for concave functions. Thus f is concave if and only if F is negative semidefinite, and if F is negative definite, then f is strictly concave. The implications of strict convexity are now considered further.

A set $S \subseteq E^n$ is *nowhere dense* in E^n if for every nonempty open set $A \subseteq E^n$ there is a nonempty open subset $A' \subseteq A$ such that $A' \cap S = \varnothing$.

Lemma B.5-3 *Let g be continuous on D and set $S = \{x: g(x) = 0$, where x is in D\}. Then S contains no nonempty, open subset if and only if S is nowhere dense in E^n.*

PROOF:

If S is nowhere dense in E^n, then clearly S cannot contain a nonempty, open subset. Conversely, suppose S contains no nonempty, open subset. Let

$A \subseteq E^n$ be nonempty and open. If $A \cap D = \varnothing$, choose $A' = A$. Then since $S \subseteq D$, $S \cap A' = \varnothing$.

If $A \cap D \neq \varnothing$, then $A \cap \Delta \neq \varnothing$, where Δ is the interior of D. Now there must exist an x in $A \cap \Delta$ such that $g(x) \neq 0$, for otherwise $A \cap \Delta$ would be an open subset of S. Since g is continuous, there is an open neighborhood $N_x \subseteq A \cap \Delta$ on which $g(x) \neq 0$. Therefore, $N_x \cap S = \varnothing$ and $N_x \subseteq A$.

Q.E.D.

Lemma B.5-4 *Let* $h = (h^1, \ldots, h^n)$ *be a continuously differentiable vector of functions, each defined on* D. *If* h *is* 1:1, *then the Jacobian of* h *[denoted by* $J_h(x)$*] cannot vanish on any open subset of* D.

PROOF:

Let S be an open subset of D. If $J_h(x) = 0$ on S, then the components of h are functionally dependent on compact subsets of S [16, p. 183]. Let C be such a compact subset which contains an open set C'. Then $h(C')$ is nowhere dense in E^n [16, p. 183]. But h is 1:1 and continuous on C, so h^{-1} must be continuous on $h(C)$ [16, p. 166]. Therefore, $h(C')$ must be open and this is a contradiction.

Q.E.D.

Theorem B.5-5 *If* f *is strictly convex on an open, convex set* D, *then, except possibly on a nowhere dense subset, its Hessian matrix is positive definite on* D.

PROOF:

By Theorem B.5-1, the Hessian matrix $F(x)$ is positive semidefinite on D. Hence it is positive definite where its determinant does not vanish. Let $h = (f_1, \ldots, f_n)$, where the f_i are partial derivatives of f. Then, by Lemma B.1-5, h is 1:1. Hence Lemmas B.5-3 and B.5-4 imply that the Jacobian of h, namely the determinant of $F(x)$, can vanish on at most a nowhere dense subset of D.

Q.E.D.

Theorem B.5-5 cannot be strengthened to assert that F is positive definite everywhere for the same reason that Corollary B.2-8(b) could not be strengthened to $f''(x) > 0$ on D. Furthermore, its converse holds without further qualification only when $n = 1$ [i.e., when Theorem B.5-5 and Corollary B.2-8(b) are identical]. To see that this is not true in general, suppose $n = 2$, $D = \{(x_1, x_2): x_2 < 0\}$, and

$$f(x) = x_1^2(1 + e^{x_2}).$$

Now the determinant of f's Hessian matrix is

$$|F(x)| = 2x_1^2 e^{x_2}(1 - e^{x_2}),$$

which is positive throughout D except on the line $x_1 = 0$ where it vanishes. Hence F satisfies the conclusion of Theorem B.5-5. But if x' and x'' are any distinct points of D whose first coordinate is zero, then $f(x') = f(x'') = 0$ and $f_i(x'') = 0$ for $i = 1, 2$. Therefore by Lemma B.1-2, f cannot be strictly convex. Additional qualifications are now introduced to obtain a valid converse of Theorem B.5-5.

A vector α *annihilates* $F(x)$ at x provided

$$\sum_{j=1}^{n} f_{ij}(x)\alpha_j = 0, \quad i = 1, \ldots, n.$$

Let $\Gamma(t)$ be any smooth curve parametrized by t.[17] The *tangent vector* of Γ at $t = t^0$ is the vector $\gamma(t^0)$ consisting of the derivatives of the n components of Γ with respect to t.

Lemma B.5-6 *If f is strictly convex on D, then for any smooth curve $\Gamma \subseteq D$, the tangent vector of Γ does not annihilate F on any nonempty, open subset of Γ.*

PROOF:

Let f be strictly convex on D and suppose $\Gamma \subseteq D$ is a smooth curve such that there exists a nonempty, open subset $B \subseteq \Gamma$ on which the tangent vector of Γ annihilates F. Parametrize Γ between any x^0 in B and distinct y in Γ as follows: $x = \Gamma(t)$ for $0 \le t \le 1$, where $y = \Gamma(0)$ and $x^0 = \Gamma(1)$. Because B is open there exists a closed interval $[t', 1]$ on which $\Gamma(t') \ne \Gamma(1)$ and $\Gamma(t)$ is in B for $0 \le t' \le t \le 1$. Set $x' = \Gamma(t')$ and note that $x' \ne x^0$. Application of the fundamental theorem for line integrals [2, p. 280] now yields

$$f_i(x^0) - f_i(x') = \int_{t'}^{1} \sum_{j=1}^{n} f_{ij}(\Gamma(t))\gamma_j(t)dt, \quad i = 1, \ldots, n.$$

By supposition, the integrand is zero. Hence $f_i(x^0) = f_i(x')$, contrary to Lemma B.1-5.

Q.E.D.

Lemma B.5-7 *If $F(x)$ is positive semidefinite on D, and if there is no straight-line segment Γ in D containing a nonempty, open (in Γ) subset B on which the tangent vector to Γ annihilates F, then F is strictly convex.*

[17] See Apostol [2, p. 233].

PROOF:

Since D is convex it contains the line segment Γ joining any distinct x^0 and x' in D. Parametrize Γ by its arc length s and let u be unit vectors tangent to Γ whose directions run from x' to x^0. Set $|x' - x^0| = \delta$. Then

$$\sum_{i=1}^{n} [f_i(x^0) - f_i(x')](x_i^0 - x_i') = \delta \sum_{i=1}^{n} [f_i(x^0) - f_i(x')]u_i$$

$$= \delta \sum_{i=1}^{n} \left[\int_0^\delta \sum_{j=1}^{n} f_{ij}(\Gamma(s))\gamma_j(s)ds \right]u_i,$$

and since Γ is linear and parametrized by its arc length,

$$= \delta \int_0^\delta \left[\sum_{i,j=1}^{n} f_{ij}(\Gamma(s))u_i u_j \right]ds.$$

By hypothesis the above integrand must be nonnegative everywhere and positive at some s^0 between zero and δ. But it is also continuous and thus positive on a subinterval of $[0, \delta]$ containing s^0. Therefore, the integral itself is positive, and by Lemma B.1-4, f is strictly convex.

Q.E.D.

Lemma B.5-8   *If F is positive semidefinite on D and if for any straight-line segment $\Gamma \subseteq D$ the set of points $B \subseteq L$ on which the tangent to Γ annihilates F is nowhere dense in Γ, then f is strictly convex.*

This lemma is an obvious consequence of Lemmas B.5-3 and B.5-1. The following two theorems are equally obvious consequences of Lemmas B.5-6 and B.5-8.

Theorem B.5-9   *For f to be strictly convex on D it is necessary and sufficient that F be positive semidefinite on D and for any straight-line segment $\Gamma \subseteq D$ the set of points in Γ at which the tangent vector of Γ annihilates F be nowhere dense in Γ.*

Theorem B.5-10   *For f to be strictly convex on D it is necessary and sufficient that F be positive semidefinite on D and for any smooth curve $\Gamma \subseteq D$ the set of points in Γ at which the tangent vector of Γ annihilates F be nowhere dense in Γ.*

B.6 SUPPORT FUNCTIONS[18]

In this section support functions of convex sets are defined and their properties studied. Throughout, K will denote a given, closed bounded,

[18] This section is based on Bonnesen and Fenchel [6, pp. 15–28]. © Springer-Verlag, Berlin, 1934. Translated and reprinted by permission of Springer-Verlag.

convex subset of E^n. Let u be a direction in E^n. Then the inner-product equation $u \cdot x = c$, for each scalar c, defines a hyperplane in E^n. The *supporting plane* of K with respect to u (written $T_{K,u}$) is the plane normal to u and tangent to K; i.e., $T_{K,u} = \{x: u \cdot x = c, \text{ where } u \cdot y \le c \text{ for all } y \text{ in } K \text{ and } u \cdot y = c \text{ for at least one } y \text{ in } K\}$. Note that $T_{K,u}$ is uniquely defined for each u. A supporting plane of K is called *regular* whenever it has only one point in common with K.

Let $A = \{u: |u| = 1\}$ and let B be the set of boundary points of K. Define the (possibly multivalued) function g mapping A into B by $g(u) = T_{K,u} \cap K$.

Lemma B.6-1 *If K has only regular supporting planes, then g is single valued and continuous.*

PROOF:

If K has only regular supporting planes, then g is clearly single valued. Consider a sequence $\{u_n\}$ in A converging to u^0 in A. Let $x_n = g(u_n)$ and $x^0 = g(u^0)$. Since B is compact and contains each x_n, the sequence $\{x_n\}$ has a limit point x' in B. Hence there is a subsequence $\{x_{n_r}\}$ converging to x' [16, p. 38].

Now x' in B implies that

$$u^0 \cdot x' < u^0 \cdot x^0.$$

On the other hand,

$$u_{n_r} \cdot x^0 \le u_{n_r} \cdot x_{n_r},$$

where $x_{n_r} = g(u_{n_r})$. Passing to the limit and noting $\{u_{n_r}\}$ converges[19] to u^0,

$$u^0 \cdot x^0 \le u^0 \cdot x'.$$

Thus

$$u^0 \cdot x^0 = u^0 \cdot x',$$

whence x' is in T_{K,u^0}. But g is single valued and hence $x' = x^0$. Since this argument is valid for all limit points of $\{x_n\}$, the latter must converge to x^0 and g is therefore continuous.

Q.E.D.

The *support function* H_K of K is defined by

$$H_K(u) = \max_K u \cdot x,$$

for all u in E^n, where the maximum is taken over all x in K. Thus for each u^0 the support function "picks out" the supporting plane T_{K,u^0}, viz., $u^0 \cdot x = H_K(u^0)$. Since K is compact, $u \cdot x$ achieves its maximum on K so H_K is well defined and single valued. Also, if $|u^0| = 1$, then $H_K(u^0)$ gives the length of the normal from the origin to T_{K,u^0}. An example is illustrated in Figure B.1.

---

[19] This follows since $\{u_n\}$ converges uniquely to u^0. See Rudin [16, p. 36].

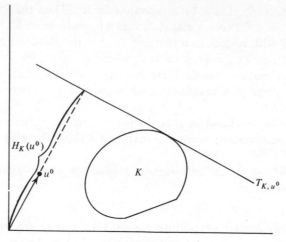

FIGURE B.1

Note that if K and the origin lie on the same side of T_{K,u^0}, then $H_K(u^0) > 0$. If T_{K,u^0} separates K and the origin, $H_K(u^0) < 0$, and $H_K(u^0) = 0$ if and only if the origin is a point of T_{K,u^0}.

The *half-space* $E_{K,u}$ is given by $E_{K,u} = \{x: u \cdot x \leq H_K(u)\}$ for each u in E^n.

Lemma B.6-2 $K = \bigcap_{E^n} E_{K,u}$, *where the intersection is taken over all u in E^n.*

PROOF:

If x is in K, then $u \cdot x \leq H_K(u)$ for each u. Hence x is in every $E_{K,u}$, so $K \subseteq \bigcap_{E^n} E_{K,u}$. Conversely, if x^0 is in $E_{K,u}$ for all u, then x^0 is in K. For if not, it follows from the separating hyperplane theory [14, pp. 397–398] that there exists a vector u' for which $u' \cdot x^0 > H_K(u')$, contrary to the hypothesis that x^0 is in $E_{K,u'}$.

Q.E.D.

Lemma B.6-3   *The support function of a set containing a single point is a linear function of u.*

PROOF:

If $K = \{x^0\}$, then for any u,

$$H_K(u) = \max_K u \cdot x = u \cdot x^0,$$

which is linear in u.

Q.E.D.

Lemma B.6-4 (a) *If $K' = K + a$, where a is some vector in E^n, then $H_{K'}(u) \le H_K(u) + u \cdot a$ for all u.*
(b) *If L is compact and convex and if $K \subseteq L$, then $H_K(u) \le H_L(u)$ for all u.*

PROOF:
To prove (a) note that

$$H_{K'}(u) = \max_{K'} u \cdot x = \max_K u \cdot (x + a)$$

$$= \max_K u \cdot x + u \cdot a$$

$$= H_K(u) + u \cdot a.$$

The proof of (b) is trivial.

Q.E.D.

Lemma B.6-5 *$H_K(u)$ is homogeneous-subadditive (and hence convex[20]) on E^n.*

PROOF:
For $\lambda \ge 0$ and any u in E^n,

$$H_K(\lambda u) = \max_K (\lambda u) \cdot x = \lambda \max_K u \cdot x = \lambda H_K(u).$$

For any u and v in E^n,

$$H_K(u + v) = \max_K (u + v) \cdot x \le \max_K u \cdot x + \max_K v \cdot x$$

$$\le H_K(u) + H_K(v).$$

Q.E.D.

Lemma B.6-6 *Let H be any homogeneous-subadditive function defined on E^n and set $K = \bigcap_{E^n} \{x : u \cdot x \le H(u)\}$ where the intersection is taken over all u in E^n. Then*
(a) *$K \ne \varnothing$.*
(b) *K is compact and convex.*
(c) *H is the support function of K.*

PROOF:
If $H(u) = u \cdot x^0$ for some x^0 and all u, then $K = \{x^0\}$ and, by Lemma B.6-3, H is the support function of K. The general case in which this supposition is not valid is now considered.

(a) Let $u^1, \ldots, u^r$ be linearly independent directions of linearity of H. Note that $0 \le r \le n$. If $r = n$, then by Corollary B.3-7, H is linear in u so $K \ne \varnothing$ by the above. If $r = n - 1$, let u^n be an arbitrary direction which is linearly independent of $u^1, \ldots, u^r$. Now, as in Lemma B.4-6, the right directional derivative $H'(u^n; u)$ exists for all u in E^n. Write $\bar{H}(u) = H'(u^n; u)$.

---

[20] That H_K is convex alone follows from Lemma B.1-6.

Then by Lemmas B.3-9 and B.3-10, $u^1, \ldots, u^n$ are n linearly independent directions of linearity of $\bar{H}$. Therefore, by the argument given above for the case $r = n$,

$$\bigcap_{E^n} \{x : u \cdot x \le \bar{H}(u)\} \ne \varnothing.$$

But by Lemma B.3-10, $\bar{H}(u) \le H(u)$ for all u. Hence

$$K = \bigcap_{E^n} \{x : u \cdot x \le H(u)\} \ne \varnothing.$$

Using the same argument successively for $r = n - 2$, $r = n - 3, \ldots$, and finally $r = 0$, proves the first assertion.

(b) Let x and y be in K. Then $u \cdot x \le H(u)$ and $u \cdot y \le H(u)$ for all u. If $0 \le \theta \le 1$, then for all u,

$$\begin{aligned} u \cdot (\theta x + [1 - \theta]y) &= \theta(u \cdot x) + [1 - \theta](u \cdot y) \\ &\le \theta H(u) + [1 - \theta]H(u) \\ &= H(u). \end{aligned}$$

Therefore, $\theta x + [1 - \theta]y$ is in K, so K is convex.

Since $\{x : u \cdot x \le H(u)\}$ is closed for each u, K is closed [16, p. 27]. To show that K is bounded and hence compact, note that H is convex. By Theorem B.4-5, H is continuous on $A = \{u : |u| = 1\}$. Hence there exists a number M such that $H(u) \le M$ for all u in A. Therefore,

$$K \subseteq \{x : u \cdot x \le M, \text{ where } u \text{ is in } A\}.$$

Now if $x \ne 0$ and x is in K, then $x/|x|$ is in A and hence $(x/|x|) \cdot x \le M$. Thus

$$|x| = \frac{x}{|x|} \cdot x \le M,$$

so K is bounded.

(c) To prove the last assertion, it suffices to show that for each u there is an x in K such that $u \cdot x = H(u)$. Thus let u^0 be given. By Lemmas B.3-8–B.3-10, for all u, $H'(u^0; u)$ exists and $H'(u^0; u) \le H(u)$. Then, letting $K' = \bigcap_{E^n} \{x : u \cdot x \le H'(u^0; u)\}$, where the intersection is taken over all u in E^n, gives $K' \subseteq K$. Now by (a) above, $K' \ne \varnothing$ and so there is an x^0 in K' such that

$$u \cdot x^0 \le H'(u^0; u),$$

for all u. Setting $u = u^0$ and then $u = -u^0$ yields

$$-H'(u^0; -u^0) \le u^0 \cdot x^0 \le H'(u^0; u^0).$$

Since $H(u^0) = -H'(u^0; -u^0) = H'(u^0; u^0)$ by Lemma B.3-10,

$$u^0 \cdot x^0 = H(u^0).$$

Q.E.D.

Now define the set $k = K \cap T_{K,u^0}$ for a given direction u^0. Then since K is closed, bounded, and convex, k is also.

Lemma B.6-7   *Let u^0 in E^n be given. Then*

$$H_k(u) = H_K'(u^0; u),$$

for all u in E^n.

PROOF:

Let x be in k. Then since x is in T_{K,u^0},

(B.6-8) $u^0 \cdot x = H_K(u^0),$

and since x is in K,

(B.6-9) $u \cdot x \leq H_K(u),$

for all u. Let v be an arbitrary direction and set $u = u^0 + tv$, where $t > 0$. Then, from (B.6-9),

$$u^0 \cdot x + (tv) \cdot x \leq H_K(u^0 + tv),$$

and using (B.6-8) this becomes

$$v \cdot x \leq \frac{H_K(u^0 + tv) - H_K(u^0)}{t}.$$

Therefore, for all v,

$$v \cdot x \leq H_K'(u^0; v),$$

so, since x was in k,

(B.6-10) $k \subset \bigcap_{E^n} \{x : v \cdot x \leq H_K'(u^0; v)\},$

where the intersection is taken over all v in E^n.

Now suppose x is in the right-hand intersection of (B.6-10). Then for all v in E^n,

(B.6-11) $v \cdot x \leq H_K'(u^0; v).$

Setting $v = u^0$ and then $v = -u^0$ and using an argument identical to that at the end of Lemma B.6-6 shows that

$$u^0 \cdot x = H_K(u^0),$$

so x is in T_{K,u^0}. But (B.6-11) and Lemma B.3-10 imply

$$v \cdot x \leq H_K(v)$$

for all v. Therefore, by Lemma B.6-2, x is in K. It follows that x is in k and

$$k = \bigcap_{E^n} \{x : v \cdot x \leq H_K'(u^0; v)\}.$$

Since $H_K'(u^0; v)$ is a homogeneous-subadditive function of v (Lemma B.3-8), the conclusion now follows from Lemma B.6-6.

Q.E.D.

Theorem B.6-12   *Let K be compact and convex. If K has only regular supporting planes, then $H_K(u)$ has partial derivatives H_{K_i} and*

$$H_{K_i}(u) = x_i, \quad i = 1, \ldots, n,$$

for all u in E^n, where $x = (x_1, \ldots, x_n)$ is the unique contact point of K and $T_{K,u}$. These partial derivatives are continuous except on possibly a set of zero measure in E^n and, in particular, they are continuous on the subset $A = \{u: |u| = 1\}$.

PROOF:

If K has only regular supporting planes, then for each u^0, the set $k = \{x^0\}$, where x^0 is the unique point of contact of K and T_{K,u^0}. By Lemmas B.6-3 and B.6-7,

$$v \cdot x^0 = H_k(v) = H_K'(u^0; v),$$

for all v. Hence H_K' is linear in v on E^n, so by Lemma B.3-1, for all v,

$$v \cdot x^0 = H_K'(u^0; v) = \sum_{i=1}^{n} H_{K_i}(u^0)v_i.$$

Therefore,

$$H_{K_i}(u^0) = x_i^0, \quad i = 1, \ldots, n.$$

By Corollary B.4-12, the H_{K_i} are continuous except on possibly a set of zero measure and by Lemma B.6-1 they are continuous on A.

Q.E.D.

B.7 QUASI-CONCAVITY

The function f defined on a convex set D is called *strictly quasi-concave* provided that for all distinct x' and x'' in D, if $f(x') = f(x'')$, then for every θ between 0 and 1,

(B.7-1) $$f(\theta x' + (1 - \theta)x'') > f(x'').$$

Relaxing $>$ to permit possible equality in (B.7-1), f is referred to as just *quasi-concave*. An equivalent definition is stated below without proof.

Lemma B.7-2   *f is strictly quasi-concave if and only if for all distinct x' and x'' in D, if $f(x') \geq f(x'')$, then for every θ between 0 and 1, $f(\theta x' + (1 - \theta)x'') > f(x'')$.*

Quasi-concavity means either convexity or concavity (or both) of the level surfaces of f, depending on the signs of the partial derivatives, f_i. If, for example, $f_i > 0$ for $i = 1, \ldots, n$, on D, then, as in Chapter 3, the level surfaces are convex throughout their domain. In this case it is rather easy to characterize quasi-concavity in terms of the derivatives of f by using results already proved in the text. Thus for twice-differentiable f denote its *bordered Hessian* by

$$F^*(x) = \begin{bmatrix} 0 & f_1(x) & \cdots & f_n(x) \\ f_1(x) & & & \\ \vdots & & F(x) & \\ f_n(x) & & & \end{bmatrix},$$

where F is the Hessian as defined in Section B.5. Let F^k be obtained from F^* by deleting its last $n - k$ rows and columns. One characterization is now as follows.

Theorem B.7-3 *Suppose f is twice continuously differentiable with $f_i(x) > 0$ for $i = 1, \ldots, n$, on an open, convex set D. Then f is quasi-concave if and only if for all x in D and any permutation of the rows and columns of F^*,*

$$|F^k(x)| \begin{cases} \leq 0, & \text{if } k \text{ is odd,} \\ \geq 0, & \text{if } k \text{ is even,} \end{cases}$$

where $k = 1, \ldots, n$. Furthermore, if f is strictly quasi-concave, then these inequalities are strict on at least a dense, open subset of D.

PROOF.

The first assertion follows by combining the discussion at the beginning of Section B.5 and the argument of Theorem 3.1-7 and Lemma 3.1-9. The second assertion is contained in Theorem 3.1-10.

Q.E.D.

It is clear that to strengthen Theorem B.7-3 so necessary and sufficient conditions for strict quasi-concavity are obtained, use must be made of Theorem B.5-9 or B.5-10. From the relationship between definite quadratic forms under linear constraints and signs of the $|F^k|$, Theorem B.7-3 is seen to be equivalent to [8, pp. 298–299]:

Theorem B.7-4 *Suppose f is twice continuously differentiable with $f_i(x) > 0$ for $i = 1, \ldots, n$, on an open convex set D. Then f is quasi-concave if and only if for all x in D,*

$$yF(x)y' \leq 0,$$

for every 1 by n vector y such that $\sum_{i=1}^{n} f_i(x)y_i = 0$. Furthermore, if f is strictly quasi-concave, then the above inequality is strict on at least a dense, open subset of D, for every $y \neq 0$ satisfying $\sum_{i=1}^{n} f_i(x)y_i = 0$.

Although the hypothesis that $f_i > 0$ for $i = 1, \ldots, n$, on D is not required for the conclusions of the last two theorems to hold, weaker results are not pursued here.[21]

[21] A more general version of Theorem B.7-3 may be found in Arrow and Enthoven [3, p. 797].

An interesting question is concerned with the relationship of concave to quasi-concave functions. Obviously every concave function is quasi-concave, but not conversely. On the other hand, if a function f is quasi-concave but not concave, there may exist an increasing transformation, T [i.e., $T(\mu') > T(\mu'')$ if and only if $\mu' > \mu''$] such that $T(f(x))$ is concave. Necessary and sufficient conditions for this property are now derived.[22]

Write $\varphi(x) = T(f(x))$, where T is defined on the range of f. Both T and f are required to be twice continuously differentiable and the derivatives of the former are written T' and T''. The derivatives of φ therefore exist and are continuous up to the second order,

(B.7-5) $$\varphi_i = T'f_i,$$

(B.7-6) $$\varphi_{ij} = T''f_if_j + T'f_{ij},$$

where $i, j = 1, \ldots, n$, and arguments of the functions have been eliminated to simplify notation.

Lemma B.7-7 *If φ is concave on D, then at each x, $f_i \neq 0$ for at least one $i = 1, \ldots, n$, except if and where f has a global maximum, μ^0. Furthermore, $T'(\mu) > 0$ for $\mu \neq \mu^0$.*

PROOF:

By adjusting Lemma B.1-2 for concave functions, it is clear that φ can have critical points only where it attains a global maximum. At any other point some $\varphi_i \neq 0$, and hence from (B.7-5), $f_i \neq 0$ and $T' \neq 0$. Since T is increasing, f and φ must have maximums at the same points and $T'(\mu) > 0$ for $\mu \neq \mu^0$.

Q.E.D.

Thus when φ is concave, critical points can occur in D only where both f and φ have global maxima and T' may vanish.

For each x in D, consider the quadratic forms

$$Q_f(y) = \sum_{i,j=1}^{n} f_{ij}y_iy_j,$$

the restriction of Q_f to the hyperplane $\sum_{i=1}^n f_iy_i = 0$, denoted by $Q_f^*(y)$, and, for noncritical x only,

(B.7-8) $$Q_\varphi(y) = Q_f(y) + \gamma\left(\sum_{i=1}^n f_iy_i\right)^2,$$

where

$$\gamma = \frac{T''}{T'}.$$

[22] The argument comes from Fenchel [9, pp. 127–137].

Let their characteristic polynomials be, respectively,

$$C_f(\lambda) = S_n^f - S_{n-1}^f \lambda + \cdots + (-1)^n S_0^f \lambda^n,$$

$$C_f^*(\lambda) = S_{n-1}^* - S_{n-2}^* \lambda + \cdots + (-1)^{n-1} S_0^* \lambda^{n-1},$$

$$C_\varphi(\lambda) = S_n^\varphi - S_{n-1}^\varphi \lambda + \cdots + (-1)^n S_0^\varphi \lambda^n,$$

where S_i^f, S_i^*, and S_i^φ for $i \neq 0$ are the elementary symmetric functions of appropriate characteristic roots and $S_0^f = S_0^* = S_0^\varphi = 1$. That Q_φ is essentially the quadratic form associated with the Hessian of φ and that C_f^* has degree $n - 1$ will become clear later.

Lemma B.7-9 *For each $i = 1, \ldots, n$, and noncritical x in D,*

$$S_i^\varphi = S_i^f + \gamma a S_{i-1}^*,$$

where $a = \sum_{i=1}^n f_i^2$.

PROOF:

Writing C_φ in its determinantal form,

$$C_\varphi(\lambda) = |f_{ij} - \lambda \delta_{ij} + \gamma f_i f_j|,$$

where $f_{ij} - \lambda \delta_{ij} + \gamma f_i f_j$ is the term in the ith row and jth column, and

$$\delta_{ij} = \begin{cases} 1, & \text{if } i = j, \\ 0, & \text{if } i \neq j. \end{cases}$$

By manipulation of rows and columns this becomes

$$\begin{vmatrix} 1 & 0 \\ f_i & f_{ij} - \lambda \delta_{ij} + \gamma f_i f_j \end{vmatrix} = \begin{vmatrix} 1 & -\gamma f_j \\ f_i & f_{ij} - \lambda \delta_{ij} \end{vmatrix},$$

and hence

(B.7-10) $$C_\varphi(\lambda) = C_f(\lambda) - \gamma \begin{vmatrix} 0 & f_j \\ f_i & f_{ij} - \lambda \delta_{ij} \end{vmatrix}.$$

Now the characteristic roots of Q_f^* are all minimum values with respect to y of $Q_f(y)$ constrained by $\sum_{i=1}^n f_i y_i = 0$, $\sum_{i=1}^n y_i^2 = 1$, and subject to additional restrictions which are not necessary to elucidate here [11, pp. 127–128]. To find them differentiate the Lagrangean expression

$$\sum_{i,j=1}^n f_{ij} y_i y_j + 2\eta \sum_{i=1}^n f_i y_i - \lambda \left(\sum_{i=1}^n y_i^2 - 1 \right),$$

where 2η and λ are multipliers, thereby obtaining

(B.7-11) $$\sum_{j=1}^n f_{ij} y_j + \eta f_i - \lambda y_i = 0, \quad i = 1, \ldots, n,$$

(B.7-12)
$$\sum_{j=1}^{n} f_j y_j = 0,$$

(B.7-13)
$$\sum_{i=1}^{n} y_i^2 = 1.$$

If (y^0, η^0, λ^0) is a solution of this system, then multiplying (B.7-11) by y_i^0, summing over i, and using (B.7-12) and (B.7-13) yields

$$\sum_{i,j=1}^{n} f_{ij} y_i^0 y_j^0 = \lambda^0.$$

Thus the characteristic roots of Q_f^* are the values of λ which solve (B.7-11)–(B.7-13) along with appropriate y and η. Since, in particular, (B.7-11) and (B.7-12) have a solution, it follows that

(B.7-14)
$$\begin{vmatrix} 0 & f_j \\ f_i & f_{ij} - \lambda\delta_{ij} \end{vmatrix} = 0,$$

whence the characteristic roots of Q_f^* are also the roots of the polynomial on the left side of (B.7-14).

Note that the coefficient of λ^n in (B.7-14) vanishes. The coefficient of λ^{n-1} is obtained by dividing the polynomial by λ^{n-1} and taking its limit as λ approaches infinity. Applying this technique to the determinant in (B.7-14) gives

$$\begin{vmatrix} 0 & f_j \\ f_i & -I \end{vmatrix} = (-1)^n \sum_{i=1}^{n} f_i^2 = -(-1)^{n-1}a,$$

where $-I$ is the identity matrix with 1 replaced by -1. Therefore,

$$C_f^*(\lambda) = -\frac{1}{a}\begin{vmatrix} 0 & f_j \\ f_i & f_{ij} - \lambda\delta_{ij} \end{vmatrix},$$

and so, from (B.7-10),

$$C_\varphi(\lambda) = C_f(\lambda) + \gamma a C_f^*(\lambda).$$

The conclusion is now evident.

Q.E.D.

Theorem B.7-15 *Let f be twice continuously differentiable on an open convex set D. Suppose there exists a twice continuously differentiable transformation T such that $\varphi(x) = T(f(x))$ is concave. Then for each x in D, $Q_f^*(y)$ is negative semidefinite, and if $k - 1$ is its rank, the rank of $Q_f(y)$ is at most k.*

PROOF:

If x is a critical point so that $f(x)$ is a maximum (Lemma B.7-7), then the necessary conditions of maximization imply Q_f is negative semidefinite. Furthermore, for this x, $Q_f(y) = Q_f^*(y)$ and hence the theorem is obvious.

Otherwise, from (B.7-5), (B.7-6), and the remarks following Theorem B.5-2, since φ is concave and twice continuously differentiable,

$$\sum_{i,j=1}^{n} \varphi_{ij} y_i y_j = T' Q_\varphi(y)$$

is negative semidefinite on D. Hence Q_φ is also. But (B.7-8) implies $Q_\varphi(y)$ and $Q_f^*(y)$ are identical for y such that $\sum_{i=1}^{n} f_i y_i = 0$. Thus the first part of the theorem is proved. Furthermore, since the characteristic roots of Q_φ are all nonpositive,

(B.7-16)
$$S_i^\varphi \begin{cases} \leq 0, & \text{if } i \text{ is odd}, \\ \geq 0, & \text{if } i \text{ is even}, \end{cases}$$

where $i = 1, \ldots, n$.

Let

$$\lambda_1 \leq \lambda_2 \leq \cdots \leq \lambda_n,$$

$$\lambda_1^* \leq \lambda_2^* \leq \cdots \leq \lambda_{n-1}^*,$$

be the respective characteristic roots of Q_f and Q_f^*. Because Q_f^* is obtained by constraining Q_f,

$$\lambda_i \leq \lambda_i^* \leq \lambda_{i+1}, \quad i = 1, \ldots, n-1$$

[10, p. 324]. Thus if the rank of Q_f^* is $k-1$,

$$\lambda_i^* \begin{cases} < 0, & \text{if } i = 1, \ldots, k-1, \\ = 0, & \text{if } i = k, \ldots, n-1, \end{cases}$$

$$\lambda_i \begin{cases} < 0, & \text{if } i = 1, \ldots, k-1, \\ \leq 0, & \text{if } i = k, \\ = 0, & \text{if } i = k+1, \ldots, n-1, \\ \geq 0, & \text{if } i = n. \end{cases}$$

Note that when $k = n$, the conclusion of the theorem clearly holds. Otherwise, with $k < n$, $S_k^* = 0$, and

$$S_{k+1}^f = \lambda_n \prod_{i=1}^{k} \lambda_i \begin{cases} \leq 0, & \text{if } k \text{ is odd}, \\ \geq 0, & \text{if } k \text{ is even}. \end{cases}$$

But (B.7-16) and Lemma B.7-9 with $i = k+1$ now imply $S_{k+1}^f = 0$ so that either λ_k or λ_n or both must vanish. Therefore, the rank of Q_f is at most k.

Q.E.D.

Corollary B.7-17 *Let $f_i > 0$ for $i = 1, \ldots, n$, on D. Then the hypotheses of Theorem B.7-15 imply that f is quasi-concave.*

The above corollary follows immediately from the fact, as asserted in Theorem B.7-15, that Q_f^* is negative semidefinite and the first part of Theorem B.7-4. Actually, as suggested by the remark following Theorem B.7-4, its conclusion follows without the hypothesis that $f_i > 0$ for $i = 1, \ldots, n$, on D, but proof is not given here.

Theorem B.7-18 *Let f be twice continuously differentiable on an open, convex set D. Suppose there exists a twice continuously differentiable transformation T such that $\varphi(x) = T(f(x))$ is concave. Then for each μ in the range of f which is not a maximum value,*

$$\frac{T''(\mu)}{T'(\mu)} \le \inf_{f(x)=\mu} \left(-\frac{S_k^f}{aS_{k-1}^*} \right),$$

where $k - 1$ is the rank of Q_f^* at x and the infimum is taken over all x in D such that $f(x) = \mu$.

PROOF:

Let noncritical x in D be fixed, $f(x) = \mu$, and $k - 1$ be the rank of Q_f^*. Since $S_i^f = S_{i-1}^* = 0$ for $i > k$, from (B.7-16) and Lemma B.7-9 it follows that $\gamma \le \bar{\gamma}$, where

$$\bar{\gamma} = \min_{1 \le 2i+1 \le k} \left(-\frac{S_{2i+1}^f}{aS_{2i}^*} \right).$$

Suppose the minimum is attained for $i = i^0$ and consider the characteristic polynomial of Q_φ with γ replaced by $\bar{\gamma}$:

$$\bar{S}_n^\varphi - \bar{S}_{n-1}^\varphi \lambda + \cdots + (-1)^n \bar{S}_0^\varphi \lambda^n,$$

where the $\bar{S}_j^\varphi$ are the corresponding elementary symmetric functions. Now Lemma B.7-9 certainly holds when $\bar{S}_j^\varphi$ and $\bar{\gamma}$ are interchanged with S_j^φ and γ. Hence for $i = i^0$,

$$\bar{S}_{2i^0+1}^\varphi = S_{2i^0+1}^f + \bar{\gamma} a S_{2i^0}^* = 0,$$

so by the properties of elementary symmetric functions, $\bar{S}_j^\varphi = 0$ for all $j \ge 2i^0 + 1$. Since, in particular, $k \ge 2i^0 + 1$,

$$\gamma \le \bar{\gamma} = -\frac{S_k^f}{aS_{k-1}^*}.$$

But this must be true for all x in D such that $f(x) = \mu$ and, therefore,

$$\frac{T''(\mu)}{T'(\mu)} = \gamma \le \inf_{f(x)=\mu} \left(-\frac{S_k^f}{aS_{k-1}^*} \right).$$

Q.E.D.

Several of the above necessary conditions for the existence of a concave φ (derived by transforming an arbitrary f) are also, in a sense, sufficient.

Theorem B.7-19 *Let f be twice continuously differentiable on an open set D. Assume that $Q_f^*(y)$ is negative semidefinite. Let T be any twice continuously differentiable transformation such that*

(a) *$T' > 0$ except at a possible maximum value, μ^0, of f.*
(b) *For all $\mu \neq \mu^0$,*

$$\frac{T''(\mu)}{T'(\mu)} \leq \inf_{f(x)=\mu} \left(-\frac{S_k^f}{a S_{k-1}^*} \right),$$

where $k - 1$ is the rank of Q_f^* at x.

Then $\varphi(x) = T(f(x))$ is concave on D.

PROOF:

In view of the discussion following Theorem B.5-2, it is only required to show that

(B.7-20)
$$\sum_{i,j=1}^{n} \varphi_{ij} y_i y_j$$

is negative semidefinite on D. If $f(x) = \mu^0$, the maximum value, then since T is increasing, φ also has a maximum at x. Negative semidefiniteness of (B.7-20) is now a trivial consequence of the necessary conditions for maximization.

For noncritical x, (B.7-20) reduces to $T' Q_\varphi(y)$. But from hypothesis (b) and (B.7-8), $Q_\varphi(y) \leq Q_\varphi'(y)$, where

$$Q_\varphi'(y) = Q_f(y) - \frac{S_k^f}{a S_{k-1}^*} \left(\sum_{i=1}^{n} f_i y_i \right)^2,$$

and $k - 1$ is the rank of Q_f^* at x. Thus it remains to show the negative semidefiniteness of Q_φ'. Applying Lemma B.7-9 to the elementary symmetric functions, S_i' of Q_φ',

$$S_i' = S_i^f - \frac{S_k^f}{S_{k-1}^*} S_{i-1}^*, \quad i = 1, \ldots, n.$$

As before, $S_k' = 0$ and hence $S_i = 0$ for $i = k, \ldots, n$. The rank of Q_φ' is therefore at most $k - 1$. However, Q_φ' constrained by $\sum_{i=1}^{n} f_i y_i = 0$ is identical to Q_f^*, the latter having $k - 1$ nonpositive roots by hypothesis. The same property clearly holds for Q_φ', which is, therefore, negative semidefinite.

Q.E.D.

Once again, if $f_i > 0$ for each i, the hypothesis of Theorem B.7-19 implies (by Theorem B.7-4) that f is quasi-concave. That quasi-concavity alone is not sufficient for the existence of a concave $\varphi(x) = T(f(x))$ is demonstrated by the following example.[23] Let $n = 2$ and

$$f(x) = (x_1 - 1) + [(1 - x_1)^2 + 4(x_1 + x_2)]^{1/2},$$

on $D = \{x : x > 0\}$. Setting $\beta(x) = [(1 - x_1)^2 + 4(x_1 + x_2)]^{-1/2}$, $\beta > 0$ on D and

$$f_1(x) = 1 + (x_1 + 1)\beta(x),$$
$$f_2(x) = 2\beta(x).$$

As in Theorem 3.1-7, the level curves have slopes

$$-\frac{f_1(x)}{f_2(x)} = \tfrac{1}{2}(\mu + 2),$$

where $f(x) = \mu$. Hence they are nonparallel straight lines and f is quasi-concave. In addition, the Hessian determinant

$$|F(x)| = -4\beta(x)^4 < 0,$$

on D. Therefore, Q_f has rank 2.

Because of Theorem B.7-15, to show that no increasing transformation of f is concave, it now suffices to prove the rank of Q_f^* vanishes. From the proof of Lemma B.7-9, however, this may be accomplished by demonstrating that the only root of

(B.7-21)
$$\begin{vmatrix} 0 & f_j \\ f_i & f_{ij} - \lambda\delta_{ij} \end{vmatrix}$$

is $\lambda = 0$. But straightforward calculation reduces (B.7-21) to

$$\lambda\{[1 + (x + 1)\beta(x)]^2 + 4\beta(x)^2\},$$

which can be zero only when $\lambda = 0$.

C. Miscellaneous Theorems

In the following paragraphs several unrelated results are presented which are used in the text. No detailed development leading up to them is given.

1. Let $y = f(x)$ be a vector-valued function defined on an open, convex set D. Suppose f is twice, continuously differentiable and has a single valued inverse g. Denote the Jacobian determinants by $|J_f(x)|$ and $|J_g(y)|$, respectively.

---

[23] The example is due to Arrow and Enthoven [3, p. 781].

Theorem C-1 *Let x^0 be in D and $y^0 = f(x^0)$. If $|J_f(x^0)| = 0$, then $|J_g(y^0)|$ cannot be finite.*

PROOF:

Suppose $|J_g(y^0)|$ is finite. Then the standard textbook argument [16, pp. 180–181] shows that

$$|J_g(y^0)|\,|J_f(x^0)| = 1.$$

It follows that $|J_f(x^0)| \neq 0$, which is a contradiction.

Q.E.D.

2. Let f be a single-valued function defined on an open, connected subset D, of the Euclidean plane. As usual, partial derivatives are denoted by subscripts.

Theorem C-2 (Young) *If f_1 and f_2 have differentials at some x^0 in D, then*

$$f_{12}(x^0) = f_{21}(x^0).$$

PROOF:

Consider the function

$$F(h, k) = g(h, k) - g(0, k),$$

where

$$g(v, k) = f(x_1^0 + v, x_2^0 + k) - f(x_1^0 + v, x_2^0).$$

Since f_1 has a differential at x^0, it is continuous there, and hence exists in some neighborhood N of x^0 [2, p. 110]. Thus by holding k fixed and applying the mean value theorem, for each h such that $(x_1^0 + h, x_2^0 + k)$ is in N, there exists a number θ between 0 and 1 for which

$$F(h, k) = g_1(\theta h, k)h$$
$$= [f_1(x_1^0 + \theta h, x_2^0 + k) - f_1(x_1^0 + \theta h, x_2^0)]h.$$

Let $\epsilon > 0$ be given. From the differentiability of f, there is a subneighborhood, N', of N on which

$$|f_1(x_1^0 + \theta h, x_2^0 + k) - f_1(x^0) - f_{11}(x^0)\theta h - f_{12}(x^0)k| < \epsilon\sqrt{\theta^2 h^2 + k^2},$$

and

$$|f_1(x_1^0 + \theta h, x_2^0) - f_1(x^0) - f_{11}(x^0)\theta h| < \epsilon\theta|h|.$$

Using this and the above,

$$|F(h, k) - f_{12}(x^0)hk| = |[f_1(x_1^0 + \theta h, x_2^0 + k) - f_1(x^0) - f_{11}(x^0)\theta h - f_{12}(x^0)k]h$$
$$- [f_1(x_1^0 + \theta h, x_2^0) - f_1(x^0) - f_{11}(x^0)\theta h]h|$$
$$< \epsilon|h|\sqrt{\theta^2 h^2 + k^2} + \epsilon|h|^2\theta.$$

Thus

$$\left|\frac{F(h, k)}{hk} - f_{12}(x^0)\right| < \epsilon\sqrt{\theta^2 \frac{h^2}{k^2} + 1} + \epsilon\theta\frac{|h|}{|k|}.$$

Letting h and k approach zero in such a manner that $|h/k|$ is always less than some positive constant, δ, and noting that ϵ is arbitrary,

$$\lim_{(h,k) \to (0,0)} \frac{F(h, k)}{hk} = f_{12}(x^0).$$

If δ is also chosen so that $|k/h| < \delta$, an analogous argument shows that

$$\lim_{(h,k) \to (0,0)} \frac{F(h, k)}{hk} = f_{21}(x^0),$$

which completes the proof.

Q.E.D.

The generalization of this theorem to functions of more than two variables is immediate.

3. Let D be a connected set and f a single-valued, continuous function defined on it. Suppose ρ is a probability measure on D. Integration is understood to be in the sense of Lebesque.

Theorem C-3 *If f is integrable, then there exists an x^0 in D such that*

$$\int_D f(x)d\rho = f(x^0).$$

PROOF:

Suppose the contrary: $\int_D f(x)d\rho \neq f(x)$ for all x in D. Let

$$S_1 = \left\{ x: \int_D f(x)d\rho > f(x) \right\},$$

$$S_2 = \left\{ x: \int_D f(x)d\rho < f(x) \right\}.$$

Then $S_1 \cup S_2 = D$, $S_1 \cap S_2 = \varnothing$, and since f is continuous, S_1 and S_2 are both open. But since D is connected, this implies either S_1 or S_2 must be empty. Suppose $S_2 = \varnothing$. Then for all x in D,

$$\int_D f(x)d\rho > f(x),$$

whence integration yields the contradiction,

$$\int_D f(x)d\rho > \int_D f(x)d\rho.$$

Q.E.D.

REFERENCES

[1] Alexandroff, A. D., "Almost Everywhere Existence of the Second Differential of a Convex Function and Some Properties of Convex Surfaces Connected with It," *Leningrad State University Annals*, Math. Ser., v. 6 (1939), pp. 3–35.

[2] Apostol, T. M., *Mathematical Analysis* (Reading, Mass.: Addison-Wesley, 1957).

[3] Arrow, K. J., and A. C. Enthoven, "Quasi-Concave Programming," *Econometrica* (1961), pp. 779–800.

[4] Bernstein, B., and R. A. Toupin, "Some Properties of the Hessian Matrix of a Strictly Convex Function," *Journal für die Reine und Angewendte Mathematik*, Band 210, Heft 1/2 (1962), pp. 65–72.

[5] Birkhoff, G., *Lattice Theory*, rev. ed. (New York: American Mathematical Society, 1948).

[6] Bonnesen, T., and Fenchel, W., *Theorie der konvexen Körper* (New York: Chelsea, 1948).

[7] Bourbaki, N., *Eléments de mathématique*, première partie, livre IV (Paris: Hermann, 1949).

[8] Debreu, G., "Definite and Semidefinite Quadratic Forms," *Econometrica* (1952), pp. 295–300.

[9] Fenchel, W., "Convex Cones, Sets, and Functions," Department of Mathematics, Princeton University, Princeton, N.J., 1953.

[10] Gantmacher, F. R., *The Theory of Matrices*, v. 1 (New York: Chelsea, 1959).

[11] Gel'fand, I. M., *Lectures on Linear Algebra* (New York: Interscience, 1961).

[12] Graves, L. M., *The Theory of Functions of Real Variables*, 2nd. ed. (New York: McGraw-Hill, 1956).

[13] Halmos, P. R., *Naive Set Theory* (Princeton, N.J.: Van Nostrand, 1960).

[14] Karlin, S., *Mathematical Methods and Theory in Games, Programming and Economics*, v. 1 (Reading, Mass.: Addison-Wesley, 1959).

[15] Kelley, J. L., *General Topology* (Princeton, N.J.: Van Nostrand, 1955).

[16] Rudin, W., *Principles of Mathematical Analysis* (New York: McGraw-Hill, 1953).

Answers
to
Exercises

2.1 Assume (2). Then

$$x' \oslash x'' \Leftrightarrow x' \gtrsim x'' \text{ and } x'' \not\gtrsim x'$$
$$\Leftrightarrow u(x') \geq u(x'') \text{ and } u(x'') \ngtr u(x')$$
$$\Leftrightarrow u(x') > u(x'').$$

Assume (1). Then

(a) If $x' \oslash x''$, then $u(x') > u(x'')$.
(b) If $x' \ominus x''$ and $u(x') \neq u(x'')$, then (1) would be violated. Hence $u(x') = u(x'')$.

2.2 Let $[x]$ denote the equivalence class containing x under $\ominus$. Then for any x and z in $\bar{E}$ such that $x \gtrsim z$, either $[x] = [z]$ or $x' \oslash z'$ for all x' in $[x]$ and z' in $[z]$. Define the relation ρ by $[x] \, \rho \, [z]$ if and only if $x \gtrsim z$. Then the set of all equivalence classes G is a chain under ρ.

Let K be the set of all points of $\bar{E}$ with rational coordinates. Set $K' = \{[y] : y \text{ is in } K\}$. Then K' is countable. To show it is order-dense in G, let $[x^0]$ and $[z']$ be any distinct classes. Suppose $x^0 \oslash z'$. Since $L_{x^0}^<$ is open, there is a neighborhood N of z' such that $x^0 \oslash z$ for all z in N. Choose y in $N \cap K$ such that $y > z'$. Then $x^0 \oslash y$ and $y \oslash z'$ because $\oslash$ is increasing. Therefore, $[x^0] \, \rho \, [y]$ and $[y] \, \rho \, [z']$.

Applying Theorem A-2 (Cantor), there is a real-valued function u such that $[x] \, \rho \, [z]$ if and only if $u([x]) \geq u([z])$. Define

$$u(x') = u([x])$$

for all x' in $[x]$. Then for any x and z in $\bar{E}$, $x \gtrsim z$ if and only if $u(x) \geq u(z)$.

2.3   Since $\circleddash$ is continuous and $x'_{(n)} > x''_{(n)}$ implies $(x'_{(n)}, 0) \circleddash (x''_{(n)}, 0)$ for all positive $x'_{(n)}$ and $x''_{(n)}$, it follows that every indifference surface intersects E^*.

To show that if $x \geq q^k$ for some q^k, then $C_x^{=}$ intersects uniquely each Q_i, where $i \geq k$, let $D = \cup C_x^{=}$, where the union is taken over all $C_x^{=}$ such that $x \geq \bar{q}^k$ and $C_x^{=} \cap Q_k$ is not empty. Continuity and quasi-linearity now imply $D = \{x : x \geq \bar{q}^k\}$, from which the conclusion is immediate.

2.4   Choose $0 \leq \alpha \leq 1$, $\beta = 1 - \alpha$, and $x = x''$. Then for any α, substitution in the definition of linearity implies $\alpha x' + (1 - \alpha)x'' \circleddash x''$, so indifference surfaces must be linear. The surfaces are parallel since setting $\beta = 0$ in the definition implies $\alpha x' \circleddash \alpha x''$. Direction cosines of the normal are positive because $\circleddash$ is increasing.

When $\circleddash$ is homothetic, increasing quantities along distinct rays from the origin in the same proportion from any fixed indifference surface leaves the consumer equally well off.

2.5   Let $\{z^k\}$ be a sequence of points converging to z^0. Then there exists a sequence $\{x^k\}$ such that $z_i^k = v^i(x_{\bar{\imath}}^k)$, all i and k. Since the sets $\{x_{\bar{\imath}} : v^i(x_{\bar{\imath}}) > z_i\}$ are unique for each z_i, $\{x^k\}$ can be chosen so as to converge to some x^0. By continuity of the v^i,

$$(2.5\text{-a}) \qquad\qquad \lim_{k \to \infty} v^i(x_{\bar{\imath}}^k) = v^i(x_{\bar{\imath}}^0) = z^0.$$

But u is also continuous and hence

$$\lim_{k \to \infty} V(z^k) = \lim_{k \to \infty} u(x^k) = u(x^0),$$

which, from (2.5-a), equals $V(z^0)$.

2.6 $u(x) = V(v^1(x_{\bar{1}}), \ldots, v^{\pi}(x_{\bar{\pi}}))$ on $\bar{E}$, where each v^i is an additive function of the components of $x_{\bar{\imath}}$ whenever N_i contains more than two elements.

3.1   Differentiating $w_1^2 = -u_1/u_2$ with respect to x_1,

$$w_{11}^2 = -\frac{1}{(u_2)^2}[u_2 u_{11} - u_1 u_{21} + (u_2 u_{12} - u_1 u_{22})w_1^2].$$

Now substitute for w_1^2 and factor out $-1/u_2$.

3.2   Write $\varphi(x) = T(u(x))$, where the derivative of T is $T' > 0$. Then the partial derivatives $\varphi_i = T'u_i$ and hence the inverse demand function f defined in (3.1-18) is not changed by T.

3.3   From the definition of the Slutsky functions (3.2-7),

$$\sum_{j=1}^{n} P_j s_{ij}^* = \sum_{j=1}^{n} P_j(h_j^{*i} + h^* h_M^{*i}) = \sum_{j=1}^{n} P_j h_j^{*i} + M h_M^{*i} = 0,$$

by Euler's theorem.

3.4   Assumptions 3.1-1, 3.1-2, and 3.1-4 are obvious. Next, note that $|U(x)| > 0$ on E. From Exercise 3.1, $w_{11}^2 > 0$, so indifference curves are strictly convex (Corollary B.2-8). This proves 3.1-3. The demand functions are

$$h^1(p, m) = \frac{m}{2p - 1 + (1 - p + p^2)^{1/2}},$$

and $h^2(p, m) = m - ph^1(p, m)$, where $p = P_1/P_2$, $m = M/P_2$. (The denominator of h^1 is always positive.) That h is differentiable everywhere on Γ follows either from direct computation of the derivatives or the fact that $|U(x)| > 0$ on E.

3.5 Differentiating the budget constraint $P \cdot h^*(P, M) = M$ with respect to M gives $\sum_{i=1}^{n} P_i h_M^{*i} = 1$, from which the conclusion is immediate.

3.6 The demand functions are

$$h^{*1}(P, M) = \frac{2P_2 - M}{P_1} + 2,$$

$$h^{*2}(P, M) = 2\frac{M - P_1}{P_2} - 2,$$

defined on that subset of Γ^* such that $2P_2 + P_1 - M > 0$ and $M - P_1 - P_2 > 0$. From the second inequality, $M - P_1 > 0$, so $h_2^{*2} < 0$ on this domain. The plane $2P_2 = M$ separates points in the domain at which good 1 is Giffen ($M > ?P_u$) from those at which it is not ($M < 2\Gamma_2$). An example of the former is $(\frac{1}{2}, \frac{1}{3}, 1)$ and of the latter is $(\frac{1}{2}, 3, 4)$. On the plane itself $h_1^{*1} = 0$.

3.7 Let (P^0, M^0) minimize l subject to $P \cdot x^0 = M$. Theorem 3.5-4 implies that the Lagrangean procedure is applicable. Thus there is a number α such that

$$l_i(P^0, M^0) = \alpha x_i^0, \quad i = 1, \ldots, n,$$

$$l_M(P^0, M^0) = -\alpha,$$

and hence

$$\frac{l_i(P^0, M^0)}{l_M(P^0, M^0)} = -x_i^0,$$

for all i. It now follows from Theorem 3.5-3 that $x^0 = h^*(P^0, M^0)$, so x^0 maximizes u subject to $P^0 \cdot x = M^0$.

Conversely, if x^0 maximizes u subject to $P^0 \cdot x = M^0$, then $x^0 = h^*(P^0, M^0)$. Let $(\bar{P}, \bar{M})$ minimize l subject to $P \cdot x^0 = M$ (a minimum exists since $-l$ is strictly quasi-concave by Theorem 3.5-4). Then from an argument similar to the above $h^*(P^0, M^0) = h^*(\bar{P}, \bar{M})$, so $(P^0, M^0) = (\tau\bar{P}, \tau\bar{M})$ for some $\tau > 0$. Since l is homogeneous of degree zero, the conclusion is now evident.

3.8 $l(P, M) = \left[\dfrac{M}{P_1} + \dfrac{M}{P_2}\right]^{1/2}$, $\quad \lambda^*(P, M) = \dfrac{1}{2}\left[\dfrac{1}{MP_1} + \dfrac{1}{MP_2}\right]^{1/2}$.

3.9 $\sum_{i=1}^{n} P_i h^{*i} = -(1/l_M) \sum_{i=1}^{n} P_i l_i = M$ from Euler's theorem. The second assertion follows again from Euler's theorem and Theorem 3.5-2.

3.10 Let (P, M) be in Ω^*. Then using the definition of the Slutsky functions (3.2-7) and Theorem 3.5-3,

$$s_{ij}^*(P, M) = \frac{1}{l_M^2} \left[-l_M l_{ij} + l_i l_{Mj} + (l_M l_{iM} - l_i l_{MM}) \frac{l_i}{l_M} \right],$$

for all i and j. Thus symmetry follows since the cross-partial derivatives of l are equal. Furthermore, if $\mathcal{L}$ denotes the bordered Hessian matrix of l, then with an argument identical to that of Lemma 3.1-9,

$$|S^{*k}(P, M)| = (-1)^k \left[\frac{1}{l_M(P, M)} \right]^{k+2} |\mathcal{L}^{k+1}(P, M)|, \quad k = 1, \dots, n,$$

on Ω^*, where superscripts indicate that the last $n - k$ rows and columns of S^* have been deleted as well as the last $n - k - 1$ rows and columns not containing l_{MM} of $\mathcal{L}$. Since $-l$ is strictly quasi-concave (Theorem 3.5-4), the conclusion is deduced exactly as that of Theorem 3.2-4 except that here all $|\mathcal{L}^{k+1}| \geq 0$.

3.11 Relation **a** follows from Euler's theorem while **b** and **c** are obtained by differentiation of the budget constraint.

4.1 $u(x) = x_1 x_2 x_3$.

4.2 $u(x) = \exp\left[-(1/x_1 + 1/x_2 + 1/x_3)\right]$. Note that $u(x) = 0$ on the boundary of E. Theorem 4.3-4 implies each $w(x_{(n)}, x^*)$ is defined for all $x_{(n)} > 0$, which is not true in this case.

5.1 Linear homogeneity of u implies that all derivatives u_i are homogeneous of degree zero. The conclusion now follows from the equality $w_j^n = -u_j/u_n$.

5.2 In the definition of weak separability set $V = u$ and each v^i equal to the identity function. The theory now suggests that $h^i(p, m) = m_{\bar{n}}/p_i$ for $i \neq n$ and $h^n(p, m) = m_{\bar{n}}$. But separability is hardly needed to derive this conclusion.

5.3 There are 14 different partitions with respect to which u is weakly separable:

(a) $\{1\}, \{2\}, \{3\}, \{4\}$.

(b) Three of the form $\{1, 2\}, \{3, 4\}$.

(c) Four of the form $\{1, 2, 3\}, \{4\}$.

(d) Six of the form $\{1\}, \{2\}, \{3, 4\}$.

Hence $h(p, m) = g^{\epsilon}(p, m)$ for appropriate g^{ϵ}, where $\epsilon = 1, \dots, 14$.

5.4 $s_{jr}(p, m) = \sigma^{i'i''}(p, m) h_m^j(p, m) h_m^r(p, m)$ for all j in $N_{i'}$ and r in $N_{i''}$, where, unlike Theorem 5.2-5, i' and i'' need not be distinct.

5.5 If $h_M^{*i^0} = 0$ on Γ', then τ^{i^0}, obtained from the separability theory, cannot be defined. In case (b), $h_j^{*i} = 0$ on Γ' for $i \neq j$ and hence $\tau^j = 0$ for all j. To obtain (5.3-12) would therefore require division by zero.

5.6 No. This is true only when the Bergson number $b = 0$.

5.7 $l(P, M) = \dfrac{M}{P_1} - 1 + \log P_1 - \log P_2.$

5.8 $h^{*i}(P, M) = (\alpha_i - 1)\delta_i + \alpha_i \dfrac{M}{P_i} + \alpha_i \sum_{j \neq i} \delta_j \dfrac{P_j}{P_i}.$

5.9 Assumptions 3.1-1–3.1-3 are satisfied for x in E such that

$$x_1 < \frac{\theta_{22}\alpha_1 - \theta_{12}\alpha_2}{\theta_{12}^2 - \theta_{22}\theta_{11}}, \quad x_2 < \frac{\theta_{11}\alpha_2 - \theta_{12}\alpha_1}{\theta_{12}^2 - \theta_{22}\theta_{11}}.$$

The demand function for commodity 1 is

$$h^{*1}(P, M) = \frac{\theta_{22}MP_1 + \alpha_2 P_1 P_2 - \alpha_1(P_2)^2 - \theta_{12}MP_2}{\theta_{11}(P_2)^2 - 2\theta_{12}P_1P_2 + \theta_{22}(P_1)^2},$$

and that for commodity 2 is similar.

6.1 Let $x^1, \ldots, x^r$ be any finite collection of points in $B^{\leq}(P, M)$. Then x^1 is in K_{x^1}. Suppose x^0 is in $K_{x^1}, \ldots, K_{x^{r-1}}$. If $x^0 \ominus x^r$, then x^0 is in K_{x^r}. Otherwise, if $x^r \ominus x^0$, then x^r is in all K_{x^i}. In either case $\bigcap_{i=1}^r K_{x^i}$ is not empty. This induction argument shows that any finite collection of sets K_x has a nonempty intersection. Since the K_x are closed subsets of the compact set $B^{\leq}(P, M)$, there is a point $\bar{x}$ contained[1] in all K_x. Clearly $\bar{x}$ is in $B^{=}(P, M)$ and $\bar{x} \ominus x$ for all x in $B^{\leq}(P, M)$. If there were a distinct x^* in $B^{\leq}(P, M)$ such that $x^* \ominus \bar{x}$, then by strict convexity $\theta x^* + (1 - \theta)\bar{x} \ominus \bar{x}$ for all $0 < \theta < 1$. But $\theta x^* + (1 - \theta)\bar{x}$ is in $B^{\leq}(P, M)$, which is a contradiction.

6.2 Let $P^0 \cdot x^0 = H(P^0, \mu)$ and $P' \cdot x' = H(P', \mu)$, where $P^0 > P'$. Then $H(P', \mu) \leq P' \cdot x^0 < P^0 \cdot x^0 = H(P^0, \mu)$, so H is increasing in P.

Let $P^0 \cdot x^0 = H(P^0, \mu)$ and $\alpha > 0$. Then $\alpha P^0 \cdot x^0 < \alpha P^0 \cdot x$ for all x such that $u(x) = \mu$. Therefore, $H(\alpha P^0, \mu) = \alpha H(P^0, \mu)$ and H is linearly homogeneous in P.

6.3 Where h^* is differentiable, negative semidefiniteness of S^* follows from (6.2-18) and Theorem B.5-1. Since H is linearly homogeneous in P, the H_i are homogeneous of degree zero in P. Hence if $\alpha > 0$, from (6.2-11) it follows that $h^{*i}(P, H(P, \mu)) = H_i(P, \mu) = H_i(\alpha P, \mu) = h^{*i}(\alpha P, H(\alpha P, \mu)) = h^{*i}(\alpha P, \alpha H(P, \mu))$.

6.4 $l(P, M) = -(1/M)(\sqrt{P_1} + \sqrt{P_2})^2$ and $H(P, \mu) = -(1/\mu)(\sqrt{P_1} + \sqrt{P_2})^2$. From the former $h^{*i}(P, M) = M/\sqrt{P_1}(\sqrt{P_1} + \sqrt{P_2})$ and from the latter $h^{*i}(P, H(P, \mu)) = -(\sqrt{P_1} + \sqrt{P_2})/2\mu\sqrt{P_1}$. Note that in both cases $h^{*i} > 0$. Taking the price–utility version of h^{*i} and substituting $-(1/M)(\sqrt{P_1} + \sqrt{P_2})^2$ for μ gives the price–income version.

6.5 Transitivity is obvious. Suppose $x' = h^*(P', M')$, $x'' = h^*(P'', M'')$ and $x' > x''$. Then $P' \cdot x' > P' \cdot x''$, so $x' \tilde{R} x''$ and hence $x' R x''$.

6.6 Suppose $x' \tilde{R} x''$ and $x' = h^*(P', M')$. If $x' \tilde{\bar{R}} [\theta x' + (1 - \theta)x'']$, then $P' \cdot x' < P' \cdot [\theta x' + (1 - \theta)x'']$ or $P' \cdot x' < P' \cdot x''$, contrary to $x' \tilde{R} x''$.

---

[1] J. L. Kelley, *General Topology* (Princeton, N.J.: Van Nostrand, 1955), pp. 135–136.

Hence $x' \tilde{R} [\theta x' + (1 - \theta)x'']$. By the weak axiom, $[\theta x' + (1 - \theta)x''] \bar{R} x'$. Therefore, from Lemma 6.3-3, $[\theta x' + (1 - \theta)x''] \tilde{R} x''$.

6.7 Let R be defined on $\bar{E}$.

a. If $x R x$ for some x in $\bar{E}$, then by asymmetry $x \bar{R} x$. Since this is a contradiction, R is irreflexive and $\bar{R}$ is reflexive.

b. By definition, $\bar{R}$ is total means for all x' and x'' in $\bar{E}$, either $x' \bar{R} x''$ or $x'' \bar{R} x'$ or both. This is equivalent to asymmetry of R.

c. Suppose for some x' and x'' in $\bar{E}$, $x' R x''$. If $x'' R x'$, then by transitivity $x' R x'$ contradicting irreflexivity. Hence $x'' \bar{R} x'$.

6.8 Consider the integrable case.

a. By the mean value theorem, there exists a point x^* on the line segment between x^0 and x such that

$$u(x^0) - u(x) = \sum_{i=1}^{n} u_i(x^*)(x_i^0 - x_i) = -\lambda(x^*)[\varphi(x^*) \cdot (x - x^0)].$$

If x is sufficiently close to x^0, then $\varphi(x^0) \cdot (x - x^0)$ and $\varphi(x^*) \cdot (x - x^0)$ have the same sign. Since λ is always positive, the conclusion is evident.

b. As in part (a),

$$u(x^0) - u(x) = \lambda(x^*)[\varphi(x^*) \cdot (x^0 - x^*) - \varphi(x^*) \cdot (x - x^*)],$$

where x^* is on the line between x^0 and x. Since $\overrightarrow{x^0 x}$ is a direction of nonpreference $\overrightarrow{x^0 x^*}$ is also, and hence, by 6.4-6, $\overrightarrow{x^* x^0}$ is a direction of preference. Therefore, $\varphi(x^*) \cdot (x^0 - x^*) > 0$. Now, $\overrightarrow{x^* x}$ cannot be a direction preference, too, because then 6.4-2 would imply $\varphi(x^*) = 0$, violating Theorem 6.4-8. By 6.4-2, $\overrightarrow{x^* x}$ is a direction of nonpreference, so $\varphi(x^*) \cdot (x - x^*) \le 0$. Therefore, $u(x^0) > u(x)$, since $\lambda(x^*) > 0$.

6.9 The relative saturation point is $(2, 2)$. The orthogonal path from $(0, 0)$ is the straight line $x_2 = x_1$ between these points. The orthogonal path from $(2, 0)$ is in two segments: first the curve $x_2 = \sqrt{x_1^2 - 4}$ between $(2, 0)$ and $(2\frac{1}{2}, 1\frac{1}{2})$, and second the straight line between $(2\frac{1}{2}, 1\frac{1}{2})$ and $(2, 2)$.

7.1 In case (a) $h_{\zeta_1}^{*1} = 0$, (b) $h_{\zeta_1}^{*1} < 0$, and (c) $h_{\zeta_1}^{*1} > 0$.

7.2 Let S^H be the matrix consisting of elements s_{ij}^H for $i, j = 1, \ldots, n - 1$, and suppose S^k is the corresponding Slutsky matrix for individual k. Then

$$S^H = \sum_{k=1}^{K} S^k,$$

where addition is the usual termwise operation. Hence for any vector $\psi = (\psi_1, \ldots, \psi_{n-1})$,

$$\psi S^H \psi' = \sum_{k=1}^{K} \psi S^k \psi',$$

where the prime denotes transpose. The conclusion now follows from the negative definiteness of each S^k.

7.3 $u^H(x) = x_1 x_2$.

7.4 The relationship is the same as that stated for the third (Leontief) definition of composites at the end of Section 7.3.

7.5 Since $u_n \equiv 1$, $f^i(x) = u_i(x)$ for $i = 1, \ldots, n - 1$. Hence $u_{ij}(x) = f^i_j(x)$, where $i \neq n$. This proves the first result. Since utility is cardinal, all other admissible utility functions, φ, are related to u by $\varphi(x) = T(u(x))$, where the derivatives $T' > 0$ and $T'' = 0$. Therefore, u_{ij} and φ_{ij} have identical signs and $u_{in} = \varphi_{in} = 0$.

Index